Freshman Business Connections

Fourth Edition

Karen M. Boston
Jeff S. Hood

University of Arkansas

Kendall Hunt
publishing company

Cover image courtesy of David Speer.

Photos within the Introduction and Chapters 1 and 2 provided by Karen M. Boston and Jeff S. Hood

www.kendallhunt.com
Send all inquiries to:
4050 Westmark Drive
Dubuque, IA 52004-1840

CONTENTS

The History of the Sam M. Walton College of Business

The Walton College was founded in 1926 in response to a growing demand for commercial education. Initially, designated as a "School" and headed by Charles C. Fichtner, the Walton College consisted of four professors, and offered thirty-six courses in business administration, economics and sociology. Curricula were available in accounting, banking and finance, general business, industrial management and marketing.

The Walton College's first four degrees were awarded in 1927. The Master of Science in Business Administration (MSBA) program was established in 1930; and a year later, The Association to Advance Collegiate Schools of Business (AACSB) accreditation was awarded to the undergraduate degree program. Also in 1931, the first female student graduated.

Academic programs have undergone continuous expansion. In 1950, the Doctor of Philosophy degree in economics was established; and the MSBA degree was re-designated Master of Business Administration (MBA). In 1959, the Doctor of Philosophy degree in Business Administration was established; and, the MBA degree was accredited in 1963.

In addition to the MBA, the Walton College offers a Masters of Accountancy, Masters of Information Systems, and a Masters of Arts in Economics. Undergraduate fields of specialization have been expanded to include accounting, business economics and international economics, information systems, finance and insurance, finance and banking, finance and real estate, personnel financial management, financial management and investments, marketing, retail, supply chain management, and general business. A Bachelor of Science in International Business is also offered.

Since 1926, the Walton College has added several specialized units to its structure in the areas of public service, research and outreach. They include: (1) the Center for Business and Economic Research (1943) to engage in grants and contracts for federal, state and local government research and to provide support for faculty research; (2) the Bessie Moore Center for Economic Education (1978) to provide economic education and understanding to elementary and secondary school teachers; (3) the Small Business and Technology Development Center (1979) to counsel and train small business owners and managers on sound business practices, and new business techniques; (4) the Center for Management and Executive Development (1984) to provide continuing education for middle and upper level managers; and (5) the Center for Teaching Effectiveness (1992) to enhance student learning by promoting improved teaching practices by faculty and graduate instructors in the Walton College; (6) the Supply Chain Management Research Center (1996) to provide a direct link between the private sector and University of Arkansas supply chain resources; (7) the Center for Retailing Excellence (1998) to focus on research and the development of students as future leaders in the retailing and related industries; (8) the Information Technology Research Institute (1999) to conduct multidisciplinary information technology research, promote student interest in information technology, and facilitate interaction with the business community; (9) the Garrison Financial Institute (2007) to advance financial education and knowledge through practice; (10) the Applied Sustainability Center (2007) to work with disparate partners to facilitate the rapid development of sustainable business practices and promote their application across the retail and consumer goods industries; and (11) the RFID Research Center (2005) to create and extend knowledge in RFID utilization and its impacts on business and society.

In 1978, the Walton College moved to its present location on Ozark Avenue. With the opening of the Donald W. Reynolds Center for Enterprise Development in 1998 and the Willard J. Walker Hall and J.B. Hunt Center for Academic Excellence buildings in 2007, the Walton College added state of the art facilities for students and faculty. Students have the advantage of classrooms and facilities in various buildings which the AACSB accrediting team designated as prototypical for collegiate schools of business.

In 2011, the Walton College and the Department of Accounting were reaccredited by the AACSB—The Association to Advance Collegiate Schools of Business.

The Walton College's student body consists of over 4,000 undergraduates and approximately 300 graduate students.

Similarly, the faculty of the Walton College has expanded from the initial four in 1926 to nearly 200 with permanent, full-time faculty holding the doctoral degree. The Walton College's academic program has been enhanced with the establishment of several endowed chairs and lectureships.

The leadership for the Walton College's record of achievement has been provided by the following: Dean Charles C. Fichtner (1926–1940), Dean Karl M. Scott (1941–1943), Dean Paul W. Milam (1944–1966), Acting Dean Merwyn G. Bridenstine (1966–1967), Dean John P. Owen (1967–1983), Dean Lloyd Seaton (1983–1989), Dean Stan Smith (1989–1992), Interim Dean Thomas McKinnon (1992–1993), Dean Doyle Z. Williams (1993–2005), Dean Dan L. Worrell (2005–2012) and Dean Eli Jones (2012 to present). Together, with a strong faculty and excellent students, these administrators have each forwarded the Walton College's dedication to continued academic excellence.

On October 6, 1998, the Walton Family Charitable Support Foundation made the largest upfront cash gift ever given to a public business college—$50 million—to establish the Sam M. Walton College of Business. The gift continues to provide a variety of programs and opportunities for both students and faculty.

Sam M. Walton

When Sam M. Walton, at the age of 44, opened his first Wal-Mart store in Rogers, Arkansas, in 1962, no one imagined he was introducing a retailing formula that within a generation would impact the lives of millions of people.

Under the drive, vision and inspiration of Walton, Wal-Mart's phenomenal growth and pursuit of excellence is unparalleled. Today, Sam's gamble is a global company with more than 1.8 million associates worldwide and more than 6,100 stores and wholesale clubs across 10 countries. Such achievement mirrors Walton's drive to succeed.

Samuel Moore Walton was born March 29, 1918, in Kingfisher, Oklahoma. He graduated from the University of Missouri at Columbia in 1940 with a B.A. in economics earning his expenses in high school and college by delivering newspapers.

He served as a Captain in the U.S. Army Intelligence Corps from 1942 to 1945. He gained early retail experience at J.C. Penney Co., Inc., in Iowa and operated his own variety store in Newport, Arkansas. During this time, Sam developed a deep understanding of the customer and an ability to motivate others. With the influence and encouragement of his wife, Helen, Sam opened the landmark Five & Dime in Bentonville, Arkansas in 1951. Never content, Walton began to look beyond the small variety store format; and, in 1962, he opened his first Wal-Mart in nearby Rogers. The company's early popularity exceeded expectations, resulting in a rapid state-by-state store expansion financed largely through proceeds of a public stock offering in 1971. Shareholders (which included most "associates") reaped the benefits of Wal-Mart's success. The stock split 10 times over the next 22 years, hitting an all-time high in December 1998 after increasing approximately 350 percent over the previous two years.

Sam Walton was frequently recognized for his business success and his commitment to the community. He was named "America's Most Successful Merchant" in the September 1991 cover story of *Fortune* magazine. A&E Biography produced Sam's life story in 1997 resulting in one of the most watched programs of the series.

Shortly after his death on April 5, 1992, Sam Walton received the Presidential Medal of Freedom from President George Bush, the highest honor the

country bestows on its private citizens. Walton along with Helen and the entire family received the prestigious 1997 National Patriots Award for "exemplifying the ideals that make this country strong." In presenting the award, the Congressional Medal of Honor Society citation read: "From building America's economic strength, to defending our country's freedoms, to generously helping others in need, the Walton family has served the nation and its citizens with humility and honor." In 1998, *Time Magazine* and CBS News recognized Sam Walton as one of the 20 most influential business geniuses of the 20th century.

CHAPTER 1

Academic Advising and Academic Planning

Courtesy of David Speer

Statement of Shared Purpose

Vision Statement

The Sam M. Walton College of Business is a nationally competitive business school that connects people with organizations and scholarship with practice by combining excellent student learning experiences with quality research serving Arkansas and the world.

Core Values

- **Excellence:** We strive for excellence in all we do.
- **Professionalism:** We believe organizational practices must be built on an ethical foundation and high standards of professional behavior.
- **Innovation:** We value creativity, innovation, and entrepreneurial spirit.
- **Collegiality:** We believe in working together to examine situations and ideas from diverse perspectives.

Mission Statement

The Walton College, the flagship business school of the state of Arkansas, has a three-fold mission: **TEACHING: Educate** a diverse population of students in bachelor's, master's, and doctoral programs to be tomorrow's business, community, and academic leaders; **RESEARCH: Discover** and disseminate knowledge through our research to support excellence and innovation in organizations; and **SERVICE: Share** our business expertise in support of our state, our professions, and the academic community.

Organization and Facilities

The Walton College offers degree programs for undergraduate students and for graduate students at both the master's and doctoral levels. The college has been a member of and accredited by AACSB International—The Association to Advance Collegiate Schools of Business since 1931. The accounting program was accredited separately in 1986 at both the bachelor's and master's level. The master's degree in the business administration program was approved in 1963. Accreditation by and membership in AACSB signifies commitment by the college to the goals of promoting and actualizing the highest standards of business education.

Walton College is located in four modern buildings designed to be a functional home for the on-campus programs. These attractive facilities house fully equipped classrooms for business classes, state-of-the-art computer laboratories for both class and individual use, faculty and administrative offices, an honors program study area with computer access, a Career Center, and large study rooms equipped for individual as well as group studying.

The library of the college is part of the general University Libraries and is housed in Mullins Library. The business and economics collection comprises approximately 55,000 volumes and makes this library one of the best in the region. Walton College also operates centers for research, outreach, and public service. Information about these centers may be found in the University Centers and Research Units section of this catalog. Walton College centers include the following:

- Applied Sustainability Center
- Bessie B. Moore Center for Economic Education
- Center for Business and Economic Research
- Center for Management and Executive Development
- Center for Retailing Excellence
- Garrison Financial Institute
- Information Technology Research Institute
- RFID Research Center
- Supply Chain Management Research Center
- Small Business and Technology Development Center
- Tyson Center for Faith and Spirituality in the Workplace

University of Arkansas Advising Mission Statement

Academic advising is an active, ongoing exchange between the advisors and students grounded in teaching and learning. Advising is based on students gaining accurate and appropriate information and direction to help make their educational experience relevant, coherent, and meaningful. It is a process that assists students in connecting with the University of Arkansas, making thoughtful decisions related to their academic experiences, and maximizing their educational and career opportunities. Quality academic advising is essential to achieving the University's vision.

ADVISING is a partnership.

While procedures may vary among schools and colleges, all successful academic advising should include the following:

- A mutual responsibility between advisor and student with the student possessing final responsibility for successful completion of a degree.
- Respect for students' ethnic and racial heritage, age, gender, culture, national origin, sexual orientation, and religion, as well as their physical, learning, and psychological abilities.
- A developmental and educational process that occurs over time.
- Consideration of individual students' interests, abilities, and needs.
- A collaborative effort to connect students to campus resources and services.
- Reasonable availability and accessibility of advisors.
- Interpretation of University of Arkansas, college, and departmental rules and regulations.
- A student's understanding of the purpose and nature of the university core courses.
- Recommendation of appropriate courses.
- A student's understanding of and progress toward academic requirements.
- General information regarding career options and opportunities, with appropriate referrals as necessary.
- An understanding of and adherence to laws and regulations that relate to academic advising.
- Adherence to the highest principles of ethical behavior.

Walton College Advisor and Student Expectations

Students can expect that their academic advisor will . . .

Provide accurate information
Educate students on the Walton College curriculum and academic policies
Treat students with respect
Be on time for scheduled appointments
NOT make students' schedules for them
Assist students with making good academic choices
Refer students to other campus resources as needed
NOT recommend teachers or classes based on difficulty
Keep accurate student records
Respect the privacy of students
Refer to students by name
NOT tolerate threatening or inappropriate behavior

Advisors expect that Walton College students will . . .
Arrive on time for advising appointments
Treat advisors with respect
Use appropriate language in the Undergraduate Programs Office
Know their University Student ID Number
Be prepared for their advising sessions
Follow through with advisors' recommendations
Make sure that the University has their accurate contact information
Turn cell phones or pagers to silent when meeting with an advisor
Make all attempts to solve academic issues themselves before asking family or friends
    to become involved
Abide by the University of Arkansas Student Code of Conduct
NOT ask advisors to request exceptions on their behalf
Make advance appointments to see an advisor

Q. How are advisors assigned? A. When students take WCOB 1111 Business Connections, their instructor is their advisor for the first two semesters. After that, students may **make appointments** to see any of the professional advisors in the Undergraduate Programs Office. To help with the success of your academic advising session and your academic career it is your responsibility to:

- Schedule an advising appointment EARLY each semester, (479) 575-4622. As a general rule advisors do not advise via email or by telephone.
- Be on time for your appointments: students who are more than 10 minutes late will be rescheduled.
- Review your curriculum prior to meeting with your advisor.
- Write down your questions.
- Have a copy of your schedule handy.
- Know your Student ID Number.
- KEEP AND BRING YOUR ADVISING WORKSHEETS.
- Keep copies of all academic records, transcripts, relevant e-mails and petitions.
- Be aware of pre-requisites and co-requisites.
- Read your Catalog of Studies.
- Consult your advisor before making drastic changes to an agreed upon schedule.
- Take responsibility for your academic career.

Undergraduate Degree Programs

Undergraduate students may pursue curricula leading to one of the following degrees: Bachelor of Science in Business Administration (B.S.B.A), Bachelor of Science in International Business (B.S.I.B.). In each of these degree programs, the pre-business requirements must be completed before students may enroll in upper division business courses. Students in Walton College may pursue an academic minor in business or in the J. William Fulbright College of Arts and Sciences. Walton College also offers business minors for business and non-business students. Degree programs and minors are outlined on subsequent pages.

Admission to the Sam M. Walton College of Business

All students admitted to the University of Arkansas, Fayetteville, are eligible for admission to the Sam M. Walton College of Business. Students will be required to follow the degree program requirements set forth in the catalog corresponding to the student's first semester in Walton College, not the first semester of enrollment at the University of Arkansas.

College Scholarships

High school graduates who expect to enroll in the Walton College are encouraged to apply for scholarships made available to freshmen by individuals, business firms, and organizations. Also available to freshmen, regardless of degree program, are freshmen academic scholarships. Current Walton College students may apply for both college and departmental scholarships beginning in January of each year for the following academic year. Information on these financial awards may be secured from the University Scholarship Office and the Walton College Undergraduate Programs Office.

Honors Program

Walton College honors program consists of two components: the four-year Walton Scholars Program and the Departmental Scholars Program. Students participating in the honors program will be eligible to graduate *Cum Laude, Magna Cum Laude*, or *Summa Cum Laude*.

Students who do not participate in the honors program are eligible to graduate with distinction, a classification separate from the *Cum Laude* awards. Honors program students will receive priority for participation in the Arkansas Cooperative Education Program, SAKE, the portfolio management class, and financial support for study-abroad programs. They also have access to an honors study area.

Eligibility for the Honors Program

Admission will be offered to incoming freshmen with an ACT of 28 (or 1240 SAT) or higher and a high school GPA of 3.75. Students are required to maintain a cumulative GPA of 3.50 to remain in the program.

Requirements for Walton Scholars Program

1. Complete 17 hours in honors courses with a minimum of 6–9 hours completed from the following honors business courses: ECON 2013H, ECON 2023H, BLAW 2013H, WCOB 1033H, or WCOB 2053H. The remaining honors hours may be selected from the University Core. Completing honors sections of courses in the Fulbright College will fulfill this requirement. MATH 2564 may be used as honors credit towards completion of the 17 required honors hours. Students must complete a minimum of 12 honors hours within the first 30 hours at the Fayetteville campus.

2. Demonstrate proficiency in a foreign language. This requires 0 to 12 hours of course work. Students may demonstrate proficiency by completing the 2013-level course in any foreign language. Students whose native language is not English must complete a 2013-level course other than their native language from Arabic, Chinese, French, German, Italian, Japanese, or Spanish or COMM 2303 and 2323. Students must

complete a foreign language or communications course within the first 90 hours at the Fayetteville campus.

3. Students must also complete MATH 2554 with a grade of "C" within the first 45 hours at the Fayetteville campus prior to taking upper level business classes.

4. Complete of the following honors courses in Walton College:

   a. Two three-hour college colloquium courses chosen from the following: WCOB 3003H (may be repeated for up to 6 hours of credit) ACCT 4003H, ECON 4003H, FINN 3003H, MGMT 4003H, ISYS 4003H, MKTG 4003H, SCMT 4003H or other business honors colloquium courses offered irregularly. One three-hour colloquium must be completed within the first 90 hours at the Fayetteville campus.

   b. A three-hour thesis (WCOB 4993H): The thesis is a major independent writing project under the leadership of a Walton College or University of Arkansas faculty member and arises from a research project, business plan, business competition, or internship.

5. Complete an alternate honors capstone course MGMT 3013H, Strategic Management, which should be completed within the first 90 hours at the Fayetteville campus.

Requirements for the Departmental Scholars Program

1. Complete nine hours of honors courses in the University Core and demonstrate proficiency in a foreign language by completing a 2003 course in any foreign language.

2. Complete six to nine hours of honors courses in Walton College to include:

   a. Two three-hour college colloquiums.

   b. A three-hour thesis.

Student Organizations in Walton College

In addition to the general university student organizations, Walton College Student Ambassadors, Study Abroad Ambassadors, and a Dean's Student Advisory Board, there are several college societies open to Walton College students. These include the following:

- Alpha Kappa Psi
- American Marketing Association
- Association of Information Technology Professionals
- Beta Alpha Psi (accounting honorary and professional)
- Beta Gamma Sigma (business honorary)
- Enactus (formerly SIFE)
- Capital Markets Group (Finance Club)
- National Association of Black Accountants
- Omicron Delta Epsilon (economics honorary)
- Phi Beta Delta (international scholars honorary)
- Society for Human Resource Management
- Transportation and Logistics Association
- Women in Logistics

Academic Regulations of Walton College

Pre-Business Requirements

Students pursuing a degree in Walton College are classified as pre-business with an intended major until all pre-business requirements are fulfilled. The following policies apply to the pre-business program: To be eligible to enroll in upper-division business courses in Walton College, a student must complete the Walton College computer competency requirement (ISYS 1120) or ISYS 1123, Business Application Knowledge and obtain at least a 2.50 (on a 4.00 scale) overall grade-point average (GPA) in addition to completing the 25 credit hours listed below of pre-business core courses (or their equivalents), also with at least a 2.50 GPA. Further, a student must complete all courses offered to meet this requirement with a grade of "C" or better or the requirement for graduation. The pre-business core courses are as follows:

ENGL 1013	COMM 1313	MATH 2053
ENGL 1023	ECON 2013	ACCT 2013
WCOB 1111	ECON 2023	ACCT 2023 or WCOB 2053
ISYS 1120 or ISYS 1123	MATH 2043	WCOB 1033

Students' records will be evaluated each semester to determine whether a student should be moved to a major and have pre-business classification removed. After receiving notification that a student has been admitted into his or her major, the student is expected to arrange for a degree check by the Undergraduate Programs Office to ascertain remaining degree requirements.

Registration in Junior/Senior-Level Walton College Courses

Walton College students must complete the pre-business requirements prior to enrollment in junior- or senior-level courses in Walton College. Non-degree seeking students and students enrolled in other colleges are subject to the same course prerequisites as students within Walton College. Specific exceptions to this policy must be addressed to the assistant dean for undergraduate programs in the Walton College.

Business Core Requirements

Students pursuing a degree in Walton College must complete the following business core courses: All business core classes must be completed with a grade of "C" or better.

BLAW 2013	MGMT 2103	MGMT 3013
ISYS 2103	FINN 3043	
SCMT 2103	MKTG 3433	

Restrictions on General Education Electives

Only three hours total of general education electives will be allowed in Physical Education Activity (PEAC) or Dance Education Activity (DEAC) courses.

Transfer of Credit Policies

In addition to the University policies controlling the granting of credit for course work taken at other institutions, the following policies apply to transfer work applied to any undergraduate business program:

1. Transfer students considering admission to pursue a major in Walton College must have completed the pre-business courses and requirements listed above and have a 2.50 (on a 4.00 scale) cumulative grade-point average in the pre-business courses and in his or her overall grade-point average. Transfer students will be classified as pre-business students until pre-business core requirements have been completed.

2. A pre-business and overall grade-point average for courses accepted for transfer by the University of Arkansas will be calculated and used to evaluate the completion of the pre-business requirements by students transferring courses from other institutions.

3. Unless exceptions are granted at the time of admission to the University of Arkansas, transfer courses accepted by the University will not be accepted by Walton College for degree purposes unless a grade of "C" or better has been earned in each of these courses.

4. A transferred course cannot carry more degree hours than are available in a similar University of Arkansas course. For example, a four-hour principles of accounting course transfers as three degree hours.

5. Business courses completed at the freshman or sophomore level at another institution will not count as equivalents of junior- or senior-level courses offered in Walton College (University of Arkansas), and no transfer credit shall be granted for any such course(s) in Walton College.

6. At least 50 percent of program requirements in business and economics must be taken in residence.

7. MGMT 3103, 21–24 hours of upper division courses required for the completion of the major, and 3–6 hours of one additional, upper division business course required for the degree must be taken in residence at the University of Arkansas, Fayetteville.

8. Junior- or senior-level core courses in business and economics may be transferred from a school accredited by AACSB International.

9. Junior- or senior-level core courses taken at a non-AACSB International-accredited, four-year institution must either be repeated or validated by procedures specified and approved by the Assistant Dean for Undergraduate Programs.

10. Junior- or senior-level electives in business and economics taken at a non-AACSB International-accredited, four-year institution may be accepted in transfer as junior/senior business electives.

11. Junior- or senior-level courses in business taken by correspondence at AACSB International or non-AACSB International institutions may not be accepted and transferred for degree credit.

12. In cases of minors or transfer, students who take courses with different names but with similar content at different institutions or in different colleges within the University of Arkansas, may be allowed degree credit for only one of the courses (i.e., principles of economics and agricultural economics). Students pursuing degrees and minors within the Walton College must enroll in business courses as designated by his/her program of study.

13. Courses taken at any higher education institution where the course content is remedial are not acceptable for degree credit.

14. The student should be prepared to submit course descriptions, syllabi, or other course-related information for transfer course work if there is any question as to whether Walton College will grant degree credit for such work.

15. Exceptions: All requests for, exceptions to, and variations from the rules, regulations, and requirements of Walton College and the university should be made in writing to the Assistant Dean for Undergraduate Programs. Consult the Undergraduate Programs Office in Walton College for these requests.

Petition of Transfer Credit

Students who wish to petition **business classes (ex. ECON 299t)** should contact the Undergraduate Programs Office 328 for the proper forms. **Students wishing to petition any non-business classes (ex. BIOL 299t)** may download the proper forms online from the Registrar's Office at: http://reigstar.uark.edu/440.php. Forms must be returned to the Registrar's Office with class syllabus attached.

Transfer Course Equivalency Guide

There is a transfer equivalency guide online at: http://waprd.uark.edu/web-apps/regr/courseequiv/Main. It has many Colleges and Universities listed but may not list every course from every school. For questions please contact the Registrar's Office/Transfer Credit at 575-5451.

Course Loads

The normal course load in Walton College is 15 to 17 hours per semester (and six hours per summer term). Students with a 2.75 grade-point average the previous semester may take a maximum of 18 hours. Seniors may take 18 to 19 hours, if required for graduation, during their final semester. Students on academic warning are limited to a maximum course load of 12 hours. University regulations on the number of hours allowed per semester are found in the Orientation and Registration section of this catalog.

Foreign Language Concentration

An undergraduate B.S.B.A. degree-seeking student may elect to substitute 12 hours in a single upper-level foreign language for 12 to 15 hours of the 12 to 15 hours required in the junior-senior business elective block of courses for the degree requirements. Students who choose to 12 hours of foreign language, but who are pursuing majors requiring 15 hours of junior-senior business electives, must take an additional 3 hour junior-senior business elective to satisfy degree requirements.

Double Major

A student may elect to obtain a double major by completing all required courses for two majors in Walton College (but not in two concentrations within a single major). The minimum hour requirement for a double major is 138 degree credit hours to include all requirements for both majors. If there are courses common to both majors, the department chairs involved will agree upon and specify additional requirements in lieu of the common courses. The junior/senior business elective block is reduced by three hours; however, choice of the junior/senior business electives is restricted to no more than three total hours from each department that offers the two majors. Students who have elected to substitute a foreign language course of study for junior/senior business electives must complete 12 hours of junior/senior language courses. The student must notify the Undergraduate Programs Office in Walton College of intent to pursue a double major. All requirements for double majors must be completed prior to awarding of a degree.

Additional Bachelor's Degrees

Students seeking a second bachelor's degree must contact the undergraduate programs office to ascertain specific requirements. Degree candidates must meet the university's general graduation requirements. The university requires that: 1) the student take a minimum of 30 semester hours over the requirements for the first degree, and 2) the 30 hours cover a minimum of 36 weeks in residency at the Fayetteville campus. Walton College also requires that the student complete all courses in the pre-business and business core and the major and any additional business requirements (if some of these have been completed on the first degree, they are waived). It is recommended that any additional courses needed to finish the University's 30-hour requirement be junior or senior business electives. The second degree may be taken after the first is awarded, or both degrees may be awarded simultaneously after completion of all requirements for both.

College Graduation Requirements

1. **University Requirements.** Degree candidates must meet the following: the University's general entrance requirements, number of credit hours required in residence, and the "requirements for graduation," including the University Core American history, and English proficiency.

2. **Hour Requirements.** Degree candidates must satisfactorily complete the total number of semester hours specified for the curriculum in courses approved for one of the majors outlined in the succeeding pages. No less than 50 percent of the total credits must be in approved subjects other than business. **NOTE**: Not all courses offered by the University will be accepted for degree credit by Walton College. Courses falling into this category are: ENGL 0002, ENGL 0013, and MATH 0003. Developmental courses are defined as 1) any course so designated by the university, and 2) any lower-division course taken after a higher-level course is taken. Credit will not be given for duplicate course work.

3. **Grade Requirements.** Students must earn a grade of "C" or better in all pre-business core course requirements. Each student must have a 2.00 cumulative GPA in each of the following areas: a. All work completed at the University of Arkansas. b. All courses specifically designated for the major. c. All required business core courses and required economics courses.

4. **General Education Course Work.** A student's general education course work must satisfy university core requirements, additional college/program course-specific requirements, as well as these two area requirements: 1) social issues, multicultural environment, and demographic diversity, and 2) Micro and macroeconomics. If a student has not satisfied these area requirements within the fine arts and/or social sciences areas of the university core, these area requirements must be satisfied through general education electives to allow students to complete degree requirements within the hours indicated above.

5. **Residency Requirements.** Students must earn a minimum of 30 semester hours on the Fayetteville campus—this includes study abroad classes, on-line and Global Campus courses. Other courses paid toward Fayetteville campus tuition and fees

may be used with the approval. These 30 semester hours must include MGMT 3013, 21–24 hours of upper division courses required for the completion of the major, and 3–6 hours of one additional, upper division business course required for the degree program.

6. Specifically required junior or senior courses in business or economics must be taken at the University of Arkansas or at an AACSB-accredited school. At least 50 percent of the total hours in business and economics must be taken in residence.

7. **Correspondence Course Rules.** No more than 18 hours of course work taken by correspondence may apply toward a degree. These 18 hours may not include more than 12 hours of courses in economics or business, and may not include any junior- or senior-level economics or business courses without prior approval of the Assistant Dean for Undergraduate Programs.

8. **Catalog/Curriculum Changes.** Business is a dynamic profession, and the college and department curricula are updated continuously to keep pace with changes in the business world. Students entering under this catalog will be required to comply with such curricular changes to earn their degree. The total number of hours required for the degree, however, may not be increased, and all work completed in accordance with this catalog prior to the curriculum change will be applied toward the student's degree requirements. Furthermore, courses incorporated into the curriculum at a level lower than the one the student has completed are not required for that student unless there are specific prerequisites. Students entering under earlier catalogs are responsible for completing the graduation requirements as published in the catalog in effect when they entered the program. Students having interruptions of their academic programs that exceed two calendar years must complete the requirements published in the catalog in effect when they reenter the program. Exceptions to the graduation requirements must be approved by the Assistant Dean for Undergraduate Programs.

Graduation with Honors

The bachelor's degree *Summa Cum Laude* (with highest honors), *Magna Cum Laude* (with high honors), or *Cum Laude* (with honors) may be conferred only upon those students who have successfully completed the Walton College Honors Program. Both Walton Scholars and Departmental Scholars are eligible for these designations. Students whose cumulative grade-point average place them in the top 10 percent of their graduating class but who have not completed the Honors Program are eligible for the designation "With Distinction" on their official transcript. Among those students completing the Honors Program, the designations *Summa Cum Laude, Magna Cum Laude* and *Cum Laude* shall be determined as follows: **1.** Top 20 percent of students completing the Honors Program: *Summa Cum Laude* **2.** Next 30 percent of students completing the Honors Program: *Magna Cum Laude* **3.** Next 50 percent of students completing the Honors Program: *Cum Laude* No honors degree will be conferred upon a candidate who has not completed at least 50 percent of his or her degree work at the University of Arkansas or who, in the last four semesters of attendance, has a cumulative grade-point average of less than 3.00 or has received a "D" or "F" in any course in the last semester. Certain other requirements will be outlined on request by the Associate Dean for Undergraduate Studies.

Eight-Semester Degree Program Policy

The Walton College offers an eight-semester degree-completion program in each of the majors. Some majors offer several concentrations, and eight-semester programs are available for each of the concentrations at http://waltoncollege.uark.edu/advisingcenter/default.asp?show=act1014.

Academic Standing

Academic Probation, Suspension and Dismissal

A student's academic status at the university is determined at the end of each term of enrollment (fall, spring, or summer) on the basis of the student's cumulative and/or term grade-point average (GPA) and number of hours attempted. The student's academic status governs his or her re-enrollment status and determines any conditions associated with re-enrollment or denial of enrollment for a subsequent term. Normally, students are notified of their status individually by the university shortly after the end of each term. However, this policy statement is the formal notification to all students of the conditions that determine academic status and the consequences for each term, regardless of individual notification.

Good Status

Upon initial admission and during a student's first term of enrollment, except for students conditionally admitted on academic probation, the student is in good status. A student remains in, or returns to, good academic status at the end of any term when the cumulative GPA is at or above the required minimum of 2.0.

Academic Probation

When a student's cumulative grade-point average at the end of any fall, spring, or summer term is less than a 2.00 with more than three cumulative hours attempted, the student will be placed on academic probation.

First-Year Freshmen

First-year freshmen who have less than a 2.00 cumulative grade-point average at the end of their first semester of enrollment are considered at risk. During the first six weeks of their second semester, these at risk students must, at a minimum, consult with an academic adviser to develop a plan to get off of probation before being eligible to register for their third semester courses.

Removal from Academic Probation

When a student's cumulative GPA at the end of any fall, spring, or summer term is a 2.00 or above, he or she will be removed from academic probation.

Continuing on Academic Probation

The semester grade point average a student on probation must earn to continue on probation and avoid suspension depends on the cumulative grade hours attempted as outlined in the probation chart below.

Probation Chart

Cumulative Hours Attempted (excludes grades of W)	Placed on Probation If Cumulative GPA Is:	Continued on Probation If Semester GPA Is:	Removed From Probation If Cumulative GPA Is:
4-30 hours attempted	Less than 2.0	Greater than or equal to 1.8	Greater than or equal to 2.0
Greater than 30 hours attempted	Less than 2.0	Greater than or equal to 2.0	Greater than or equal to 2.0

Academic Suspension

A student on academic probation who does not earn the minimum required term GPA will be academically suspended. No student may be suspended who has not spent the prior term of enrollment on academic probation. A student on academic suspension will be on academic leave from the university for one major semester (Spring or Fall) and all contiguous summer and intersessions from the close of the term which resulted in the suspension. Thus, a student suspended at the end of the spring semester would not be eligible to enroll until the next spring semester; a student suspended at the end of the summer semester would not be eligible to enroll until the following spring term; and a student suspended at the end of a fall semester would not be eligible to enroll until the next fall semester. The first enrollment when returning from suspension may not be in an intersession.

Students who sit out for one major semester after the term of the suspension may apply for readmission to the university. A student who does not earn credit from another institution may be readmitted on academic probation following suspension. A student who earns credit from another institution(s) during or subsequent to the suspension must apply to the university for admission as a transfer student and, if readmitted, will be on academic probation following suspension. A student readmitted on probation after suspension must make a semester grade-point average of at least 2.00 for each semester, (fall, spring, or summer) until he or she is removed from probation. Failure to do so will result in academic dismissal.

Academic Dismissal

A student who returns to the university after an academic suspension is continued on probation following suspension and must make a semester grade-point average of at least 2.00 for each fall, spring, or summer term until he or she is removed from probation. Failure to do so will result in academic dismissal.

Returning after Dismissal

The duration of dismissal is indefinite, and the student may reenter the University only by favorable action of the Academic Standards Committee. A favorable decision by the committee is unlikely within two years of the dismissal. Self-paced courses taken through the Global Campus at the University of Arkansas or courses taken at another university by a student who has been academically dismissed may be submitted as evidence of academic competence on a petition to the Academic Standards Committee for readmission. It is strongly recommended that students meet with an academic adviser to develop a plan for returning from dismissal.

A student who reenters the university by favorable action of the Academic Standards Committee after an academic dismissal is continued on probation after dismissal and

must make a semester grade-point average of at least 2.00 for each semester until the cumulative GPA reaches 2.00 and he or she is removed from probation. Failure to do so will result in academic dismissal.

Individual colleges or programs have the discretion to set academic admission and continuation standards for specific programs that are higher then university standards.

Students who are on Academic Dismissal can take Correspondence/Independent Study through the University of Arkansas Global Campus (and use their Grade Forgiveness) to raise their GPA. If their cumulative GPA is not a 2.00 or higher they would still have to petition Academic Standards to be readmitted. Students should contact their Academic Advisor before enrolling in any correspondence courses. See the Department of Independent Study for application and forms at: http://globalcampus.uark.edu/.

Global Campus
Department of Independent Study
2 East Center Street
Fayetteville, AR 72701
Phone: (479) 575-3604—Fax (479) 575-7232

Correspondence Course Rules

No more than 18 hours of course work taken by correspondence may apply toward a degree. These 18 hours may not include more than 12 hours of courses in economics or business, and may not include any junior- or senior-level economics or business courses without prior approval of the Assistant Dean for Undergraduate Programs.

SAT and ACT Requirements

English

- Students who score 19 or above on the English portion of the ACT (or 470 SAT verbal) may begin the English series with ENGL 1013. Students with scores below 19 (or 470 SAT verbal) must take ENGL 0002, Basic Writing with ENGL 1013.

- Students who score 30 or above on English portion of the ACT (or 680 SAT verbal) can be exempt from (ENGL 1013, and ENGL 1023 but must complete 6 additional hours of General Education Electives.

Math

- Students who score 18 or below on the math portion of the ACT (or 460 SAT math) must take MATH 0003, Beginning and Intermediate Algebra, before taking College Algebra (MATH 1203) or College Algebra with Review (MATH 1204). Students must make a grade of "C" or better in MATH 1203 College Algebra or MATH 1204 College Algebra with Review in order to take MATH 2053 Finite Math or MATH 2043 Survey of Calculus.

- Students who score 26 or above on the math portion of the ACT (or 600 SAT math) can skip College Algebra or College Algebra with Review and start with Finite Math or Survey of Calculus. Calculus I, MATH 2554 can substitute for Survey of Calculus (MATH 2043) and Calculus II, MATH 2564 can substitute for Finite Math (MATH 2053).

Minors in the J. William Fulbright College of Arts and Sciences

Students in Walton College may pursue an academic minor in the J. William Fulbright College of Arts and Sciences. Academic minors usually consist of 15 to 18 hours of course work. The available minors and course requirements are specified in the Fulbright College section of this catalog. Students must notify the Undergraduate Programs Office in Walton College of their intention to pursue a minor as early as possible. Walton College will certify that the requirements of the minor have been satisfied by graduation and, with the assistance of the Fulbright College, will advise students on the requirements to complete a minor. The minor will be designated on the student's transcript.

Courses that are part of the University Core Requirements or the additional General Education Requirements or any other non-business course that is part of a student's course of study may also be counted for credit in a minor. For example, ANTH 1023 Introduction to Cultural Anthropology is a concentration in the B.S.B.A. social science bloc and can also be used to satisfy the requirements of the anthropology minor. Other courses in a minor can be counted as general education electives. Walton College economics majors in the business economics concentration or the international economics and business concentration may not obtain a Fulbright College minor in economics. Please check the Catalog of Studies for a complete list of Arts and Sciences Minors.

Graduate Studies

The University of Arkansas offers the following advanced degrees in business: Master of Accountancy, Master of Business Administration, Master of Arts in Economics, Master of Information Systems, and various Doctor of Philosophy in Business Administration programs. For further information about these programs and requirements for admission, see the *Graduate School Catalog* or write to the Associate Director of Graduate Admissions, 310 WJWH.

Bachelor of Science in Business Administration (BSBA)

The Bachelor of Science in Business Administration degree is offered through an educational program in the business and organizational disciplines intended to prepare individuals to make sustained contributions to organizations and society in a global, diverse, and dynamic environment. To achieve this objective the curriculum focuses on developing an individual's interdisciplinary problem-solving skills, interpersonal and communication skills, ability to adapt to changing technology, spirit of entrepreneurial innovation, and ethical and professional values.

Walton College offers work in the following eight majors for the B.S.B.A. degree. Some majors have concentrations to allow additional specialization.

Accounting (ACCT)

Economics (ECON)
Concentration I—Business Economics
Concentration II—International Economics and Business

Finance (FINN)
Concentration I—Banking
Concentration II—Financial Management/Investment
Concentration III—Insurance
Concentration IV—Real Estate
Concentration V—Personal Financial Management

General Business (GBUS)

Information Systems (ISYS)
Concentration I—Enterprise Systems
Concentration II—IT Applications Management
Concentration III—Business Analytics

Management (MGMT)
Concentration I—Human Resource Management
Concentration II—Organizational Leadership
Concentration III—Small Business and Entrepreneurship

Marketing (MKTG)

Retail (RETL)

Supply Chain Management (SCMT)
Concentration I—Transportation and Logistics
Concentration II—Retail Supply Chain Management

Students pursuing a degree in Walton College are classified as pre-business with an intended major until all pre-business requirements are fulfilled. To enroll in upper-division courses, a student must obtain at least a 2.50 (on a 4.00 scale) overall grade-point average in addition to the completion of all pre-business core courses (or equivalents), also with a minimum 2.50 GPA. Further, a student must earn a grade of "C" or better in each pre-business core course for admission into the major or for the graduation requirement.

Bachelor of Science in International Business Degree (B.S.I.B.)

The Bachelor of Science in International Business degree is intended for students who wish to learn more about the international aspects of business. It provides preparation for a broad range of careers in business, including accounting, management, marketing, economics, information systems, finance, and supply chain management. This degree is also well suited for students wishing to continue their studies in law, international affairs, or graduate education in business and economics.

This degree requires completion of the University Core and Walton College Core courses, as well as course work in international business, a single foreign language and an area of study related to that language. In addition, students must select a concentration in one of the following areas: accounting, business economics, information systems, finance, general business, management, marketing, or supply chain management.

Students pursuing a degree in Walton College are classified as pre-business with an intended major until all pre-business requirements are fulfilled. To enroll in upper-division courses, a student must obtain at least a 2.50 (on a 4.00 scale) overall grade-point average in addition to the completion of all pre-business core courses (or equivalents), also with a minimum 2.50 GPA. Further, a student must earn a grade of "C" or better in each pre-business core course for admission into the major or for the graduation requirement.

Business Minors for Business Students

The Sam M. Walton College of Business offers a variety of business minors for students desiring specific knowledge in another area of business (outside of their major) to assist them in their business careers. Students may elect to obtain a business major and a business minor by completing all required courses for both the major and the minor in the Walton College (but not a major and minor within the same discipline). Students must complete all requirements for both the major and the minor and may not use more than six hours of major courses toward minor requirements. The minor requires the completion of 15 specific hours of study. All upper-division courses applied toward the minor must be taken in residence. Students who desire to earn a Business Minor must notify the Walton College Undergraduate Programs Office of intent to pursue the minor. All requirements for the minor must be completed prior to the awarding of the student's undergraduate degree. All specific course prerequisites must be met. Each student must have a 2.00 cumulative grade point in the courses offered for the minor.

CHAPTER 2

Study Abroad and Exchange Programs

Study abroad gives you an international dimension and a global perspective. It increases your understanding of other cultures. You gain a whole new perspective on your own culture. Students returning from study abroad programs have said they enjoyed meeting new people and seeing new places. They talk of new friends, travel adventures, and of how the experience was personally rewarding and enriching.

"Twenty years from now you will be more disappointed by the things you didn't do than by the ones you did do. So throw off the bowlines, sail away from the safe harbor. Catch the trade winds in your sails. Explore. Dream. Discover."—Mark Twain

There are countless reasons why everyone should study abroad. Here are the top ten according to AllAbroad.us:

1. See the world and broaden your experience.
2. Gain a new perspective on your own country.
3. Explore your heritage.
4. Learn a language in a country where it is spoken.
5. Improve your professional and financial potential.
6. Become a full-time learner.
7. Gain new insights and outlooks through new relationships.
8. Fight stereotypes by educating others.
9. Dispel your own stereotypes.
10. Take control of your future.

During your time abroad, you will be exposed to countless different experiences that may influence the rest of your life. Some students even end up changing their major or career path as a result of the new things they learn from being abroad. Others discover a newfound passion for travel, decide they want to work abroad, or desire to learn a new language. Elaine Chao, the Secretary of Labor, explains how her experiences in different cultures have influenced her career, "Memories of living in a developing nation are part of who I am today and give me a profound understanding of the challenges of economic development." After studying abroad, you may find your travels have had a profound influence on your career or personal goals. If you wish to continue with your higher education into either a Masters or a Doctorate, study abroad experience will give you an edge on the competition. Graduate programs, law schools, and med schools all look favorably on such global experience. You never know who may be impressed by your travels.

University of Arkansas Faculty-Led Programs (http://studyabroad.uark.edu/facultyled/)

- Students travel with at least one UA faculty member and fellow students.
- All participants will be assessed off-campus tuition and/or a program fee (this fee combines other expenses; i.e., lodging, local transportation, excursions, administrative fees, insurance), which will be placed on the student's ISIS account.

See the list below for some of our current faculty-led programs focusing on business and/or language.

Summer Programs

All summer programs are taught in English. Financial aid and scholarships are available to UA students. Visiting students must apply for financial aid through their home university. Business College students should request funding from the Walton College of Business. Honors students should apply for study abroad grants through the UA Honors College. Students should contact the UA Office of Study Abroad for applications and deadlines or visit the Honors website. Applications will be considered after this date on a space available basis. A deposit is required upon acceptance into the program. Applicants must have completed a minimum of 24 hours by the beginning of the program with a cumulative GPA of 2.6 or better. One academic recommendation from a faculty member or academic advisor is also required. Applicants must also have completed ECON 2013/2023 or ECON 2143. Prospective students will be interviewed and should display an academic record demonstrating maturity.

Brazil

Rio de Janeiro is one of the most beautiful and dynamic cities in the world. It combines unrivaled natural beauty with a rich and diverse culture. This culture is expressed in Rio's music, art, cuisine, and fun loving (somewhat disorganized) approach to life and business. This attitude creates special challenges for those seeking to do business. The program will provide students with insight into the economic, business, political, and cultural environment, and trends in Brazil. During the four-week program students will be introduced to key issues in the Brazilian/American economic and business relationship. Instruction will include both classroom and extramural activities. Guest lecturers will be from the business, academic, and political community. The course will be taught in English and guided by UA faculty. There will also be field trips to businesses, cultural and historical sites, and government institutions. The program includes ten hours of preparatory instruction at UA, giving students a background in Brazil's current business, political, and cultural environment, as well as some basic communication in Portuguese. It is important that program participants recognize that Rio (like many larger cities) has potential dangers as well.

Six hours of credit are offered at the undergraduate level. The program is intended for advanced undergraduate students in the Walton College of Business as well as interested students from other UA Colleges.

Cost of the program includes a program fee and six hours of UA tuition.

The program fee includes round trip airfare, hotel accommodation, transportation from the hotel to Ibmec-Rio for classes, and most expenses during group field trips. Passport fees, most meals, books, personal travel, and incidentals are not covered by the program fee. Program fees are subject to change.

China

Students investigate the economic, business, political, and cultural environment, and trends in China and are introduced to the key issues in the Chinese/American economic and business relationship. Courses will be taught primarily by Walton College faculty, with guest lecturers and international faculty from Fudan University and Northern Jiaotong University. Classes will be visited by executive speakers from businesses such as Wal-Mart, China. Students will visit multinational companies such as Coca-Cola, Johnson and Johnson, Unilever, Hormel, and Chinese companies such as the Shanghai Stock Exchange. Students will also tour cultural sites such as the Great Wall, Forbidden City, Hangzhou Gardens, the Summer Palace, Tienanmen Square, and Mao's Memorial Hall.

Six hours of credit are offered at the undergraduate level. The program is intended for advanced undergraduate students in the Walton College of Business as well as interested students from other UA Colleges.

Cost of the program includes a program fee and six hours of UA tuition. The program fee includes group airfare from Fayetteville and transfer from Shanghai to Beijing, hotel room (double occupancy) in Shanghai and Beijing on the campuses of Fudan University and Northern Jiaotong University, meals while on cultural excursions, cultural excursions, visits to multinational companies, guest executive speakers, guest faculty speakers, and Chinese student hosts. Passport and visa fees, personal expenses, or meals while in town are not covered by the program fee. Program fees are subject to change.

Greece

The Greece study abroad program is appropriate for both the novice international traveler and the experienced traveler, and for those students who wish to study international business focused on Europe, and specifically Greece, as a part of the European Union. Students of the Greece study abroad program explore the Greek economic, business, political, and cultural environment and trends; students are introduced to the key issues in the Greek/American economic and business (e-business) relationship. This program provides students with insights into the business, political, and technological environment in the European Union, as well as a chance to experience Greek culture. During the four-week program, students will be introduced to key issues in the Greek/American economic and business relationship. Guest lecturers will be from the business, academic, and political community. Students will receive six credit hours through courses taught in English and guided by UA faculty. The program is intended for advanced undergraduate students in the Walton College of Business as well as interested students from other UA Colleges.

The program includes ten hours of preparatory instruction at UA, giving students a background in Greece's current business, political, technological, and cultural environment. There will also be field trips to businesses, cultural and historical sites, and government institutions (i.e., a four-day, three-night excursion to Santorini; visits to local businesses such as IBM, CERES Shipping, and others; plus a visit to the U.S. Embassy and the European Union, as well as an organized tour around Athens).

Cost of the program includes a program fee, which includes group internal transfers, lodging, breakfast, business visits, and the four-day/three-night island tour. Students will share hotel rooms with two to three other students during the trip. The base location is the Palmyra Beach Hotel, located in the Athens suburb of Glyfada. Airfare, passport fees, two meals per day, books, personal travel, and incidentals are not covered by the program fee. Program fees are subject to change.

Italy

The Italy summer program is unique in that students will take classes at a university made up of a consortium of universities from around the world. The program and campus is known as CIMBA (Consortium of Universities for International Studies). CIMBA offers both semester and summer study abroad programs for undergraduate students. Both programs provide students with a valuable international experience, while staying on track for graduation at their home universities. Students generally come from Consortium-member universities across the country, but students attending other institutions are welcome and often participate. Most students major in some area of business, economics, journalism, or communication studies. However, students majoring in everything from art and history to biology and engineering have participated in the programs. All classes are taught in English, thus eliminating the language barrier to learning. The CIMBA Italy program offers students the unique experience of learning abroad, while providing high-quality upper-division courses in a variety of subjects. The summer program provides an introduction to international studies for many students, while continuing to enhance the education of students already possessing international experience. Travel time, in the form of two long weekends, is built into the program to encourage students to explore Europe on their own. Students also are encouraged to participate in lectures, plant tours, and CIMBA's unique personal development opportunities to enhance their educational experience.

Six hours of credit are offered at the undergraduate level for the summer program and 15 hours for the semester. The program is intended for advanced undergraduate students in the Walton College of Business. Students will work hard during the week, but if they plan properly, they should have time to participate in extracurricular activities as well. Additionally, the professors schedule assignments so students do not have complex projects right after a long travel weekend.

Cost of the program includes a program fee. The program fee includes the application fee, six hours of UA tuition (and 15 hours for the semester), a campus fee, housing, and a meal package consisting of breakfast, lunch, and dinner each class day. The campus fee includes textbook usage, materials, technology connection, linens and towels, housekeeping, laundry tokens, a bus pass, and an activities/excursion pass. Not included are personal expenses, special trips that may be planned, airfare, or travel within Europe. Students who wish to purchase their course texts can do so for a nominal fee at the end of the summer program. All costs are based on a projected Euro rate and are subject to change.

The Consortium has a number of both merit- and need-based financial awards available for students attending CIU programs. Accepted students must contact the Consortium Office at the University of Iowa for more information. Details can be found at www.cimbaitaly.com.

Ireland

Ireland is a beautiful and welcoming country with a deep history and strong cultural ties to the United States. This study abroad is appropriate for both the novice international traveler and the experienced one. Your English is understood by everyone, though you will pick up new phrases and perhaps even a bit of their charming accent and a few words of Irish (Gaelic). Ireland is the perfect introduction to international travel.

The study abroad program will provide students with insights into Irish culture and history as well as international business and the economic environment in the European Union. University College Dublin will serve as host to the program, with several excursions planned to accounting firms, multinational companies, and destinations outside of the city, including Galway, Clonmcnoise, and Newgrange. Course Area Offered: WCOB 410V (6 credit hours): Special Topics: "Business in Ireland and the EU," COURSE INFORMATION: Accommodations: Participants will stay in student (single) housing at University College Dublin, and hotels (double) during excursions. Excursions: Students will have the opportunity to go on visits to business enterprises and cultural attractions in Dublin and the surrounding areas.

Japan

This program is designed to immerse the student in a living classroom experience with the Japanese economic system. Japan is a very beautiful and exciting country with extraordinarily friendly people. You will meet individuals from all walks of life, including several CEOs, VPs, politicians, mom and pop restaurant owners, housewives, farmers, a world renowned potter, engineers, and teachers. Students can enjoy the exciting nightlife of Tokyo, known as the Paris of the Orient, and certainly one of the world's most energetic cities. Witness the lights of Ginza at the top of the most exclusive shopping districts in the world, or visit Shibuya, the world's busiest street crossing; these are just a few of the many opportunities available to students.

The Japan study abroad program is taught in English by Dr. Robert Stapp of the Walton College of Business. Students will have audiences with top executives of multinational companies such as Sanyo, Toyota Motor Company, Mazda, Sharp, Kirin, NEC, Mitsui Engineering and Shipbuilding, Daiwa Steel, and Oyatsu, along with various attaches of the U.S. Embassy in Tokyo among others. Students will also visit the Arkansas Economic Development Commission. Cultural activities will include rice planting, pottery, a Hanshin Tigers baseball game, and martial arts such as Kendo (the way of the sword) and Kyudo (the way of the bow and arrow), Kodo (world renowned Taiko Drum Group), and Hibi Elementary School. Students will also have three nights of home stays with a Japanese family. Students will visit sites such as the Golden Pavilion, the Peace Park in Hiroshima, Todaij (the largest all-wood structure in the world, housing the largest Buddha statue in Japan),

Shinto Shrines, Himeji Castle, Matsuri Festivals, and Hiezan Temple will be explored. We will visit the following cities: Kyoto, Osaka, Nara, Hiroshima, Toyota City, Tamano City, Kameoka, Tokyo, Takayama, and Sapporo.

Six hours of credit are offered at the undergraduate level. The program is intended for advanced undergraduate students in the Walton College of Business as well as interested students from other UA Colleges. Cost of the program includes a program fee and six hours of UA tuition. The program fee includes group airfare from Fayetteville, and transfers within Japan, all lodging (double occupancy), some meals, cultural excursions, home stay with Japanese families, visits to multinational companies, guest faculty speakers, and visits to various business sites. Not included are UA tuition, passport fees, one to two meals per day, and personal expenses. Program fees are subject to change.

India

This program involves an intense study about the business environment in India. In order to appreciate the nuances of dealing with India, students are exposed to the history and culture of India, and the course culminates with a two and a half week trip to India, where many of the concepts learned in the course are personally experienced. The prep for this course includes exposing students to lectures, presentations, Indian movies, and panel discussions. Students do research that is then presented at these classes. While in India, students visit cultural sites that include the famous Taj Mahal, wildlife sanctuaries, ancient temples, activities with students at our partner schools, visits to an orphanage and NGO that we work with, and business visits to companies such as Walmart, WIPRO (one of the world's largest IT companies), and talks from individuals from business and other leadership positions. We also arrange interactions with local families to maximize your exposure to Indian culture. Several fun activities such as playing cricket are also included.

Six hours of credit are offered at the undergraduate level. The program fee includes round trip airfare from Fayetteville to Delhi, lodging (double occupancy), most meals, most excursions, health insurance, visa and administrative fees, visits to multinational companies, guest faculty speakers, and visits to various business sites. Not included are passport fees, some meals, and personal expenses. Program fees are subject to change.

Panama

Global supply chain management is increasingly important for firms as they strive to compete in today's global business environment. While supply chain management has captured the attention and interest of higher-level executives, the complexities of the global environment complicate the management task. Some of this is due to issues of sovereignty: every country has the right to impose whatever rules and requirements it wishes concerning the regulation of business within and across its borders. Cultural differences between nations further complicate the nature of business relationships and transactions. Moreover, the global transportation infrastructure presents a significant challenge, as ocean and intermodal carriers are often faced with extraordinary issues and costs to manage. Within this context, this course will address issues relating to the drivers of globalization and managing supply/demand fulfillment and transportation processes across an extended and global organization.

Community Development: Belize

In February 2006, representatives of the University visited Belize to become more familiar with the social, economic, and cultural environment of the country. Afterward, the University of Arkansas entered into a partnership with the community of Dangriga, and through Peacework for education, service, and economic development involving seven colleges and departments of the University.

University of Arkansas faculty project leaders will instruct students in a practicum in their specific fields of study, where they have the opportunity to consult with community partners to prepare and develop the projects that will take place each summer in Dangriga and throughout the year, and implement service learning projects during the first UA summer session in the community of Dangriga, a city of about 10,000 on the Caribbean coast.

The expectations are high, but the reward is a deep understanding of the challenges of working in a developing country, an amazing cultural immersion, and the experience of leadership and accomplishment as students work creatively to face unexpected roadblocks in their work.

Projects are currently being planned for the oral history, business, engineering, nutrition, literacy, and health professions. All projects will be open to students of all majors, and they can either receive credit in the project area in which they work or general humanities credits.

Accommodations: Students will be staying in a few different hotels located in Dangriga (some rooms have air-condition upgrade possibilities, most do not). Rooms are typically two to three students/room. For most meals, local women will be cooking large meals for the group dinners; vegetarian options will be available. Please note: you will want to bring bug spray and light, long sleeves to ward off any unwelcome advances by insects.

Excursions: Students will have the opportunity to participate in various cultural events around Dangriga, as well as two weekend excursions coordinated by Peacework. Typically, these excursions have been to an in-land spot as well as a coastal or island town in Belize.

Community Development: Ghana

Students will not only be living in and learning about African culture, they also will be studying and utilizing African business and governmental practices. Students will hear from business leaders of companies headquartered in Ghana (e.g. SOFTTribe) and US companies that have presence in Ghana (for example CocaCola and IBM). These leaders will represent several industries such as banking and finance, consumer products, energy, mining and technology.

Community Development: Mozambique

This unique program is an international interdisciplinary service learning project, for six credit hours, in Nampula, Mozambique, during Summer Session I. Agriculture, business, and engineering students will work together in a poultry business that is intended to be a model for sustainable economic development. Students will learn first-hand of the challenges in creating sustainable business in this challenging environment as well as to apply their skills creatively to improve the business.

This will offer tremendous capacity for not only experiential learning, but also leadership and creativity. Finally, the cultural experience will be tremendous, as students will be working side by side with local community members in this business. The expectations on students will be high, and the work will be difficult, but for uniquely dedicated students, this will hopefully be an unbelievable experience

Course Areas Offered: Projects are currently being planned for business, engineering, and agriculture. All projects will be open to students of all majors, and they can either receive credit in the project area in which they work or general humanities credits.

Excursions: Two weekend excursions to the Indian Ocean are included in the program fee. At the conclusion of the program, a two- to three-day safari in South Africa is being planned before students return to the U.S.

Community Development: Vietnam

This unique program is a NEW international service learning project (following the well-established principles of Global Community Development on campus), for 6 credit hours, in Vietnam during Summer Session I. Projects are currently being planned for agriculture, business, the humanities, & the social sciences. All majors are welcome as projects can be designed to fit a student's needs.

University of Arkansas Reciprocal Exchange Programs (http://studyabroad.uark.edu/exchange/)

- Students will be assessed tuition and fees at the same rate as a full-time course load at the University of Arkansas.
- Payment of room, board, and personal expenses vary according to program/location, but are usually equivalent to living costs paid here.
- For the more independent student traveler extra excursions may be added and cost will vary accordingly.

See the list below for some of our current opportunities to study business and/or language.

Australia

University of Newcastle (*Fall, Spring, or Academic Year*). If you are looking for an exciting and intellectually stimulating place to study—one that introduces you to the real Australia—look no further than Newcastle and the Central Coast regions in New South Wales. Newcastle combines a country setting with all the advantages of city living, while the Central Coast offers abundant beaches and easy access to Sydney. Undergraduate credit available.

Austria

Karl-Franzens Universitaet, Graz (*Fall, Spring, or Academic Year*). A full university for students who would like to take business courses in German; limited courses, usually focusing on political science or international relations, offered in English. Karl-Franzens Universitaet offers you a unique German learning experience. KFU has courses offered daily in the beautiful Styria region, where "Styrish" German is everywhere. The town of Graz is widely known for its natural beauty, with rivers, lakes, and mountains all around it. Students have the opportunity to explore the area with fellow students from KFU, the majority of who are Austrian, but who may also be from numerous countries around the world. Undergraduate and Graduate credit available.

England

University of Essex Internationalism is central to who we are and what we do. Our global community is a place that fuses ideas, cultures and a breadth of perspectives. We're about people who love to learn how, but want to challenge why. If you are tenacious, bold, inquisitive and impatient for change, welcome home. (need to fix this on the main SA web site it says: This program is currently not accepting applications.

University of Sussex From its foundation, Sussex has had an international perspective to its academic activities and its outlook. The University attracts staff and students to its campus from over 120 different countries across the world. Nearly a third of staff come from outside the UK.

Denmark

Aarhus School of Business (*Fall, Spring, or Academic Year*). A business school for students who would like exposure to a very high-quality research and research-based study program. Many courses are taught in English, as they offer full Bachelor and Master programs in business administration and communication exclusively taught in English. Undergraduate credit available.

France

NEOMA Business School, Reims NEOMA Business School thus positions itself as the preferred partner of business, answering the problems and challenges they face and helping them to improve their performance. Its mission will thus be to educate and accompany future entrepreneurs and managers, capable of responsible leadership and of going beyond prevailing models. FREN 1013 required before you go.

Germany

WHU Otto Beisheim School of Management, Koblenz (*Fall, Spring, Summer, or Academic Year*). WHU is an internationally oriented and privately financed business school. Since its establishment, WHU has proved itself to be a paragon of future-oriented research and teaching in business administration hosting about 1,000 students. WHU's international network includes more than 170 partner universities all over the world. Undergraduate and Graduate credit available.

Japan

Kansai Gaidai University, Osaka (*Academic Year*). Students will be enrolled in the Asian Studies Program at Kansai Gaidai University. Intensive Japanese language courses, plus a wide variety of liberal arts and business courses taught in English are offered. Additionally, students will participate in the Homestay Program. Kansai Gaidai University is located in Hirakata City, Osaka, and is accessible, within a one-hour train ride, to Kyoto and Nara, the ancient capitals, and Osaka, the second largest business hub in Japan. Undergraduate credit available.

Kanto Gakuin University, Yokohama (*Fall*). Students will be enrolled in intensive Japanese language courses plus some courses focusing on culture and history. Additionally, students will participate in the Homestay Program. Living with a Japanese family will provide students with not only an environment to develop their language skills, but also opportunities to understand the daily life, values, and customs of the Japanese people, which will inevitably enhance what they have acquired in the classroom. Undergraduate credit available.

Shimane University, Matsue City (*Spring or Academic Year*). Students can spend an academic year or a spring semester studying at Shimane University in Matsue. Students are able to pick from a wide variety of liberal arts and business courses offered in Japanese. Shimane Prefecture has been essentially unchanged for centuries, and provides a unique view of Japanese traditions and culture not available anywhere else. Undergraduate credit available.

South Korea

Soonchunhyang University, Asan Chungnam (*Fall, Spring, or Academic Year*). Students intern as a "cultural and language ambassador" and serve as a conversation partner attending group meetings, the language and cultural exchange center, and by living side by side with Korean students in specially designated dorms. Internship duties will be up to 15 hours/week. Undergraduate credit available.

Spain

Universidad Carlos III de Madrid, Madrid (*Fall, Spring, or Academic Year*). Exchange students can come to the University to study in Spanish or in English, as UC3M offers several Bachelor and Master programs in English. UC3M and Madrid are lively and exciting environments in which you will learn and enjoy. Undergraduate credit available.

Sweden

Jonkoping School of Business, Jonkoping (*Fall, Spring, or Academic Year*). JIBS is the most international business school in Sweden and one of the most international in the world. With over 750 international students from 75 different countries, the campus is a mini United Nations. With one-third of the students and faculty coming from countries outside Scandinavia, they host students and faculty from over 75 countries. Their programs on all three levels: Bachelor, Master, and Doctoral, are delivered in English. Undergraduate credit available.

More to come:
The Walton College is currently developing relationships with other business schools in China, Brazil, Vietnam, Russia, and Panama, so keep watching for more exchange programs in the future.

Outside Program Providers (http://study abroad.uark.edu/)

- Students will be assessed a program fee, to cover tuition and fees, by the program provider.
- Students will pay the University a small fee (usually $100–$200) to study abroad.
- Payment of room, board, and personal expenses vary according to program/location.
- For the traveler looking for additional support in-country; most providers have an office or a group of individuals overseeing each program.

Financing Your Study Abroad

There are many financial resources available; and to help you realize your dream of studying abroad, we've tried to offer you a good start to your search in this section.

"If there is one advice I can offer about scholarships it is to get started early. One of the most beneficial things I did was setting a designated time to complete scholarships. I committed my Friday evenings and Saturday mornings to searching for scholarships, writing essays, and filling out applications. I missed out on parties and other social events, but it was well worth it once I started to read my scholarship award notification letters." Thoughts from a Recent Study Abroad Student

In many cases, the scholarships and financial aid that you currently use to pay for your education may be used for study abroad.

Most UA scholarships may be applied toward study abroad costs.

- Some exceptions may apply for athletic scholarships.
- If you plan to use your UA academic scholarships, please inform the Scholarships Office that you will study abroad. Recipients of the Governor's award should contact Mary Willis at 479-575-2227.
- You may defer your scholarship disbursement to a later semester by contacting the Scholarships Office.
- Contact the administrators of any outside scholarship awards to determine if they can be applied to your study abroad costs. Usually you are able to use these scholarships if you can prove you will receive credit, which our office can provide for approved programs.

Federal financial aid may be applied toward the costs of study abroad programs that meet these criteria:

- Program is approved by Office of Study Abroad.
- Enrollment in full-time courses during the period abroad.

Federal aid includes (but is not limited to) Pell Grants, Stafford, and Perkins Loans.

- These awards may be applied to approved study abroad programs.
- Do not rule out federal aid if you have previously been unsuccessful. Study abroad can increase your education costs, which may result in a financial aid award.
- To determine if you are eligible to receive financial aid you must have a current FAFSA form completed on file. This form may be found online at: http://www.fafsa.ed.gov/ or visit the Office of Financial Aid located in Silas Hunt Hall.
- Set an appointment with your financial aid counselor to discuss your options. Be sure to bring a copy of your budget (see Budgets section) with you to this meeting.
- Students applying for summer aid may need to complete supplemental forms. Contact the Office of Financial Aid for more information.

For more information on disbursement arrangements and the process, check out the Paying for your Program section under Prepare to Go Abroad on the study abroad website (http://studyabroad.uark.edu/).

For additional information on studying abroad, please contact:

The Office of Study Abroad & International Exchange Office
http://studyabroad.uark.edu/
479.575.7582
studyabroad@uark.edu
722 West Maple Street, on the University of Arkansas Campus
Experience study abroad!

CHAPTER 3

Managing Time and Money

Learning Objectives

Read to answer these key questions:

- What are my lifetime goals?

- How can I manage my time to accomplish my goals?

- How much time do I need for study and work?

- How can I make an effective schedule?

- What are some time management tricks?

- How can I deal with procrastination?

- How can I manage my money to accomplish my financial goals?

- What are some ways to save money?

- How can I pay for my education?

- How can I use priorities to manage my time?

Success in college requires that you manage both time and money. You will need time to study and money to pay for your education. The first step in managing time and money is to think about the goals that you wish to accomplish in your life. Having goals that are important to you provides a reason and motivation for managing time and money. This chapter provides some useful techniques for managing time and money so that you can accomplish the goals you have set for yourself.

What Are My Lifetime Goals?

Setting goals helps you to establish what is important and provides direction for your life. Goals help you to focus your energy on what you want to accomplish. Goals are a promise to yourself to improve your life. Setting goals can help you turn your dreams into reality. Steven Scott, in his book *A Millionaire's Notebook,* lays out five steps in this process:

1. Dream or visualize.

2. Convert the dream into goals.

3. Convert your goals into tasks.

4. Convert your task into steps.

5. Take your first step, and then the next.[1]

As you begin to think about your personal goals in life, make your goals specific and concrete. Rather than saying, "I want to be rich," make your goal something that you can break into specific steps. You might want to start learning about money management or begin a savings plan. Rather than setting a goal for happiness, think about what brings you happiness. If you want to live a long and healthy life, think about the health habits that will help you to accomplish your goal. You will need to break your goals down into specific tasks to be able to accomplish them.

Here are some criteria for successful goal setting:

1. **Is it achievable?** Do you have the skills, abilities, and resources to accomplish this goal? If not, are you willing to spend the time to develop the skills, abilities, and resources needed to achieve this goal?

2. **Is it realistic?** Do you believe you can achieve it? Are you positive and optimistic about this goal?

3. **Is it specific and measurable?** Can it be counted or observed? The most common goal mentioned by students is happiness in life. What is happiness, and how will you know when you have achieved it? Is happiness a career you enjoy, owning your own home, or a travel destination?

4. **Do you want to do it?** Is this a goal you are choosing because it gives you personal satisfaction, rather than meeting a requirement or an expectation of someone else?

5. **Are you motivated to achieve it?** What are your rewards for achieving it?

6. **Does the goal match your values?** Is it important to you?

7. **What steps do you need to take to begin?** Are you willing to take action to start working on it?

8. **When will you finish this goal?** Set a date to accomplish your goal.

"A goal is a dream with a deadline."
Napoleon Hill

Write a paragraph about your lifetime goals. Use any of these questions to guide your thinking:

- What is your career goal? If you do not know what your career goal is, describe your preferred work environment. Would your ideal career require a college degree?

- What are your family goals? Are you interested in marriage and family? What would be your important family values?

- What are your social goals (friends, community, and recreation)?

- When you are older and look back on your life, what are the three most important life goals that you want to have accomplished?

A Goal or a Fantasy?

One of the best questions ever asked in my class was, "What is the difference between a goal and a fantasy?" As you look at your list of lifetime goals, are some of these items goals or fantasies? Think about this question as you read the following scenario:

When Linda was a college student, she was walking through the parking lot, noticed a beautiful red sports car, and decided that it would become a lifetime goal for her to own a similar car one day. However, with college expenses and her part-time job, it was not possible to buy the car. She would have to be content with the used car that her dad had given her so that she could drive to college. Years passed by, and Linda now has a good job, a home, and a family. She is reading a magazine and sees a picture of a similar red sports car. She cuts out this picture and tapes it to the refrigerator. After it has been on the refrigerator for several months, her children ask her why the picture is on the refrigerator. Linda replies, "I just like to dream about owning this car." One day, as Linda is driving past a car dealership, she sees the red sports car on display and stops in for a test drive. To her surprise, she decides that she does not like driving the car. It doesn't fit her lifestyle, either. She enjoys outdoor activities that would require a larger car. Buying a second car would be costly and reduce the amount of money that the family could spend on vacations. She decides that vacations are more important than owning the sports car. Linda goes home and removes the picture of the red sports car from the refrigerator.

There are many differences between a goal and a fantasy. A fantasy is a dream that may or may not become a reality. A goal is something that we actually plan to achieve. Sometimes we begin with a fantasy and later it becomes a goal. A fantasy can become a goal if steps are taken to achieve it. In the preceding example, the sports car is a fantasy until Linda actually takes the car for a test drive. After driving the car, she decides that she really does not want it. The fantasy is sometimes better than the reality. Goals and fantasies change over a lifetime. We set goals, try them out, and change them as we grow and mature and find out what is most important in life. Knowing what we think is important, and what we value most, helps us make good decisions about lifetime goals.

What is the difference between a goal and a fantasy? A goal is something that requires action. Ask yourself if you are willing to take action on the goals you have set for yourself. Begin to take action by thinking about the steps needed to accomplish the goal. Then take the first step and continue. Change your goals if they are no longer important to you.

"Vision without action is a daydream. Action without vision is a nightmare."
Japanese Proverb

"In life, as in football, you won't go far unless you know where the goalposts are."

Arnold Glasgow

Write a paragraph about how you will accomplish one of your important lifetime goals. Start your paragraph by stating an important goal from the previous journal entry. What is the first step in accomplishing this goal? Next, list some additional steps needed to accomplish it. How can you motivate yourself to begin taking these steps?

For example:

One of my important lifetime goals is _____. The first step in accomplishing this goal is . . . Some additional steps are . . . I can motivate myself to accomplish this goal by . . .

The ABCs of Time Management

Using the **ABCs of time management** is a way of thinking about priorities. Priorities are what you think is important. An **A priority** is a task that relates to your lifetime goal. For example, if my goal is to earn a college degree, studying becomes an A priority. This activity would become one of the most important tasks that I could accomplish today. If my goal is to be healthy, an A priority would be to exercise and plan a healthy diet. If my goal is to have a good family life, an A priority would be to spend time with family members. Knowing about your lifetime goals and spending time on those items that are most important to you will help you to accomplish the goals that you have set for yourself. If you do not spend time on your goals, you may want to look at them again and decide which ones are fantasies that you do not really value or want to accomplish.

A **B priority** is an activity that you have to do, but that is not directly related to your lifetime goal. Examples of B priorities might be getting out of bed, taking a shower, buying groceries, paying bills, or getting gas for the car. These activities are less important, but still are necessary for survival. If I do not put gas in the car, I cannot even get to school or work. If I do not pay the bills, I will soon have financial difficulties. While we often cannot postpone these activities in order to accomplish lifetime goals, we can learn efficient time management techniques to accomplish these tasks quickly.

A **C priority** is something that I can postpone until tomorrow with no harmful effect. For example, I could wait until tomorrow or another day to wash my car, do the laundry, buy groceries, or organize my desk. As these items are postponed, however, they can move up the list to a B priority. If I cannot see out of my car window or have no clean clothes to wear, it is time to move these tasks up on my list of priorities.

Have you ever been a victim of "**C fever**"? This is an illness in which we do the C activities first and do not get around to doing the A activities that are connected to lifetime goals. Tasks required to accomplish lifetime goals are often ones that are more difficult, challenge our abilities, and take some time to accomplish. These tasks are often more difficult than the B or C activities. The C activities can fill our time and exhaust the energy we need to accomplish the A activities. An example of C fever is the student who cleans the desk or organizes the CD collection instead of studying. C fever is doing the endless tasks that keep us from accomplishing goals that are really important to us. Why do we fall victim to C fever? C activities are often easy to do and give us a sense of accomplishment. We can see immediate progress without too much effort. I can wash my car and get a sense of accomplishment and satisfaction in my shiny clean car. The task is easy and does not challenge my intellectual capabilities.

ACTIVITY

Setting Priorities

To see how the ABCs of time management work, read the profile of Justin, a typical college student, below.

Justin is a 19-year-old college student who plans to major in physical therapy. He is athletic and values his good health. He cares about people and likes helping others. He has a part-time job working as an assistant in the gym, where he monitors proper use of the weightlifting machines. Justin is also a member of the soccer team and practices with the team every afternoon.

Here is a list of activities that Justin would like to do today. Label each task as follows:

A if it relates to Justin's lifetime goals
B if it is something necessary to do
C if it is something that could be done tomorrow or later

_____ Get up, shower, get dressed	_____ Study for biology test that is tomorrow
_____ Eat breakfast	_____ Meet friends for pizza at lunch
_____ Go to work	_____ Call girlfriend
_____ Go to class	_____ Eat dinner
_____ Visit with friends between classes	_____ Unpack gear from weekend camping trip
_____ Buy a new battery for his watch	_____ Watch football game on TV
_____ Go shopping for new gym shoes	_____ Play video games
_____ Attend soccer practice	_____ Do math homework
_____ Do weightlifting exercises	

While Justin is the only one who can decide how to spend his time, he can take some steps toward accomplishing his lifetime goal of being healthy by eating properly, exercising, and going to soccer practice. He can become a physical therapist by studying for the biology test and doing his math homework. He can gain valuable experience related to physical therapy by working in the gym. He cares about people and likes to maintain good relationships with others. Any tasks related to these goals are high-priority A activities.

What other activities are necessary B activities? He certainly needs to get up, shower, and get dressed. What are the C activities that could be postponed until tomorrow or later? Again, Justin needs to decide. Maybe he could postpone shopping for a new watch battery and gym shoes until the weekend. He would have to decide how much time to spend visiting with friends, watching TV, or playing video games. Since he likes these activities, he could use them as rewards for studying for the biology test and doing his math homework.

How to Estimate Study and Work Time

Students are often surprised at the amount of time necessary for study to be successful in college. A general rule is that you need to study two hours for every hour spent in a college class. A typical weekly schedule of a full-time student would look like this:

Typical College Schedule

> 15 hours of attending class
> +30 hours of reading, studying, and preparation
> _____
> 45 hours total

A full-time job involves working 40 hours a week. A full-time college student spends 45 hours or more attending classes and studying. Some students will need more than 45 hours a week if they are taking lab classes, need help with study and learning skills, or are taking a heavy course load.

Some students try to work full-time and go to school full-time. While some are successful, this schedule is extremely difficult.

The Nearly Impossible Schedule

> 15 hours attending class
> 30 hours studying
> +40 hours working
> _____
> 85 hours total

This schedule is the equivalent of having two full-time jobs! Working full-time makes it very difficult to find the time necessary to study for classes. Lack of study causes students to do poorly on exams and to doubt their abilities. Such a schedule causes stress and fatigue that make studying difficult. Increased stress can also lead to problems with personal relationships and emotional problems. These are all things that lead to dropping out of college.

Many students today work and go to college. Working during college can provide some valuable experience that will help you to find a job when you finish college. Working can teach you to manage your time efficiently and give you a feeling of independence and control over your own future. Many people need to work to pay for their education. A general guideline is to work no more than 20 hours a week if you plan to attend college full-time. Here is a workable schedule.

Part-Time Work Schedule

> 12 hours attending class
> 24 hours studying
> +20 hours working
> _____
> 56 hours total

A commitment of 56 hours a week is like having a full-time job and a part-time job. While this schedule takes extra energy and commitment, many students are successful with it. Notice that the course load is reduced to 12 hours. This schedule involves taking one less class per semester. The class missed can be made up in summer school, or the time needed to graduate can be extended. Many students take five years to earn the bachelor's degree because they work part-time. It is better to take longer to graduate than to drop out of college or to give up because of frustration. If you must work full-time, consider reducing your course load to one or two courses. You will gradually reach your goal of a college degree.

Part-Time Student Schedule

        6 hours attending class
       12 hours studying
    +40 hours working
       58 hours total

Add up the number of hours you are attending classes, double this figure for study time, and add to it your work time, as in the above examples. How many hours of commitment do you have? Can you be successful with your current level of commitment to school, work, and study?

To begin managing your schedule, use the weekly calendar located at the end of this chapter to write in your scheduled activities such as work, class times, and athletics.

> "The bad news is time flies. The good news is you're the pilot."
> Michael Althsuler

Schedule Your Success

If you have not used a schedule in the past, consider trying a schedule for a couple of weeks to see if it is helpful in completing tasks and working toward your lifetime goals. There are several advantages to using a schedule:

- It gets you started on your work.
- It helps you avoid procrastination.
- It relieves pressure because you have things under control.
- It frees the mind of details.
- It helps you find time to study.
- It eliminates the panic caused by doing things at the last minute.
- It helps you find time for recreation and exercise.

Once you have made a master schedule that includes classes, work, and other activities, you will see that you have some blanks that provide opportunities for using your time productively. Here are some ideas for making the most of your schedule:

1. Fill in your study times. Use the time immediately before class for previewing and the time immediately after class for reviewing. Remember that you need to study two hours or more for each hour spent in a college class.

2. Break large projects such as a term paper or test into small tasks and begin early. Double your time estimates for completion of the project. Larger projects often take longer than you think. If you finish early, use the extra time for something fun.

3. Use the daylight hours when you are most alert for studying. It may take you longer to study if you wait until late in the day when you're tired.

4. Think about your day and see if you can determine when you are most alert and awake. Prime time differs with individuals, but it is generally earlier in the day. Use the prime time when you are most alert to accomplish your most challenging tasks. For example, do your math homework during prime time. Wash your clothes during nonprime time, when you are likely to be less alert.

5. Set priorities. Make sure you include activities related to your lifetime goals.

6. Allow time for sleep and meals. It is easier to study if you are well rested and have good eating habits.

7. Schedule your time in manageable blocks of an hour or two. Having every moment scheduled leads to frustration when plans change.

> "The only thing even in this world is the number of hours in a day. The difference in winning or losing is what you do with these hours."
> Woody Hayes

8. Leave some time unscheduled to use as a shock absorber. You will need unscheduled time to relax and to deal with unexpected events.

9. Leave time for recreation, exercise, and fun.

Return to the schedule at the end of this chapter. After you have written in classes, work times, and other scheduled activities, use the scheduling ideas listed earlier to write in your study times and other activities related to your lifetime goals. Leave some unscheduled time to provide flexibility in the schedule.

If You Dislike Schedules

Some personality types like more freedom and do not like the structure that a schedule provides. There are alternatives for those who do not like to use a schedule. Here are some additional ideas.

1. A simple and fast way to organize your time is to use a to-do list. Take an index card or small piece of paper and simply write a list of what you need to do during the day. You can prioritize the list by putting an A or star by the most important items. Cross items off the list as you accomplish them. A list helps you focus on what is important and serves as a reminder not to forget certain tasks.

2. Another idea is to use monthly or yearly calendars to write down important events, tasks, and deadlines. Use these calendars to note the first day of school, when important assignments are due, vacations, and final exams. Place the calendars in a place where they are easily seen.

3. Alan Lakein, who wrote a book titled *How to Get Control of Your Time and Your Life*, suggests a simple question to keep you on track.[2] Lakein's question is, "What is the best use of my time right now?" This question works well if you keep in mind your goals and priorities.

4. Use reminders and sticky notes to keep on track and to remind yourself of what needs to be done each day. Place the notes in a place where you will see them, such as your computer, the bathroom mirror, or the dashboard of your car.

5. Some families use their refrigerators as time management devices. Use the refrigerator to post your calendars, reminders, goals, tasks, and to-do lists. You will see these reminders every time you open the refrigerator.

6. Invent your own unique ideas for managing time. Anything will work if it helps to accomplish your goals.

Manage Your Time with a Web Application

There are thousands of new web applications available to organize your life. You can use a web application on your phone, laptop, computer, or other mobile device to:

- Create a to-do list or schedule.
- Send reminders when assignments are due.
- Organize your calendar and plan your tasks.
- Organize your study time and plan assignments.
- Avoid procrastination.
- Create a virtual assistant to keep you organized.

Time Management, Part I

Test what you have learned by selecting the correct answers to the following questions.

1. The most important difference between a goal and a fantasy is

    a. imagination.
    b. procrastination.
    c. action.

2. An A priority is

    a. related to your lifetime goals.
    b. something important.
    c. something you have to do.

3. A general rule for college success is that you must spend ___ hours studying for every hour spent in a college class.

    a. one
    b. four
    c. two

4. For a workable study schedule,

    a. fill in all the blank time slots.
    b. leave some unscheduled time to deal with the unexpected.
    c. plan to study late at night.

5. To complete a large project such as a term paper,

    a. break the project into small tasks and begin early.
    b. schedule large blocks of time the day before the paper is due.
    c. leave time for exercise, recreation, and fun before beginning on the project.

How did you do on the quiz? Check your answers: 1. c, 2. a, 3. c, 4. b, 5. a

Time Management Tricks

Life is full of demands for work, study, family, friends, and recreation. Time management tricks can help you get started on the important tasks and make the most of your time. Try the following techniques when you are feeling frustrated and overwhelmed.

Divide and Conquer

When large tasks seem overwhelming, think of the small tasks needed to complete the project and start on the first step. For example, suppose you have to write a term paper. You have to take out a paper and pencil, log onto your computer, brainstorm some ideas, go to the library to find information, think about your main ideas, and write the first sentence. Each of these steps is manageable. It's looking at the entire project that can be intimidating.

I once set out hiking on a mountain trail. When I got to the top of the mountain and looked down, I enjoyed a spectacular view and was amazed at how high I had climbed. If I had thought about how high the mountain was, I might not have attempted the hike. I climbed the mountain by taking it one step at a time. That's the secret to completing any large project: break it into small, manageable parts, then take the first step and keep going.

Learning a small part at a time is also easy and helps with motivation for learning. While in college, carry around some material that you need to study. Take advantage of

> **Time Management Tricks**
>
> - Divide and conquer
> - Do the first small step
> - 80/20 rule
> - Aim for excellence, not perfection
> - Make learning fun
> - Take a break
> - Study in the library
> - Learn to say no

five or ten minutes of time to study a small part of your material. In this way you make good use of your time and enhance memory by using distributed practice. Don't wait until you have large blocks of uninterrupted study time to begin your studies. You may not have the luxury of large blocks of time, or you may want to spend that time in other ways.

Do the First Small Step

The most difficult step in completing any project is the first step. If you have a challenging project to do, think of a small first step and complete that small step. Make the first step something that you can accomplish easily and in a short amount of time. Give yourself permission to stop after the first step. However, you may find that you are motivated to continue with the project. If you have a term paper to write, think about some small step you can take to get started. Log onto your computer and look at the blank screen. Start writing some ideas. Type the topic into a computer search engine and see what information is available. Go to the library and see what is available on your topic. If you can find some interesting ideas, you can motivate yourself to begin the project. Once you have started the project, it is easier to continue.

The 80/20 Rule

Alan Lakein is noted for many useful time management techniques. One that I have used over the years is the 80/20 rule. Lakein says, "If all items are arranged in order of value, 80 percent of the value would come from only 20 percent of the items, while the remaining 20 percent of the value would come from 80 percent of the items."[3] For example, if you have a list of ten items to do, two of the items on the list are more important than the others. If you were to do only the two most important items, you would have accomplished 80 percent of the value. If you are short on time, see if you can choose the 20 percent of the tasks that are the most valuable. Lakein noted that the 80/20 rule applies to many situations in life:

- 80 percent of file usage is in 20 percent of the files.
- 80 percent of dinners repeat 20 percent of the recipes.
- 80 percent of the washing is done on the 20 percent of the clothes worn most frequently.
- 80 percent of the dirt is on the 20 percent of the floor used most often.

Think about how the 80/20 rule applies in your life. It is another way of thinking about priorities and figuring out which of the tasks are C priorities. This prioritizing is especially important if you are short on time. The 80/20 rule helps you to focus on what is most important.

Aim for Excellence, Not Perfection

Are you satisfied with your work only if it is done perfectly? Do you put off a project because you cannot do it perfectly? Aiming for perfection in all tasks causes anxiety and procrastination. There are times when perfection is not necessary. Dave Ellis calls this time management technique "It Ain't No Piano."[4] If a construction worker bends a nail in the framing of a house, it does not matter. The construction worker simply puts in another nail. After all, "it ain't no piano." It is another matter if you are building a fine cabinet or finishing a piano. Perfection is more important in these circumstances. We need to ask: Is the task important enough to invest the time needed for perfection? A final term paper needs to be as perfect as we can make it. A rough draft is like the frame of a house that does not need to be perfect.

In aiming for excellence rather than perfection, challenge yourself to use perspective to see the big picture. How important is the project and how perfect does it need to be? Could your time be better invested accomplishing other tasks? This technique requires flexibility and the ability to change with different situations. Do not give up if you cannot complete a project perfectly. Do the best that you can in the time available. In some situations, if life is too hectic, you may need to settle for completing the project and getting it in on time rather than doing it perfectly. With this idea in mind, you may be able to relax and still achieve excellence.

Make Learning Fun by Finding a Reward

Time management is not about restriction, self-control, and deprivation. If it is done correctly, time can be managed to get more out of life and to have fun while doing it. Remember that behavior is likely to increase if followed by a reward. Think about activities that you find rewarding. In our time management example with Justin who wants to be a physical therapist, he could use many tasks as rewards for completing his studies. He could meet friends for pizza, call his girlfriend, play video games, or watch TV. The key idea is to do the studying first and then reward the behavior. Maybe Justin will not be able to do all of the activities we have mentioned as possible rewards, but he could choose what he enjoys most.

Studying first and then rewarding yourself leads to peace of mind and the ability to focus on tasks at hand. While Justin is out having pizza with his friends, he does not have to worry about work that he has not done. While Justin is studying, he does not have to feel that he is being deprived of having pizza with friends. In this way, he can focus on studying while he is studying and focus on having a good time while relaxing with his friends. It is not a good idea to think about having pizza with friends while studying or to think about studying while having pizza with friends. When you work, focus on your work and get it done. When you play, enjoy playing without having to think about work.

> "Don't say you don't have enough time. You have exactly the same number of hours per day that were given to Helen Keller, Pasteur, Michelangelo, Mother Teresa, Leonardo da Vinci, Thomas Jefferson, and Albert Einstein."
>
> H. Jackson Browne

Take a Break

If you are overwhelmed with the task at hand, sometimes it is best to just take a break. If you're stuck on a computer program or a math problem, take a break and do something else. As a general rule, take a break of 10 minutes for each hour of study. During the break, do something totally different. It is a good idea to get up and move around. Get up and pet your cat or dog, observe your goldfish, or shoot a few baskets. If time is really at a premium, use your break time to accomplish other important tasks. Put your clothes in the dryer, empty the dishwasher, or pay a bill.

Study in the Library

If you are having difficulty with studying, try studying at school in the library. Libraries are designed for studying, and other people are studying there as well. It is hard to do something else in the library without annoying the librarian or other students. If you can complete your studying at school, you can go home and relax. This may be especially important if family, friends, or roommates at home easily distract you.

Learn to Say No Sometimes

Learn to say no to tasks that you do not have time to do. Follow your statement with the reasons for saying no: you are going to college and need time to study. Most people will understand this answer and respect it. You may need to say no to yourself as well. Maybe you cannot go out on Wednesday night if you have a class early on Thursday morning. Maybe the best use of your time right now is to turn off the TV or get off the Internet and study for tomorrow's test. You are investing your time in your future.

Dealing with Time Bandits

Time bandits are the many things that keep us from spending time on the things we think are important. Another word for a time bandit is a time waster. In college, it is tempting to do many things other than studying. We are all victims of different kinds of bandits.

Here are some ideas for keeping time bandits under control:

- **Schedule time for other people.** Friends and family are important, so we do not want to get rid of them! Discuss your goal of a college education with your friends and family. People who care about you will respect your goals. You may need to use a Do Not Disturb sign at times. If you are a parent, remember that you are a role model for your children. If they see you studying, they are more likely to value their own education. Plan to spend quality time with your children and the people who are important to you. Make sure they understand that you care about them.

ACTIVITY

Put a checkmark next to the items that waste your time. Add your own personal time wasters at the end of the list.

_____ TV	_____ Phone	_____ Sleeping in
_____ Other electronic devices	_____ Household chores	_____ Shopping
_____ Daydreaming	_____ Roommates	_____ Being easily distracted
_____ Social networking	_____ Video games	_____ Studying at a bad time
_____ Saying yes when you mean no	_____ Partying	_____ Reading magazines
_____ Friends	_____ Children	_____ Studying in a distracting place
_____ Internet	_____ iPod	_____ Movies
_____ Social time	_____ Waiting time	_____ Commuting time (travel)
_____ Family	_____ Girlfriend, boyfriend, spouse	

List some of your personal time bandits here.

_____

_____

- **Remember the rewards.** Many of the time bandits listed above make good rewards for completing your work. Put the time bandits to work for you by studying first and then enjoying a reward. Enjoy the TV, Internet, iPod, video games, or phone conversations after you have finished your studies. Aim for a balance of work, study, and leisure time.
- **Use your prime time wisely.** Prime time is when you are most awake and alert. Use this time for studying. Use non-prime time for the time bandits. When you are tired, do household chores and shopping. If you have little time for household chores, you might find faster ways to do them. If you don't have time for shopping, you will notice that you spend less and have a better chance of following your budget.
- **Remind yourself about your priorities.** When time bandits attack, remind yourself of why you are in college. Think about your personal goals for the future. Remember that college is not forever. By doing well in college, you will finish in the shortest time possible.
- **Use a schedule.** Using a schedule or a to-do list is helpful in keeping you on track. Make sure you have some slack time in your schedule to handle unexpected phone calls and deal with the unplanned events that happen in life. If you cannot stick to your schedule, just get back on track as soon as you can.

Journal Entry #3

Write a paragraph about how you will manage your time to accomplish your goal of a college education. Use any of these questions to guide your thinking:

- What are your priorities?
- How will you balance school, work, and family/friends?
- What are some time management tools you plan to use?
- How can you deal with time bandits?

Dealing with Procrastination

Procrastination means putting off things until later. We all use delaying tactics at times. Procrastination that is habitual, however, can be self-destructive. Understanding some possible reasons for procrastination can help you use time more effectively and be more successful in accomplishing goals.

Why Do We Procrastinate?

There are many psychological reasons for procrastinating. Just becoming aware of these may help you deal with procrastination. If you have serious difficulty managing your time for psychological reasons, visit the counseling center at your college or university. Do you recognize any of these reasons for procrastination in yourself or others?

- **Fear of failure.** Sometimes we procrastinate because we are afraid of failing. We see our performance as related to how much ability we have and how worthwhile we are as human beings. We may procrastinate in our college studies because of doubts about our ability to do the work. Success, however, comes from trying and learning from mistakes. There is a popular saying: falling down is not failure, but failing to get up or not even trying is failure.

- **Fear of success.** Most students are surprised to find out that one of the reasons for procrastination is fear of success. Success in college means moving on with your life, getting a job, leaving a familiar situation, accepting increased responsibility, and sometimes leaving friends behind. None of these tasks is easy. An example of fear of success is not taking the last step required to be successful. Students sometimes do not take the last class needed to graduate. Some good students do not show up for the final exam or do not turn in a major project. If you ever find yourself procrastinating on an important last step, ask yourself if you are afraid of success and what lies ahead in your future.

- **Perfectionism.** Some people who procrastinate do not realize that they are perfectionists. Perfectionists expect more from themselves than is realistic and more than others expect of themselves. There is often no other choice than to procrastinate because perfectionism is usually unattainable. Perfectionism generates anxiety that further hinders performance. Perfectionists need to understand that perfection is seldom possible. They need to set time limits on projects and do their best within those time limits.

- **Need for excitement.** Some students can only be motivated by waiting until the last minute to begin a project. These students are excited and motivated by playing a game of "Beat the Clock." They like living on the edge and the adrenaline rush of responding to a crisis. Playing this game provides motivation, but it does not leave enough time to achieve the best results. Inevitably, things happen at the last minute to make the game even more exciting and dangerous: the printer breaks, the computer crashes, the student gets ill, the car breaks down, or the dog eats the homework. These students need to start projects earlier to improve their chances of success. It is best to seek excitement elsewhere, in sports or other competitive activities.

- **Excellence without effort.** In this scenario, students believe that they are truly outstanding and can achieve success without effort. These students think that they can go to college without attending classes or reading the text. They believe that they can pass the test without studying. They often do not succeed in college the first semester, which puts them at risk of dropping out of school. They often return to college later and improve their performance by putting in the effort required.

- **Loss of control.** Some students fear loss of control over their lives and procrastinate to gain control. An example is students who attend college because others (such as parents) want them to attend. Procrastination becomes a way of gaining control over the situation by saying, "You can't make me do this." They attend college but accomplish nothing. Parents can support and encourage education, but students need to choose their own goals in life and attend college because it is an important personal goal.

Tips for Dealing with Procrastination

When you find yourself procrastinating on a certain task, think about the consequences. Will the procrastination lead to failing an exam or getting a low grade? Think about the rewards of doing the task. If you do well, you can take pride in yourself and celebrate your success. How will you feel when the task is completed? Will you be able to enjoy your leisure time without guilt about not doing your work? How does the task help you to achieve your lifetime goals?

Maybe the procrastination is a warning sign that you need to reconsider lifetime goals and change them to better suit your needs.

Procrastination Scenario

George is a college student who is on academic probation for having low grades. He is required to make a plan for improving his grades in order to remain in college. George tells the counselor that he is making poor grades because of his procrastination. He is an accounting major and puts off doing homework because he dislikes it and does not find it interesting. The counselor asks George why he had chosen accounting as a major. He replies that accounting is a major that is in demand and has a good salary. The counselor suggests that George consider a major that he would enjoy more. After some consideration, George changes his major to psychology. He becomes more interested in college studies and is able to raise his grades to stay in college.

Most of the time, you will reap benefits by avoiding procrastination and completing the task at hand. Jane Burka and Lenora Yuen suggest the following steps to deal with procrastination:

1. Select a goal.

2. Visualize your progress.

3. Be careful not to sabotage yourself.

4. Stick to a time limit.

5. Don't wait until you feel like it.

6. Follow through. Watch out for excuses and focus on one step at a time.

7. Reward yourself after you have made some progress.

8. Be flexible about your goal.

9. Remember that it does not have to be perfect.[5]

Time Management, Part II

Test what you have learned by selecting the correct answers to the following questions.

1. To get started on a challenging project,

    a. think of a small first step and complete it.
    b. wait until you have plenty of time to begin.
    c. wait until you are well rested and relaxed.

2. If you are completing a to-do list of 10 items, the 80/20 rule states that

    a. 80% of the value comes from completing most of the items on the list.
    b. 80% of the value comes from completing two of the most important items.
    c. 80% of the value comes from completing half of the items on the list.

3. It is suggested that students aim for

    a. perfection.
    b. excellence.
    c. passing.

4. Sometimes students procrastinate because of

    a. fear of failure.
    b. fear of success.
    c. all of the above.

5. Playing the game "Beat the Clock" when doing a term paper results in

    a. increased motivation and success.
    b. greater excitement and quality work.
    c. increased motivation and risk.

How did you do on the quiz? Check your answers: 1. a, 2. b, 3. b, 4. c, 5. c

Journal Entry #4

Write a paragraph about how you will avoid procrastination. Consider these ideas when thinking about procrastination: fear of failure, fear of success, perfectionism, need for excitement, excellence without effort, and loss of control. How will you complete your assignments on time?

Managing Your Money

To be successful in college and in life, you will need to manage not only time, but money. One of the top reasons that students drop out of college is that they cannot pay for their education or that they have to work so much that they do not have time for school. Take a look at your lifetime goals. Most students have a goal related to money, such as becoming financially secure or becoming wealthy. If financial security or wealth is one of your goals, you will need to begin to take some action to accomplish that goal. If you don't take action on a goal, it is merely a fantasy.

> "Education costs money, but then so does ignorance."
>
> Claus Moser

How to Become a Millionaire

Save regularly. Frances Leonard, author of *Time Is Money*, cites some statistics on how much money you need to save to become a millionaire.[6] You can retire with a million dollars by age 68 by saving the following amounts of money at various ages. These figures assume a 10 percent return on your investment.

At age 22, save $87 per month
At age 26, save $130 per month
At age 30, save $194 per month
At age 35, save $324 a month

Notice that the younger you start saving, the less money is required to reach the million-dollar goal. (And keep in mind that even a million dollars may not be enough money to save for retirement.) How can you start saving money when you are a student struggling to pay for college? The answer is to practice money management techniques and to begin a savings habit, even if the money you save is a small amount to buy your books for next semester. When you get that first good job, save 10 percent of the money. If you are serious about becoming financially secure, learn about investments such as real estate, stocks and bonds, and mutual funds. Learning how to save and invest your money can pay big dividends in the future.

Think thrifty. Money management begins with looking at your attitude toward money. Pay attention to how you spend your money so that you can accomplish your financial goals such as getting a college education, buying a house or car, or saving for the future. The following example shows how one woman accomplished her financial goals through being thrifty. Amy Dacyczyn, author of *The Tightwad Gazette*, says, "A lot of people get a thrill out of buying things. Frugal people get a rush from the very act of saving. Saving can actually be fun—we think of it almost as a sport."[7] She noticed that people were working harder and harder for less and less. Amy Dacyczyn had the goals of marriage, children, and a New England farmhouse to live in. She wanted to stay home and take care of her six children instead of working. In seven years, she was able to accomplish her goals with her husband's income of $30,000 a year. During this time, she saved $49,000 for the down payment on a rural farmhouse costing $125,000. She also paid cash for $38,000 worth of car, appliance, and furniture purchases while staying at home with her children. How did she do this? She says that she just started paying attention to how she was spending her money.

To save money, Amy Dacyczyn made breakfast from scratch. She made oatmeal, pancakes, and muffins instead of purchasing breakfast cereals. She saved $440 a year in this way. She purchased the family clothing at yard sales. She thought of so many ideas to save money that she began publishing *The Tightwad Gazette* to share her money-saving ideas with others. At $12 per subscription, she grosses a million dollars a year!

Managing Your Money

- Monitor your spending
- Prepare a budget
- Beware of credit and interest
- Watch spending leaks

Challenge yourself to pay attention to how you spend your money, and make a goal of being thrifty in order to accomplish your financial goals. With good money management, you can work less and have more time for college and recreational activities.

Budgeting: The Key to Money Management

It is important to control your money, rather than letting your money control you. One of the most important things that you can do to manage your money and begin saving is to use a budget. A budget helps you become aware of how you spend your money and will help you make a plan for how you would like to spend your money.

Monitor how you spend your money. The first step in establishing a workable budget is to monitor how you are actually spending your money at the present time. For one month, keep a list of purchases with the date and amount of money spent for each. You can do this on a sheet of paper, on your calendar, on index cards, or on a money management application for your phone. If you write checks for items, include the checks written as part of your money monitor. At the end of the month, group your purchases in categories such as food, gas, entertainment, and credit card payments, and add them up. Doing this will yield some surprising results. For example, you may not be aware of just how much it costs to eat at a fast-food restaurant or to buy lunch or coffee every day.

Prepare a budget. One of the best tools for managing your money is a budget. At the end of this chapter, you will find a simple budget sheet that you can use as a college student. After you finish college, update your budget and continue to use it. Follow these three steps to make a budget:

1. Write down your income for the month.
2. List your expenses. Include tuition, books, supplies, rent, telephone, utilities (gas, electric, water, cable TV), car payments, car insurance, car maintenance (oil, repairs), parking fees, food, personal grooming, clothes, entertainment, savings, credit card payments, loan payments, and other bills. Use your money monitor to discover how you are spending your money and include categories that are unique to you.
3. Subtract your total expenses from your total income. You cannot spend more than you have. Make adjustments as needed.

Beware of credit and interest. College students are often tempted to use credit cards to pay for college expenses. This type of borrowing is costly and difficult to repay. It is easy to pull out a plastic credit card and buy items that you need and want. Credit card companies earn a great deal of money from credit cards. Jane Bryant Quinn gives an example of the cost of credit cards.[8] She says that if you owe $3,000 at 18 percent interest and pay the minimum payment of $60 per month, it will take you 30 years and 10 months to get out of debt! Borrowing the $3,000 would cost about $22,320 over this time! If you use a credit card, make sure you can pay it off in one to three months. It is good to have a credit card in order to establish credit and to use in an emergency.

Watch those spending leaks. We all have spending problem areas. Often we spend small amounts of money each day that add up to large spending leaks over time. For example, if you spend $3 on coffee each weekday for a year, this adds up to $780 a year!

If you eat lunch out each weekday and spend $8 for lunch, this adds up to $2,080 a year. Here are some common areas for spending leaks:

- Fast food and restaurants
- Entertainment and vacations
- Clothing
- Miscellaneous cash
- Gifts

To identify your spending problem areas, write down all of your expenditures for one month. Place a three-by-five card in your wallet or use your phone to monitor your cash expenditures. At the end of the month, organize your expenditures into categories and total them up. Then ask yourself if this is how you want to spend your money.

Need More Money?

You may be tempted to work more hours to balance your budget. Remember that to be a full-time college student, it is recommended that you work no more than 20 hours per week. If you work more than 20 hours per week, you will probably need to decrease your course load. Before increasing your work hours, see if there is a way you can decrease your monthly expenses. Can you make your lunch instead of eating out? Can you get by without a car? Is the item you are purchasing a necessity, or do you just want to have it? These choices are yours.

1. **Check out financial aid.** All students can qualify for some type of financial aid. Visit the Financial Aid Office at your college for assistance. Depending on your income level, you may qualify for one or more of the following forms of aid.

   - **Loans.** A loan must be paid back. The interest rate and terms vary according to your financial need. With some loans, the federal government pays the interest while you are in school.

   - **Grants.** A grant does not need to be repaid. There are both state and federal grants based on need.

   - **Work/study.** You may qualify for a federally subsidized job depending on your financial need. These jobs are often on campus and provide valuable work experience for the future.

   The first step in applying for financial aid is to fill out the Free Application for Federal Student Aid (FAFSA). This form determines your eligibility for financial aid. You can obtain this form from your college's financial aid office or over the Internet at www.fafsa.ed.gov.

   Here are some other financial aid resources that you can obtain from your financial aid office or over the Internet.

   - **Student Guide.** The Student Guide, published by the U.S. Department of Education, describes in detail the kinds of financial aid available and eligibility requirements; it is available over the Internet at studentaid.ed.gov/students/publications/student_guide/index.html.

   - **How to apply for financial aid.** Learn how to apply for federal financial aid and scholarships at www.finaid.org.

   - **Student Gateway.** Visit the new Student Gateway to the U.S. Government, which has information about planning and paying for your education, at www.students.gov/STUGOVWebApp/index.jsp.

> "Money is, in some respects, like fire; it is a very excellent servant, but a terrible master."
> P. T. Barnum

> "Empty pockets never held anyone back. Only empty heads and empty hearts can do that."
> Norman Vincent Peale

2. **Apply for a scholarship.** Applying for a scholarship is like having a part-time job, only the pay is often better, the hours are flexible, and you can be your own boss. For this part-time job, you will need to research scholarship opportunities and fill out applications. There are multitudes of scholarships available, and sometimes no one even applies for them. Some students do not apply for scholarships because they think that high grades and financial need are required. While many scholarships are based on grades and financial need, many are not. Any person or organization can offer a scholarship for any reason they want. For example, scholarships can be based on hobbies, parent's occupation, religious background, military service, and personal interests, to name a few.

There are several ways to research a scholarship. As a first step, visit the financial aid office on your college campus. This office is staffed with persons knowledgeable about researching and applying for scholarships. Organizations or persons wishing to fund scholarships often contact this office to advertise opportunities.

You can also research scholarships through your public or college library. Ask the reference librarian for assistance. You can use the Internet to research scholarships as well. Use a search engine such as yahoo.com and simply type in the keyword *scholarships*. The following websites index thousands of scholarships:

- Federal Student Aid Scholarship Wizard at studentaid2.ed.gov/getmoney/scholarship/scholarship_search_select.asp?13817
- fastweb.com
- princetonreview.com/college/finance
- college-scholarships.com
- guaranteed-scholarships.com
- collegenet.com/mach25
- studentscholarshipsearch.com
- collegeboard.com/paying

To apply for scholarships, start a file of useful material usually included in scholarship applications. You can use this same information to apply for many scholarships.

- Three current letters of recommendation
- A statement of your personal goals
- A statement of your financial need
- Copies of your transcripts
- Copies of any scholarship applications you have filled out

Be aware of scholarship scams. You do not need to pay money to apply for a scholarship. No one can guarantee that you will receive a scholarship. Use your college scholarship office and your own resources to research and apply for scholarships.

The Best Ideas for Becoming Financially Secure

Financial planners provide the following ideas as the best ways to build wealth and independence.[9] If you have financial security as your goal, plan to do the following:

1. **Use a simple budget to track income and expenses.** Do not spend more than you earn.
2. **Have a financial plan.** Include goals such as saving for retirement, purchasing a home, paying for college, or taking vacations.

3. **Save 10 percent of your income.** As a college student, you may not be able to save this much, but plan to do it as soon as you get your first good-paying job. If you cannot save 10 percent, save something to get in the habit of saving. Save to pay for your tuition and books.

4. **Don't take on too much debt.** Be especially careful about credit cards and consumer debt. Credit card companies often visit college campuses and offer high-interest credit cards to students. It is important to have a credit card, but pay off the balance each month. Consider student loans instead of paying college fees by credit card.

5. **Don't procrastinate.** The earlier you take these steps toward financial security, the better.

Tips for Managing Your Money

Keeping these guidelines in mind can help you to manage your money.

- Don't let friends pressure you into spending too much money. If you can't afford something, learn to say no.
- Keep your checking account balanced or use online banking so you will know how much money you have.
- Don't lend money to friends. If your friends cannot manage their money, your loan will not help them.
- Use comparison shopping to find the best prices on the products that you buy.
- Get a part-time job while in college. You will earn money and gain valuable job experience.
- Don't use shopping as a recreational activity. When you visit the mall, you will find things you never knew you needed and will wind up spending more money than intended.
- Make a budget and follow it. This is the best way to achieve your financial goals.

Do What Is Important First

The most important thing you can do to manage time and money is to spend it on what is most important. Manage time and money to help you live the life you want. How can you do this? Author Stephen Covey wrote a book titled *The Seven Habits of Highly Effective People.* One of the habits is "Put first things first." Covey suggests that in time management, the "challenge is not to manage our time but to manage ourselves."[10]

How can you manage yourself? Our first thoughts in answering this question often involve suggestions about willpower, restriction, and self-control. Schedules and budgets are seen as instruments for self-control. It seems that the human spirit resists attempts at control, even when we aim to control ourselves. Often the response to control is rebellion. With time and money management, we may not follow a schedule or budget. A better approach to begin managing yourself is to know your values. What is important in your life? Do you have a clear mental picture of what is important? Can you describe your values and make a list of what is important to you? With your values and goals in mind, you can begin to manage both your time and your money.

When you have given some thought to your values, you can begin to set goals. When you have established goals for your life, you can begin to think in terms of what is most important and establish your priorities. Knowing your values is essential in making decisions about how to invest your time and money. Schedules and budgets are merely tools for helping you accomplish what you have decided is important. Time and money management is not about restriction and control, but about making decisions regarding what is important in your life. If you know what is important, you can find the strength to say no to activities and expenditures that are less important.

As a counselor, I have the pleasure of working with many students who have recently explored and discovered their values and are highly motivated to succeed. They are willing to do what is important first. I recently worked with a young couple who came to enroll in college. They brought their young baby with them. The new father was interested in environmental engineering. He told

me that in high school, he never saw a reason for school and did just the minimum needed to get by. He was working as a construction laborer and making a living, but did not see a future in the occupation. He had observed an environmental engineer who worked for the company and decided that was what he wanted for his future. As he looked at his new son, he told me that he needed to have a better future for himself and his family.

He and his wife decided to do what was important first. They were willing to make the sacrifice to attend school and invest the time needed to be successful. The father planned to work during the day and go to school at night. Later, he would go to school full-time and get a part-time job in the evening. His wife was willing to get a part-time job also, and they would share in taking care of the baby. They were willing to manage their money carefully to accomplish their goals. As they left, they added that their son would be going to college as well.

How do you get the energy to work all day, go to school at night, and raise a family? You can't do it by practicing self-control. You find the energy by having a clear idea of what you want in your life and focusing your time and resources on the goal. Finding what you want to do with your life is not easy either. Many times people find what they want to do when some significant event happens in their lives.

Begin to think about what you want out of life. Make a list of your important values and write down your lifetime goals. Don't forget about the people who are important to you, and include them in your priorities. Then you will be able to do what is important first.

> "Fathers send their sons to college either because they went to college or because they didn't."
> L. L. Henderson

Journal Entry #5

What is your plan for managing your money? Consider these ideas when thinking about your plan: monitoring how you spend your money, using a budget, applying for financial aid and scholarships, saving money, and spending money wisely.

JOURNAL ENTRIES

Managing Time and Money

Go to http://www.collegesuccess1.com/JournalEntries.htm for Word files of the Journal Entries

Success over the Internet

Visit the *College Success Website* at http://www.collegesuccess1.com/

The *College Success Website* is continually updated with new topics and links to the material presented in this chapter. Topics include:

- Suggestions for time management
- How to overcome procrastination
- How to deal with perfectionism
- Goal setting
- Goal setting in sports
- Goal setting and visualization
- Scholarship websites
- Recognizing scholarship scams
- Financial aid websites

Ask your instructor if you need any assistance in accessing the *College Success Website*.

Notes

1. Quoted in Rob Gilbert, ed., *Bits and Pieces,* November 4, 1999, 15.

2. Alan Lakein, *How to Get Control of Your Time and Your Life* (New York: Peter H. Wyden, 1973).

3. Ibid., 70–71.

4. Dave Ellis, *Becoming a Master Student* (Boston: Houghton Mifflin, 1998).

5. Jane Burka and Lenora Yuen, *Procrastination* (Reading, MA: Addison-Wesley, 1983).

6. Frances Leonard, *Time Is Money* (Addison-Wesley), cited in the *San Diego Union Tribune,* October 14, 1995.

7. Amy Dacyczyn, *The Tightwad Gazette II* (Villard Books), cited in the *San Diego Union Tribune,* February 20, 1995.

8. Jane Bryant Quinn, "Money Watch," *Good Housekeeping*, November 1996, 80.

9. Robert Hanley, "Breaking Bad Habits," *San Diego Union Tribune,* September 7, 1992.

10. Stephen R. Covey, *The Seven Habits of Highly Effective People* (New York: Simon and Schuster, 1990), 150.

My Lifetime Goals: Brainstorming Activity

Name _____ Date _____

1. Think about the goals that you would like to accomplish in your life. At the end of your life, you do not want to say, "I wish I would have _____." Set a timer for five minutes and write whatever comes to mind about what you would like to do and accomplish over your lifetime. Include goals in these areas: career, personal relationships, travel, and financial security or any area that is important to you. Write down all your ideas. The goal is to generate as many ideas as possible in five minutes. You can reflect on which ones are most important later. You may want to do this as part of a group activity in your class.

Look over the ideas you wrote above and highlight or underline the goals that are most important to you.

2. Ask yourself what you would like to accomplish in the next five years. Think about where you want to be in college, what you want to do in your career, and what you want to do in your personal life. Set a timer and write whatever comes to mind in five minutes. The goal is to write down as many ideas as possible.

Again, look over the ideas you wrote and highlight or underline the ideas that are most important to you.

3. What goals would you like to accomplish in the next year? What are some steps that you can begin now to accomplish your lifetime goals? Consider work, study, leisure, and social goals. Set your timer for five minutes and write down your goals for the next year.

Review what you wrote and highlight or underline the ideas that are most important to you. When writing your goals, include fun activities as well as taking care of others.

Looking at the items that you have highlighted or underlined, make a list of your lifetime goals using the form that follows. Make sure your goals are specific enough so that you can break them into steps you can achieve.

Name _____ Date _____

Using the ideas that you brainstormed in the previous exercise, make a list of your lifetime goals. Make sure your goals are specific and concrete. Begin with goals that you would like to accomplish over a lifetime. In the second section, think about the goals you can accomplish over the next one to three years.

Long-Term Goals (lifetime goals)

Short-Term Goals (one to three years)

What are some steps you can take now to accomplish intermediate and long-term goals?

Name _____ Date _____

Look at your list of lifetime goals. Which one is most important? Write the goal here:

Answer these questions about the goal you have listed above.

1. What skills, abilities, and resources do you have to achieve this goal? What skills, abilities, and resources will you need to develop to achieve this goal?

2. Do you believe you can achieve it? Write a brief positive statement about achieving this goal.

3. State your goal in specific terms that can be observed or counted. Rewrite your goal if necessary.

4. Write a brief statement about how this goal will give you personal satisfaction.

5. How will you motivate yourself to achieve this goal?

6. What are your personal values that match this goal?

7. List some steps that you will take to accomplish this goal.

8. When will you finish this goal?

9. What roadblocks will make this goal difficult to achieve?

10. How will you deal with these roadblocks?

Name _____   Date _____

Copy the following schedule to use in future weeks or design your own schedule. Fill in this schedule and try to follow it for at least one week. First, fill in scheduled commitments (classes, work, activities). Next, fill in the time you need for studying. Put in some tasks related to your lifetime goals. Leave some blank time as a shock absorber to handle unexpected activities.

Time	Monday	Tuesday	Wednesday	Thursday	Friday	Saturday	Sunday
7 A.M.							
8							
9							
10							
11							
Noon							
1 P.M.							
2							
3							
4							
5							
6							
7							
8							
9							
10							
11							

Name _____ Date _____

Using a to-do list is an easy way to remind yourself of important priorities each day. This chart is divided into three areas representing types of tasks that college students need to balance: academic, personal, and social.

Weekly To-Do List

	Monday	Tuesday	Wednesday	Thursday	Friday
Academic					
Personal					
Social					

Name _____   Date _____

Before completing this analysis, use the schedule form to create a master schedule. A master schedule blocks out class and work times as well as any regularly scheduled activities. Looking at the remaining time, write in your planned study times. It is recommended that you have two hours of study time for each hour in class. For example, a three-unit class would require six hours of study time. A student with 12 units would require 24 hours of study time. You may need more or fewer hours, depending on your study skills, reading skills, and difficulty of courses.

1. How many units are you enrolled in?

2. How many hours of planned study time do you have?

3. How many hours do you work each week?

4. How many hours do you spend in relaxation/social activities?

5. Do you have time planned for exercise?

6. Do you get enough sleep?

7. What are some of your time bandits (things that take up your time and make it difficult to accomplish your goals)?

Write a few discovery statements about how you use your time.

8. Are you spending enough time to earn the grades you want to achieve? Do you need to spend more time studying to become successful?

9. Does your work schedule allow you enough time to study?

10. How can you deal with your time bandits?

11. How can you use your time more effectively to achieve your goals?

Name _____ Date _____

This circle represents 24 hours. Each piece is six hours. Draw a slice of pie to represent how much time you spend on each of these activities in a typical day: sleeping, attending classes, studying, work, family, friends, and other activities.

Thinking about your values is the first step in setting goals. How you spend your time determines whether you will accomplish these goals. Are you using your time to accomplish your goals? Make some intention statements for the future on how you want to spend your time.

I intend to:

The College Student's Tightwad Gazette

Name _____ Date _____

List five ideas for saving money that could be included in a publication called *The College Student's Tightwad Gazette*.

1. _____

2. _____

3. _____

4. _____

5. _____

Get together with other students in the class and come up with five additional ideas that college students can use to save money or increase income.

1. _____

2. _____

3. _____

4. _____

5. _____

List five ways that college students can have fun without spending much money.

1. _____

2. _____

3. _____

4. _____

5. _____

Name _____ Date _____

Before you complete this budget, monitor your expenses for one month. Write down all expenditures and then divide them into categories that have meaning for you. Then complete the following budget and try to follow it for at least two months. Do this exercise on your own, since it is likely to contain private information.

College Student Monthly Budget

Monthly income for _____ (month)	
Income from job _____	
Money from home _____	**Total Income** [ ]
Financial aid _____	
Other _____	
Budgeted Monthly Expenses:	**Actual Monthly Expenses:**
Total Budgeted [ ]	**Total Actual**

Total Income [ ]   **Minus Total Budgeted** [ ]   **Equals** [ ]

CHAPTER 4

Higher-Level Thinking
Moving Beyond Basic Knowledge to Critical and Creative Thinking

Learning Goal

To increase awareness of what it means to think at a higher level and how higher-level thinking can be used to achieve excellence in college and beyond.

ACTIVATE YOUR THINKING | *Reflection* **4.1**

To me, critical thinking means . . .

(At a later point in this chapter, we'll discuss critical thinking and ask you to flash back to the response you made here.)

What Is Higher-Level Thinking?

The term *higher-level thinking* (or *higher-order thinking*) refers to a more advanced level of thought than that used for learning basic skills and acquiring factual knowledge. Higher-level thinking involves reflecting on the knowledge you've acquired and taking additional mental action on it, such as evaluating its validity, integrating it with something else you've learned, or creating new ideas.

Contestants performing on TV quiz shows such as *Jeopardy!* or *Who Wants to Be a Millionaire?* respond to questions asking for knowledge about who, what, when, and where. If game-show contestants were asked higher-level thinking questions, they'd be responding to questions such as "Why?" "How?" and "What if?"

> **Remember**
>
> *The focus of higher-level thinking is not just to answer questions, but also to question answers.*

As its name implies, higher-level thinking involves raising the bar and jacking up your thinking to levels that go beyond merely remembering, reproducing, or regurgitating factual information. "Education is what's left over after you've forgotten all the facts" is an old saying that carries a lot of truth. Studies show that students' memory of facts learned in college often fades with time (Pascarella & Terenzini, 1991, 2005). Memory for factual information has a short lifespan; the ability to think at a higher level is a durable, lifelong learning skill that lasts a lifetime.

Compared to high school, college courses focus less on memorizing information and more on thinking about issues, concepts, and principles (Conley, 2005). Remembering information in college may get a grade of "C," demonstrating comprehension of that information may get you a "B," and going beyond comprehension to demonstrate higher-level thinking will earn you an "A." In national surveys of college professors teaching freshman- through senior-level courses in various fields, more than 95 percent of them report that the most important goal of a college education is to develop students' ability to think critically (Gardiner, 2005; Milton, 1982). Similarly, college professors teaching introductory courses to freshmen and sophomores indicate that the primary educational purpose of their courses is to develop students' critical thinking skills (Higher Education Institute, 2009; Stark et al., 1990).

Simply stated, college professors are often more concerned with teaching you *how* to think than with teaching you *what* to think (i.e., what facts to remember).

© Rafael Ramirez Lee, 2013. Under license from Shutterstock, Inc.

> **Remember**
>
> *Your college professors will often expect you to do more than just retain or reproduce information; they'll ask you to demonstrate higher levels of thinking with respect to what you've learned, such as analyze it, evaluate it, apply it, or connect it with other concepts that you've learned.*

This is not to say that acquiring knowledge and basic comprehension are unimportant. They are important because they supply you with the raw material needed to manufacture higher-level thinking. Deep learning and a broad base of knowledge provide the stepping stones you need to climb to higher levels of thinking (as illustrated in **Figure 4.1**).

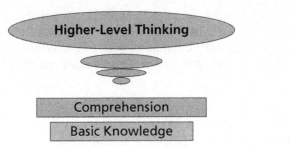

Figure 4.1 The Relationship between Knowledge, Comprehension, and Higher-Level Thinking.

Defining and Describing the Major Forms of Higher-Level Thinking

When your college professors ask you to "think critically," they're usually asking you to use one or more of the eight forms of thinking listed in the **Snapshot Summary 4.1**. As you read the description of each form of thinking, note whether or not you've heard of it before.

Snapshot Summary

4.1 Major Forms of Higher-Level Thinking

1. **Application (applied thinking).** Putting knowledge into practice to solve problems and resolve issues;
2. **Analysis (analytical thinking).** Breaking down information to identify its key parts and underlying elements;
3. **Synthesis.** Building up ideas by integrating them into a larger whole or more comprehensive system;
4. **Multidimensional thinking.** Taking multiple perspectives (i.e., viewing issues from different vantage points);

5. **Inferential reasoning.** Making arguments or judgments by inferring (stepping to) a conclusion that's supported by empirical (observable) evidence or logical consistency;
6. **Balanced thinking.** Carefully considering arguments for and against a particular position or viewpoint;
7. **Critical thinking.** Evaluating (judging the quality of) arguments, conclusions, and ideas; and
8. **Creative thinking.** Generating ideas that are unique, original, or distinctively different.

Application (Applied Thinking)

When you learn something deeply, you transform information into knowledge; when you translate knowledge into action, you're engaging in a higher-level thinking process known as *application*. Applied thinking moves you beyond simply knowing something to actually doing something with the knowledge you possess; you use the knowledge you've acquired to solve a problem or resolve an issue. For example, if you use knowledge you've acquired in a human relations course to resolve an interpersonal conflict, you're engaging in application. Similarly, when you use knowledge acquired in a math course to solve a problem that you haven't seen before, you're using applied thinking. Application is a powerful form of higher-level thinking because it allows you to transfer your knowledge to new situations or contexts and put it into practice.

Reflection 4.2

Look back at the eight forms of thinking described in the **Snapshot Summary 4.1**. Which of these forms of thinking had you heard of before? Did you use any of these forms of thinking on high school exams or assignments?

Always be on the lookout for ways to apply the knowledge you acquire to your personal life experiences and current events or issues. When you use your knowledge for the practical purpose of doing something good, such as bettering yourself or others, you not only demonstrate application, you also demonstrate *wisdom* (Staudinger, 2008).

Analysis (Analytical Thinking)

The mental process of analysis is similar to the physical process of peeling an onion. When you analyze something, you take it apart or break it down and pick out its key parts, main points, or underlying elements. For example, if you were to analyze a textbook chapter, you would go beyond reading just to cover the content; instead, you would read it to uncover the author's main ideas, detecting its core ideas and distinguishing them from background information and incidental details.

In an art course, you would use analysis to identify the components or elements of a painting or sculpture (e.g., its structure, texture, tone, and form). In the natural and social sciences, you would use analysis to identify underlying reasons or causes for natural (physical) phenomena and social events, which is commonly referred to as *causal analysis*. For instance, causal analysis of the September 11, 2001, attack on the United States would involve identifying the factors that led to the attack or the underlying reasons for why the attack took place.

Synthesis

A form of higher-level thinking that's basically the opposite of analysis is *synthesis*. When you analyze, you break information into its parts; when you synthesize, you build it up by taking separate parts or pieces of information and connect them to form an integrated whole (like piecing together parts of a puzzle). You engage in synthesis when you connect ideas presented in different courses: for instance, when you integrate ethical concepts learned in a philosophy course with marketing concepts learned in a business course to produce a set of ethical guidelines for marketing and advertising products.

Reflection **4.3**

A TV commercial for a particular brand of liquor (which shall remain nameless) once showed a young man getting out of his car in front of a house where a party is going on. The driver gets out of his car, takes out a knife, slashes his tires, and goes inside to join the party. Using the higher-level thinking skill of analysis, what would you say are the underlying or embedded messages in this commercial?

Synthesis involves more than a summary. It goes beyond just condensing information to a higher level of thinking that involves finding and forming meaningful connections across separate pieces of information and weaving them together to form a cohesive picture. When you're synthesizing, you're thinking conceptually by converting isolated facts and separate bits of information and integrating them into a *concept*—a larger system or network of related ideas.

Although synthesis and analysis are virtually opposite thought processes, they complement each other. When you analyze, you disassemble information into its key parts. When you synthesize, you reassemble information into a whole. For instance, when writing this book, we analyzed published material in many fields (e.g., psychology, history, philosophy, and biology) and identified information from parts of these fields that were most relevant to promoting the success of beginning college students. We then synthesized or reassembled these parts to create a new whole—the textbook you're now reading.

Multidimensional Thinking

When you engage in multidimensional thinking, you view yourself and the world around you from different angles or vantage points. In particular, a multidimensional thinker is able to think from four key perspectives and determine how each of them influences, and is influenced by, the issue under discussion.

1. **Person (self).** How does this issue affect me as an individual? (The perspective of person.)
2. **Place.** What impact does this issue have on people living in different countries? (The perspective of place.)
3. **Time.** How will future generations of people be affected by this issue? (The perspective of time.)
4. **Culture.** How is this issue likely to be interpreted or experienced by groups of people who share different social customs and traditions? (The perspective of culture.)

Each of these four general perspectives has specific elements embedded within it. The four major perspectives, along with the key elements that comprise each of them, are listed and described in the **Snapshot Summary 4.2**. Note how these perspectives are consistent with those developed by the liberal arts.

Snapshot Summary

4.2 | **Perspectives Associated with Multidimensional Thinking**

Perspective 1: PERSON (Perspectives on different dimension of oneself)

Key Components
- **Intellectual (cognitive):** Knowledge, style of thinking, and self-concept
- **Emotional:** Feelings, emotional adjustment, and mental health
- **Social:** Interpersonal relationships and social interactions
- **Ethical:** Values and moral convictions
- **Physical:** Health and wellness
- **Spiritual:** Beliefs about the meaning or purpose of life and the hereafter
- **Vocational (occupational)**—Means of making a living and earning an income

Perspective 2: PLACE (Perspectives beyond the self that include progressively wider social and spatial distance)

Key Components
- **Family:** Parents, children, and other relatives
- **Community:** Local communities and neighborhoods
- **Society:** Societal institutions (e.g., schools, churches, and hospitals) and groups within society (e.g., social groups differing in age, gender, race, or socioeconomic status)
- **Nation:** One's own country or place of citizenship
- **International:** Citizens of different nations and territories

- **Global:** Planet earth (e.g., its life forms and natural resources)
- **Universe:** The galaxy that includes earth, other planets, and celestial bodies

Perspective 3: TIME (Chronological perspective)

Key Components
- **Historical:** The past
- **Contemporary:** The present
- **Futuristic:** The future

Perspective 4: CULTURE (Perspective of particular groups of people who share the same social heritage and traditions)

Key Components
- **Linguistic (language):** How group members communicate via spoken and written words and through nonverbal communication (body language)
- **Political:** How the group organizes societal authority and uses it to govern itself, make collective decisions, and maintain social order
- **Economic:** How the material wants and needs of the group are met through allocation of limited resources, and how wealth is distributed among its members
- **Geographical:** How the group's physical location influences the nature of social interactions and the way its members adapt to and use their environment

(continued)

- **Aesthetic:** How the group appreciates and expresses artistic beauty and creativity through the arts (e.g., visual art, music, theater, literature, and dance)
- **Scientific:** How the group views, understands, and investigates natural phenomena through research (e.g., scientific tests and experiments)
- **Ecological:** How the group views its relationship to the surrounding biological world (e.g., other living creatures) and the physical environment
- **Anthropological:** How the group's culture originated, evolved, and developed over time

- **Sociological:** How the group's society is structured and organized into social subgroups and social institutions
- **Psychological:** How group members tend to think, feel, and interact with each other, and how their attitudes, opinions, or beliefs have been acquired
- **Philosophical:** The group's ideas or views on the nature of truth, goodness, wisdom, beauty, and the meaning or purpose of life
- **Theological:** Group members' ideas and beliefs about a transcendent, supreme being, and how they express their shared faith in a supreme being

Important human issues don't exist in isolation but as parts of complex, interconnected systems that involve the interplay of multiple factors and perspectives. For example, global warming is a current issue that involves the earth's atmosphere gradually thickening and trapping more heat due to a collection of greenhouse gases, which are being produced primarily by the burning of fossil fuels. It's theorized that this increase of manmade pollution is causing temperatures to rise (and sometimes fall) around the world and is contributing to natural disasters, such as droughts, wildfires, and dust storms (Joint Science Academies Statement, 2005; National Resources Defense Council, 2012). Understanding and addressing this issue involves interrelationships among a variety of perspectives, as depicted in **Figure 4.2**.

Person	Global warming involves us on an individual level because our personal efforts at energy conservation in our homes and our willingness to purchase energy-efficient products can play a major role in solving this problem.
Place	Global warming is an international issue that extends beyond the boundaries of one's own country to all countries in the world, and its solution will require worldwide collaboration.
Time	If the current trend toward higher global temperatures caused by global warming continues, it could seriously threaten the lives of future generations of people who inhabit our planet.
Culture	The problem of global warming has been caused by industries in technologically advanced cultures, yet the problem of rising global temperatures is likely to have its most negative impact on less technologically advanced cultures that lack the resources to respond to it (Joint Science Academies Statement, 2005). To prevent this from happening, technologically advanced cultures will need to use their advanced technology to devise alternative methods for generating energy that don't release heat-trapping gases into the atmosphere.

Figure 4.2 Understanding Global Warming from Four Key Perspectives.

Addressing the issue of global warming also involves different components of our culture, including: (1) ecology: understanding the delicate interplay between humans and their natural environment, (2) science: need for research and development of alternative sources of energy, (3) economics: managing the cost incurred by industries to change their existing sources of energy, (4) politics: devising incentives or laws to encourage changes in industries' use of energy sources, and (5) international relations: collaboration between our nation and other nations that are currently contributing to this worldwide problem and that play pivotal roles in its future solution.

Briefly explain how each of the perspectives of person, place, time, and culture may be involved in causing and solving one the following problems:

1. War and terrorism

2. Poverty and hunger

3. Prejudice and discrimination

4. Any world issue of your choice

Inferential Reasoning

When people make arguments or arrive at conclusions, they do so by starting with a premise (a statement or an observation) and use it to infer (step to) a conclusion. The following sentence starters demonstrate the process of inferential reasoning:

"Because this is true, it follows that . . ."

"Based on this evidence, I can conclude that . . ."

Inferential reasoning is the primary thought process humans use to reach conclusions about themselves and the world around them. This is also the form of thinking that you will use to make arguments and reach conclusions about ideas presented in your college courses. You'll often be required to take positions and draw conclusions by supporting them with solid evidence and sound reasoning. In a sense, you'll be asked to take on the role of a courtroom lawyer trying to prove a case by supplying supporting arguments and evidence (exhibit A, exhibit B, etc.).

The following are two major ways in which you use inferential reasoning to support your points or arguments:

1. **Citing empirical (observable) evidence.** Supporting your point with specific examples, personal experiences, facts, figures, statistical data, scientific research findings, expert testimonies, supporting quotes, or statements from leading authorities in the field.

2. **Using principles of logical consistency.** Showing that your conclusion follows or flows logically from an established premise or proposition. The following is an example of logical consistency:
   * The constitution guarantees all U.S. citizens the right to vote (established premise);
   * U.S. citizens include women and people of color; therefore,
   * Granting women and people of color the right to vote was logically consistent (and constitutional).

Both empirical evidence and logical consistency can be used to support the same argument. For instance, advocates for lowering the legal drinking age to 18 have argued that: (1) in other countries where drinking is allowed at age 18, statistics show fewer binge-drinking and drunk-driving problems than in the United States (empirical evidence), and (2) 18-year-olds in the United States are considered to be legal adults with respect to such rights and responsibilities as voting, serving on juries, joining the military, and being held responsible for committing crimes; therefore, 18-year-olds should have the right to drink.

Can you think of any arguments *against* lowering the drinking age to 18 that are based on empirical (observable) evidence or logical consistency?

Unfortunately, errors can be made in the inferential reasoning process, often referred to as *logical fallacies*. Some of the more common logical fallacies are summarized in the **Snapshot Summary 4.3**. As you read each of these reasoning errors, briefly note in the margin whether you've ever witnessed it or experienced it.

Snapshot Summary

4.3 Logical Fallacies: Inferential Reasoning Errors

- **Dogmatism.** Stubbornly clinging to a personally held viewpoint that's unsupported by evidence and remaining closed-minded (non-receptive) to other viewpoints that are better supported by evidence (for instance, those who believe that America's form of capitalism is the only economic system that can work in a successful democracy, while refusing to acknowledge that there are other successful democratic countries with different types of capitalistic economies).

"Facts do not cease to exist because they are ignored."

—Aldous Huxley, English writer and author of Brave New World.

- **Selective perception.** Seeing only examples and instances that support a position while overlooking or ignoring those that contradict it (e.g., believers in astrology who only notice and point out people whose personalities happen to fit their astrological signs, while overlooking those who don't).

"A very bad (and all too common) way to misread a newspaper: To see whatever supports your point of view as fact, and anything that contradicts your point of view as bias."

—Daniel Okrent, first public editor of The New York Times and inventor of Rotisserie League Baseball, the best-known form of fantasy baseball

- **Double standard.** Having two sets of standards for judgment: a higher standard for judging others and a lower standard for judging oneself. This is the classic "do as I say, not as I do" hypocrisy (e.g., critically evaluating and challenging the opinions of others but not our own).
- **Wishful thinking.** Thinking that something is true not on the basis of logic or evidence, but because the person wants it to be true (for instance, a teenage girl who believes she will not become pregnant, even though she and her boyfriend always have sex without using any form of contraception).

"Belief can be produced in practically unlimited quantity and intensity, without observation or reasoning, and even in defiance of both by the simple desire to believe."

—George Bernard Shaw, Irish playwright and Nobel Prize winner for literature

- **Hasty generalization.** Reaching a conclusion prematurely on the basis of a limited number of instances or experiences (e.g., concluding that people belonging to a group are all or nearly all "that way" on the basis of personal experiences with only one or two individuals).
- **Jumping to a conclusion.** Making a leap of logic to reach a conclusion that's based on only one reason or factor while ignoring other possible reasons and contributing factors (e.g., immediately concluding that "I must be a real loser" after being rejected for a date or a job)
- **Glittering generality.** Making a positive general statement without supplying details or evidence to back it up (e.g., writing a letter of recommendation describing someone as a "wonderful person" with a "great personality" but not providing any reasons or evidence to support these claims).
- **Straw man argument.** Distorting an opponent's position and then attacking it (e.g., attacking an opposing political candidate for supporting censorship and restricting civil liberties when the opponent supported only a ban on violent pornography).
- **Ad *hominem* argument.** Aiming an argument at the person rather than the person's argument (e.g., telling a younger person, "You're too young and inexperienced to know what you're talking about," or telling an older person, "You're too old-fashioned to understand this issue"). Literally translated, the term *ad hominem* means "to the man."
- **Red herring.** Bringing up an irrelevant issue that disguises or distracts attention from the real issue being discussed or debated (e.g., responding to criticism of former President Richard Nixon's

involvement in the Watergate scandal by arguing, "He was a good president who accomplished many good things while he was in office"). The term *red herring* derives from an old practice of dragging a herring—a strong-smelling fish—across a trail to distract the scent of pursuing dogs. (In the example, Nixon's effectiveness as a president is an irrelevant issue or a red herring; the real issue being discussed is Nixon's behavior in the Watergate scandal.)

- **Smoke screen.** Intentionally disguising or covering up true reasons or motives with reasons that confuse or mislead others (e.g., opposing gun control legislation by arguing that it is a violation of the constitutional right to bear arms without revealing that the opponent of the legislation is receiving financial support from gun manufacturing companies).

- **Slippery slope.** Using fear tactics by arguing that not accepting a position will result in a "domino effect"—one bad thing happening after another, like a series of falling dominoes (e.g., "If someone experiments with marijuana, it will automatically lead to loss of motivation, harder drugs, and withdrawal from college").

- **Rhetorical deception.** Using deceptive language to conclude that something is true without providing reasons or evidence (e.g., glibly making statements such as: "Clearly this is . . ." "It is obvious that . . ." or "Any reasonable person can see . . ." without explaining why it's so clear, obvious, or reasonable).

- **Circular reasoning (a.k.a. "begging the question").** Drawing a conclusion that's merely a rewording or restatement of one's position without any supporting reasons or evidence, leaving the original question still unanswered and the issue still unsolved. This form of reasoning basically draws conclusion logically by claiming "it's true because it's true" (e.g., "Stem cell research shouldn't be legal because it shouldn't be done").

- **Appealing to authority or prestige.** Believing that if an authority figure or celebrity says it's true then it must be true or should be done (e.g., buying product X simply because a famous actor or athlete uses it, or believing that if someone in authority, such as the U.S. president, says something should be done, then it must be the right or best thing to do).

- **Appealing to tradition or familiarity.** Concluding that if something has always been thought to be true or has always been done in a certain way, then it must be true or the best way to do it (e.g., "This is the way it's always been done, so it must be right").

- **Appealing to popularity or the majority (a.k.a. jumping on the bandwagon).** Believing that if it's popular or held by the majority of people, it must be true (e.g., "So many people believe in psychics, it has to be true; they can't all be wrong").

- **Appealing to emotion.** Believing in something based on the emotional intensity experienced when the claim is made, rather than the quality of reasoning or evidence used to support the claim (e.g., "If I feel strongly about something, it must be true"). The expressions "Always trust your feelings" and "Just listen to your heart" may not always lead to the most accurate conclusions and the best decisions because they could be driven more by emotion than by reason.

"Political talk shows have become shouting matches designed to push emotional hot buttons and drive us further apart. We desperately need to exchange ideas with one another rationally and courteously."

—David Boren, president of the University of Oklahoma and longest-serving chairman of the U.S. Senate Intelligence Committee

Note: For evaluations of the factual accuracy of statements made by politicians in TV ads, debates, speeches, interviews, and news releases, go to www.factcheck.org or www.politifact.com.

Reflection **4.6**

Glance back at the reasoning errors summarized in the Snapshot Summary 4.3. Identify the two most common errors you've witnessed or experienced.

What was the situation in which these errors took place?

Why do you think they occurred?

Author's Experience Soon after my wife and I were married, we moved to a new city and tried to find a place to live. We got up early one morning, skipped breakfast, and drove to the town where we were planning to move. We were determined to find an apartment to rent before lunch, but we found ourselves still driving around town from place to place in the middle of the afternoon. By this time, both of us were famished because we hadn't eaten anything since the night before; we decided to stop looking for a place to live and start looking for a place to eat.

Unfortunately, we had about as much luck finding a place to eat as we did finding a place to live. It was approaching 4 p.m. and we were now beginning to hear lion-like growls coming from our stomachs. While I was driving, my wife suddenly elbowed me (hard) and exclaimed, "Joe, look—fried chicken!" She pointed to a flashing sign in the distance; I couldn't read the sign clearly, but figured her long-range vision was better than me. So, I hit the accelerator and sped up to get there as fast as was legally possible. As we continued down the road, I still couldn't see any flashing sign that read "fried chicken." Finally, I did see a sign flashing sign and thought to myself, "That must be it!" However, as I drove closer and closer to the flashing sign, it became clearer and clearer to me that it didn't spell FRIED CHICKEN at all. Instead, it was a sign flashing the words: FREE CHECKING! FREE CHECKING!

We had a great laugh about my wife's perceptual error. She wasn't joking when she first saw the flashing sign in the distance; she really did think it was flashing the words "fried chicken." That experience proved to me beyond a doubt that human beings engage in selection perception—we tend to see what we *want* (or hope) to see, rather than reality.

Joe Cuseo

Reflection 4.7

Have you ever had the experience of seeing what you hoped or expected to see, rather than seeing things accurately (objectively)? Or, have you ever observed this happen to someone else?

What was the situation?

Why do you think that you (or the person you observed) did not view the situation accurately or objectively?

Balanced Thinking

Balanced thinking involves seeking out and carefully considering evidence for and against a particular position. The process of supporting a position with evidence is technically referred to as *adduction*; when you adduce, you offer reasons for a position. The process of arguing against a position by presenting contradictory evidence or reasons is called *refutation*; when you refute, you provide a rebuttal by supplying evidence *against* a particular position. The opposing position's stronger arguments are acknowledged, and its weaker ones are refuted (Fairbairn & Winch, 1996).

Balanced thinking involves both adduction and refutation. The goal of a balanced thinker is not to stack up evidence for one position or the other, but to be an impartial investigator who looks at supporting and opposing evidence for both sides of an issue and attempts to reach a conclusion that's not biased or one-sided. Thus, the first step in the process of seeking truth should not be to immediately jump in and take an either-or (for or against) stance on a debatable issue. Instead, your first step should be to look at arguments for and against each position, acknowledge the strengths and weaknesses of both sides of the argument, and identify what additional information may still be needed to make a fair judgment or reach a reasonable conclusion.

Balanced thinking requires more than just adding up the number of arguments for and against a position; it also involves weighing the strength of those arguments, because arguments can vary in terms of their level of importance and degree of support. When evaluating arguments, ask yourself, "How sure am I about the conclusion made by this argument?" Determine whether the evidence is:

1. **Definitive.** So strong or compelling that a definite conclusion should be reached;

2. **Suggestive.** Strong enough to suggest that a tentative conclusion may be reached; or

3. **Inconclusive.** Too weak to reach any conclusion.

> *Remember*
>
> *A characteristic of balanced thinking is being mindful of the weight (degree of importance) you assign to different arguments and articulating how their weight has been factored into your final conclusion (e.g., in a written report or class presentation).*

In some cases, after you review both supporting and contradictory evidence for opposing positions, balanced thinking may lead you to suspend judgment and to withhold making a firm decision that favors one position over the other. A balanced thinker may occasionally reach the following conclusions: "Right now, I can't be sure; the evidence doesn't strongly favor one position over the other," or "More information is needed before I can make a final judgment or reach a firm conclusion." This isn't being wishy-washy: these are legitimate conclusions to draw, as long as they are informed conclusions supported by sound reasons and solid evidence. In fact, it's better to hold an undecided but informed viewpoint based on balanced thinking than to hold a definite opinion that's uninformed, biased, or based on emotion—such as the opinions offered loudly and obnoxiously by people on radio and TV talk shows.

Reflection 4.8

Consider the following positions:

1. Course requirements should be eliminated; college students should be allowed to choose the classes they want to take for their degree.

2. Course grades should be eliminated; college students should take classes on a pass-fail basis.

Using balanced thinking, identify one or more arguments *for* and *against* each of these positions.

> *Remember*
>
> *When you combine balanced thinking with multidimensional thinking, you become a more complex and comprehensive thinker who is capable of viewing any issue from opposing sides and different angles.*

"The more you know, the less sure you are."
Voltaire,
French historian,
philosopher, and
advocate for civil liberty

"Too often we enjoy the comfort of opinion without the discomfort of thought."
John F. Kennedy,
35th president of the
United States

"I always seemed to stand in the no man's land between opposing arguments, yearning to be won over by one side or the other but finding instead degrees of merit in both. But in time I came to accept, even embrace, what I called 'my confusion.' I preferred to listen rather than speak; to inquire, not crusade."
"In Praise of the 'Wobblies'" by Ted Gup, journalist who has written for *Time Magazine*, *National Geographic*, and *The New York Times*

Critical Thinking

Critical thinking is a form of higher-level thinking that involves *evaluation* or *judgment*. The evaluation can be either positive or negative: for example, a movie critic can give a good (thumbs up) or bad (thumbs down) review of a film. However, critical thinking involves much more than simply stating, "I liked it," or "I didn't like it." Specific reasons or evidence must be supplied to support the critique; failure to do so makes the criticism unfounded—i.e., it has no foundation or basis of support.

Reflection 4.9

Flash back to the journal entry at the start of this chapter. How does your response to the incomplete sentence compare with the definition of critical thinking we just provided?

How are they similar?

How do they differ?

(If you wrote that critical thinking means "being critical" or negatively criticizing something or somebody, don't feel bad. Many students think that critical thinking has this negative meaning or connotation.)

Critical thinking is used to evaluate many things besides films, art, or music: it's also used to judge the quality of ideas, beliefs, choices, and decisions—whether they be your own or those of others. It's also a skill that's highly valued by professors teaching students at all stages in the college experience and all subjects in the college curriculum (Higher Education Institute, 2009; Stark et al., 1990). By working on developing these skills now, you'll significantly improve your academic performance throughout your college experience. You can start developing the mental habit of critical thinking by regularly asking yourself the following questions as criteria for evaluating any idea or argument:

1. **Validity (truthfulness).** Is it true or accurate?

2. **Morality (ethics).** Is it fair or just?

3. **Beauty (aesthetics).** Is it beautiful or artistic?

4. **Practicality (usefulness).** Can it be put to use for practical purposes?

5. **Priority (order of importance or effectiveness).** Is it the best option or alternative?

When I teach classes or give workshops, I often challenge students or participants to debate me on either politics or religion. For their debate topic, I ask them to choose a political party affiliation, a religion or a branch of religion, or a stance on a social issue for which there are political or religious viewpoints. The ground rules are as follows: they choose the topic for debate; they can only use facts to pose their argument, rebuttal, or both; and they can only respond in a rational manner, without letting emotions drive their answers. This exercise usually reveals that the topics people feel strongly about are often topics that they have not critically evaluated. People often say they are Democrat, Republican, independent, and so on, and argue from this position. However, few of them have taken the time to critically examine whether their stated affiliation is actually consistent with their personal viewpoints. For example, they almost always answer "no" to the following questions: "Have you read the core document (e.g., party platform) that outlines the party stance?" and "Have you engaged in self-examination of your party affiliation through reasoned discussions with others who say they have the same or a different political affiliation?"

— *Aaron Thompson*

Creative Thinking

When you think creatively, you generate something new or different, whether that may be a novel idea, strategy, or work product. Creative thinking leads you to ask the question, "Why not?" (e.g., "Why not do it a different way?"). It could be said that when you think critically you look "inside the box" and evaluate the quality of its content. When you think creatively, you look "outside the box" to imagine other packages containing different content.

Any time you combine two existing ideas to generate a new idea, you're engaging in creative thinking. Creative thinking can be viewed as an extension or higher form of synthesis, whereby parts of separate ideas are combined or integrated to create a final product that turns out to be different (and better) than what previously existed (Anderson & Krathwohl, 2001). Even in the arts, what's created isn't totally original or unique. Instead, artistic creativity typically involves a combination or rearrangement of previously existing elements to generate a new "whole"—a final product that is distinctive or noticeably different. For instance, hard rock was created by combining elements of blues and rock and roll, and folk rock took form when Bob Dylan combined musical elements of acoustic blues and amplified rock (Shelton et al., 2003). Robert Kearns (subject of the film *Flash of Genius*) combined preexisting mechanical parts to create the intermittent windshield wiper (Seabrook, 2008).

Creative and critical thinking are two of the most important forms of higher-level thinking, and they work well together. We use creative thinking to ask new questions and generate new ideas; we use critical thinking to evaluate or critique the ideas we create (Paul & Elder, 2004). A creative idea must not only be different or original: it must also be effective (Sternberg, 2001; Runco, 2004). If critical thinking reveals that the quality of what we've created is poor, we then shift back to creative thinking to generate something new and improved. Or, we may start by using critical thinking to evaluate an old idea or approach and come to the judgment that it's not very good. This unfavorable evaluation naturally leads to and turns on the creative thinking process, which tries to come up with a new idea or different approach that's better than the old one.

"The principal mark of genius is not perfection but originality, the opening of new frontiers."
Arthur Koestler,
Hungarian novelist
and philosopher

"The blues are the roots. Everything else are the fruits."
Willie Dixon,
blues songwriter;
commenting on how all
forms of contemporary
American music contain
elements of blues music,
which originated among
African American slaves

Brainstorming is a problem-solving process that effectively illustrates how creative and critical thinking complement each other. The steps or stages involved in the process of brainstorming are summarized in **Do It Now! 4.1**. As the brainstorming process suggests, creativity doesn't just happen suddenly or effortlessly, like the so-called stroke of genius; instead, it takes considerable mental effort (Paul & Elder, 2004; De Bono, 2007). Although creative thinking initially involves some spontaneous and intuitive leaps; it also involves careful reflection and evaluation of whether any of those leaps actually land you on a good idea.

4.1   DO IT **NOW**!

The Process of Brainstorming

1. List as many ideas as you can, generating them rapidly without stopping to evaluate their validity or practicality. Studies show that worrying about whether an idea is correct often blocks creativity (Basadur, Runco, & Vega, 2000). So, at this stage of the process, just let your imagination run wild; don't worry about whether the idea you generate is impractical, unrealistic, or outrageous.

2. Use the ideas on your list as a springboard to trigger additional ideas, or combine them to create new ideas.

3. After you run out of ideas, review and critically evaluate the list of ideas you've generated and eliminate those that you think are least effective.

4. From the remaining list of ideas, choose the best idea or best combination of ideas.

Note: The first two steps in the brainstorming process involve *divergent thinking*—a form of creative thinking that allows you to go off in different directions and generate diverse ideas. In contrast, the last two steps in the process involve *convergent thinking*—a form of critical thinking in which you converge (focus in) and narrow down the ideas, evaluating each of them for their effectiveness.

Author's Experience

Several years ago, I was working with a friend to come up with ideas for a grant proposal. We started out by sitting at his kitchen table, exchanging ideas while sipping coffee; then we both got up and began to pace back and forth, walking all around the room while bouncing different ideas off each other. Whenever a new idea was thrown out, one of us would jot it down (whoever was pacing closer to the kitchen table at the moment).

After we ran out of ideas, we shifted gears, slowed down, and sat down at the table again to critique each of the ideas we'd just generated during our "binge-thinking" episode. After some debate, we finally settled on an idea that we judged to be the best of all the ideas we produced, and we used this idea for the grant proposal.

Although I wasn't fully aware of it at the time, the stimulating thought process we were using was called brainstorming because it involved both of its key stages: we first engaged in creative thinking—our fast-paced walking and idea-production stage; we followed that with critical thinking—our slower-paced sitting and idea-evaluation stage.

Joe Cuseo

Lastly, keep in mind that creative thinking is not restricted to the arts: it can occur in all subject areas, even in fields that seek precision and definite answers. For example, in math, creative thinking may involve using new approaches or strategies for arriving at a correct solution to a problem. In science, creative thinking takes place when a scientist first uses imaginative thinking to create a hypothesis or logical hunch ("What might happen if . . . ?"), then conducts an experiment to test whether that hypothesis proves to be true.

Strategies for Developing Higher-Level Thinking Skills and Using Them to Improve Academic Performance

Thus far, this chapter has been devoted primarily to helping you get a clear idea about what higher-level thinking is and what its major forms are. The remainder of this chapter focuses on helping you develop habits of higher-level thinking and apply these habits to improve your performance in the first year of college and beyond.

1. **Cross-reference and connect any ideas you acquire in class with related ideas you acquire from your assigned reading.** When you discover information in your reading that relates to something you've learned about in class (or vice versa), make a note of it in the margin of your textbook or your class notebook. By integrating knowledge you've obtained from these two major sources, you're using synthesis—a higher-level thinking skill that you can then demonstrate on course exams and assignments to improve your course grades.

2. **When listening to lectures and completing reading assignments, pay attention not only to the content being covered, but also to the thought process that accompanies the content.** Periodically ask yourself what form of higher-level thinking your instructors are using during major segments of a class presentation and what your textbook authors are using in different sections of a chapter. The more conscious you are of the types of higher-level thinking skills you're being exposed to, the more likely you are to acquire those thinking skills and demonstrate them on exams and assignments.

3. **Periodically pause to reflect on your own thinking process.** When working on your courses, ask yourself what type of thinking you're doing (e.g., analysis, synthesis, or evaluation) during the work process. When you think about your own thinking, you're engaging in a mental process known as *metacognition*—that is, you're aware of how you're thinking while you're thinking (Flavell, 1979; Hartman, 2001). Metacognition is a mental habit that's associated with higher-level thinking and improved problem-solving skills (Halpern, 2003; Resnick, 1986).

4. **Develop habits of higher-level thinking by asking yourself higher-level thinking questions.** One simple but powerful way to think about your thinking is through self-questioning. Since questions have the power to activate and elevate your thinking and since thinking often involves talking silently to yourself, if you make an intentional attempt to ask yourself good questions, you can train your mind to think at a higher level. A good question can serve as a launching pad that propels you to higher levels of thinking in your quest to answer it. The higher the level of thinking called for by the questions you regularly ask yourself, the higher the level of thinking you will display in class discussions, on college exams, and in written assignments.

> "Imagination should give wings to our thoughts, but imagination must be checked and documented by the factual results of the experiment."
>
> Louis Pasteur, French microbiologist, chemist, and inventor of pasteurization (a method for preventing milk and wine from going sour)

> "To think is to talk to oneself."
>
> Immanuel Kant, German philosopher

> "If you do not ask the right questions, you do not get the right answers."
>
> Edward Hodnett, British poet

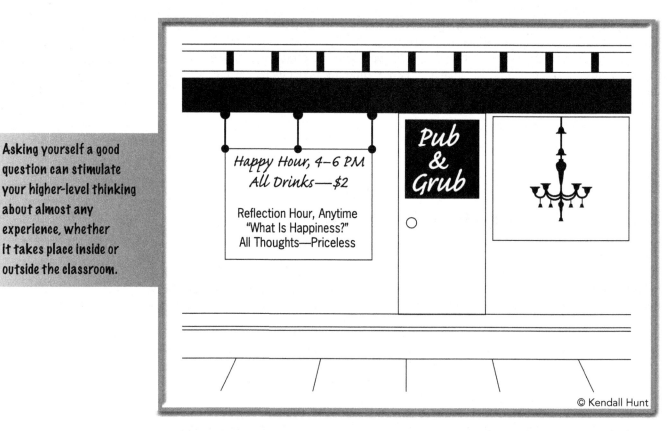

Asking yourself a good question can stimulate your higher-level thinking about almost any experience, whether it takes place inside or outside the classroom.

© Kendall Hunt

In **Do It Now! 4.2** you'll find numerous questions that have been intentionally designed to promote higher-level thinking. The questions are constructed in a way that will allow you to easily fill in the blank and apply the type of thinking called for by the question to ideas or issues being discussed in any course you may take. Considerable research indicates that students can learn to use questions such as these to improve their higher-level thinking ability in various subject areas (King, 1990, 1995; 2002).

As you read each set of trigger questions, place a checkmark next to one question in the set that could be applied to a concept or issue being covered in a course you're taking this term.

Reflection 4.10

Look back at the forms of thinking described in Snapshot Summary 4.3. Identify one question listed under each set of trigger questions in Do It Now! 4.2 and fill in the blank with an idea or issue being covered in a course you're taking this term.

Self-Questioning Strategies for Triggering Different Forms of Higher-Level Thinking

Application (applied thinking). Putting knowledge into practice to solve problems and resolve issues.

Trigger Questions

- How can this idea be used to _____?
- How could this concept be implemented to _____?
- How can this theory be put into practice to _____?
- What could be done to prevent or reduce _____?

Analysis (analytical thinking). Breaking down information into its essential elements or parts.

Trigger Questions

- What are the main ideas contained in _____?
- What are the important aspects of _____?
- What are the issues raised by _____?
- What are the major purposes of _____?
- What assumptions or biases lie hidden within _____?
- What are the reasons behind _____?

Synthesis. Integrating separate pieces of information to form a more complete product or pattern.

Trigger Questions

- How can this idea be joined or connected with _____ to create a more complete or comprehensive understanding of _____?
- How could these different _____ be grouped together into a more general class or category?
- How could these separate _____ be reorganized or rearranged to produce a more comprehensive understanding of the big picture?

Multidimensional thinking. Thinking that involves viewing yourself and the world around you from different angles or vantage points.

Trigger Questions

- How would _____ affect different dimensions of myself (emotional, physical, etc.)?
- What broader impact would _____ have on the social and physical world around me?
- How might people living in different times (e.g., past and future) view _____?

- How would people from different cultural backgrounds interpret or react to _____?
- Have I taken into consideration all the major factors that could influence _____ or be influenced by _____?

Inferential reasoning. Making an argument or judgment by inferring (stepping to) a conclusion that's supported by empirical (observable) evidence or logical consistency.

Trigger Questions Seeking Empirical Evidence

- What examples support the argument that _____?
- What research evidence is there for _____?
- What statistical data document that this _____ is true?

Trigger Questions Seeking Logical Consistency

- Since _____ is true, why shouldn't _____ also be true?
- If people believe in _____, shouldn't they practice _____?
- To make the statement that _____, wouldn't it have to be assumed that _____?

Balanced thinking. Carefully considering reasons for and against a particular position or viewpoint.

Trigger Questions

- Have I considered both sides of _____?
- What are the strengths (advantages) and weaknesses (disadvantages) of _____?
- What evidence supports and contradicts _____?
- What are arguments for and counterarguments against _____?

Trigger Questions for Adduction (arguing for a particular idea or position by supplying supporting evidence)

- What proof is there for _____?
- What are logical arguments for _____?
- What research evidence supports _____?

Trigger Questions for Refutation (arguing against a particular idea or position by supplying contradictory evidence)

- What proof is there against _____?
- What logical arguments indicate that _____ is false?
- What research evidence contradicts _____?
- What counterarguments would provide an effective rebuttal to _____?

(continued)

Critical thinking. Making well-informed evaluations or judgments.

Trigger Questions for Evaluating Validity (Truthfulness)
- Is _____ true or accurate?
- Is there sufficient evidence to support the conclusion that _____?
- Is the reasoning behind _____ strong or weak?

Trigger Questions for Evaluating Morality (Ethics)
- Is _____ fair?
- Is _____ just?
- Is this action consistent with the professed or stated values of _____?

Trigger Questions for Evaluating Beauty (Aesthetics)
- What is the artistic merit of _____?
- Does _____ have any aesthetic value?
- Does _____ contribute to the beauty of the world?

Trigger Questions for Evaluating Practicality (Usefulness)
- Will _____ work?
- How can _____ be put to good use?
- What practical benefit would result from _____?

Trigger Questions for Evaluating Priority (Order of Importance or Effectiveness)
- Which one of these _____ is the most important?
- Is this _____ the best option or choice available?
- How should these _____ be ranked from first to last (best to worst) in terms of their effectiveness?

Creative thinking. Generating ideas that are unique, original, or distinctively different.

Trigger Questions
- What could be invented to _____?
- Imagine what would happen if _____?
- What might be a different way to _____?
- How would this change if _____?
- What would be an ingenious way to _____.

Note: Save these higher-level thinking questions so that you can use them when completing different academic tasks required by your courses (e.g., preparing for exams, writing papers or reports, and participating in class discussions or study-group sessions). Try to get into the habit of periodically stepping back to reflect on your thinking process. Ask yourself what type of thinking you are doing (such as analysis, synthesis, or evaluation) and record your personal reflections in writing. You could even keep a "thinking log" or "thinking journal" to increase self-awareness of the thinking strategies you develop across time, or how your thinking strategies may vary across different courses and academic fields. This strategy will not only help you acquire higher-level thinking skills: it will also help you describe the thinking skills you have acquired during job interviews and in letters of application for career positions.

5. **To stimulate creative thinking, use the following strategies.**
   - **Be flexible.** Think about ideas and objects in unusual or unconventional ways. The power of flexible and unconventional thinking is well illustrated in the movie *Apollo 13*, which is based on the real story of an astronaut saving his life by creatively using duct tape as an air filter. The inventor of the printing press (Johannes Gutenberg) made his groundbreaking discovery while watching a machine being used to crush grapes at a wine harvest. He thought that the same type of machine could be used to press letters onto paper (Dorfman, Shames, & Kihlstrom, 1996).
   - **Be experimental.** Play with ideas, trying them out to see whether they'll work and work better than the status quo. Studies show that creative people tend to be mental risk-takers who experiment with ideas and techniques (Sternberg, 2001). Consciously resist the temptation to settle for the security of familiarity. Doing things the way they've always been done doesn't mean you're doing them the best way possible. It may mean that it's just the most habitual (and mindless) way to do them. When people cling rigidly or stubbornly to what's conventional or traditional, what they're doing is clinging to the comfort or security of what's most familiar and predictable, which blocks originality, ingenuity, and openness to change.

- **Get mobile.** Get up and move around. Studies show that the brain gets approximately 10 percent more oxygen when we stand up than it does when we're sitting down (Sousa, 2006). Since oxygen provides fuel for the brain, our ability to think creatively is stimulated when we think on our feet and move around, rather than sitting on our butts for extended periods of time.

- **Get it down.** Carry a pen and a small notepad or packet of sticky notes (or a portable electronic recording device) with you at all times to record creative ideas, because these ideas often come to mind at the most unexpected times. The process of creative ideas suddenly popping into your mind is sometimes referred to as *incubation*—just like incubated eggs can hatch at any time, ideas can suddenly hatch and pop into consciousness after you've sat on them for a while. Unfortunately, however, just as an idea can suddenly come into mind, it can just as suddenly slip out of mind when you start thinking about something else. You can prevent this from happening by having the right equipment on hand to record your creative ideas as soon as you have them.

- **Get diverse.** Seek ideas from diverse social and informational sources. Bouncing your ideas off of different people and getting their ideas about your idea is a good way to generate energy, synergy, and serendipity (accidental discoveries). Studies show that creative people venture well beyond the boundaries of their particular area of training or specialization (Baer, 1993; Kaufman & Baer, 2002). They have wide-ranging interests and knowledge, which they draw upon and combine to generate new ideas (Riquelme, 2002). Be on the lookout to combine the knowledge and skills you acquire from different subject areas and different people to create bridges to new ideas.

- **Take a break.** When working on a problem that you can't seem to solve, stop working on it for a while and come back to it later. Creative solutions often come to mind after you stop thinking about the problem. When you're trying so hard and working so intensely on a problem or challenging task, your attention may become mentally set or rigidly fixed on one aspect of it (German & Barrett, 2005; Maier, 1970). Taking your mind off of it and returning to it at a later point allows the problem to incubate in your mind at a lower level of consciousness and stress. This can sometimes give birth to a sudden solution. Furthermore, when you come back to the task later, your focus of attention is likely to shift to a different feature or aspect of the problem. This new focus may enable you to view the problem from a different angle or vantage point, which can lead to a breakthrough idea that was blocked by your previous perspective (Anderson, 2000).

- **Reorganize the problem.** When you're stuck on a problem, try rearranging its parts or pieces. Rearrangement can transform the problem into a different pattern that provides you with a new perspective. The new perspective may position you to suddenly see a solution that was previously overlooked, much like changing the order of letters in a word jumble can suddenly enable you to see the hidden scrambled word. By changing the wording of any problem you're working on, or by recording ideas on index cards (or sticky notes) and laying them out in different orders and arrangements, you may suddenly see a solution.

- If you're having trouble solving problems that involve a sequence of steps (e.g., math problems), try reversing the sequence and start by working from the end or middle. The new sequence changes your approach to the problem by forcing you to come at it from a different direction, which can sometimes provide you with an alternative path to its solution.

- **Be persistent.** Studies show that creativity takes time, dedication, and hard work (Ericsson, 2006; Ericsson & Charness, 1994). Creative thoughts often do not emerge in one sudden stroke of genius, but evolve gradually after repeated reflection and persistent effort.

"I make progress by having people around who are smarter than I am—and listening to them. And I assume that everyone is smarter about something than I am."
Henry Kaiser, successful industrialist, known as the father of American shipbuilding

"Eureka!" (Literally translated, "I have found it!")
Attributed to Archimedes, ancient Greek mathematician and inventor, when he suddenly discovered (while sitting in a bathtub) how to measure the purity of gold

"Creativity consists largely of re-arranging what we know in order to find out what we do not know."
George Keller, prolific American architect and originator of the Union Station design for elevated train stations

"Genius is 1% inspiration and 99% perspiration."
Thomas Edison, scientist and creator of more than 1,000 inventions, including the light bulb, phonograph, and motion picture camera

Summary and Conclusion

Since higher-level thinking is the number one educational goal of college professors, developing this skill is crucial for achieving academic excellence. In addition to improving academic performance in college, developing higher-level thinking skills have three other critical benefits.

Reflection **4.11**

The popularity of sticky notes is no doubt due to their versatility—you can post them on almost anything, remove them from where they were stuck (without a mess), and re-stick them somewhere else.

Think creatively for a minute. In what ways could college students use sticky notes to help complete the academic tasks they face in college? Think of as many ways as possible.

1. **Higher-level thinking is essential in today's "information age," in which new information is being generated at faster rates than at any other time in human history.** The majority of new workers in the information age will no longer work with their hands but will instead work with their heads (Miller, 2003), employers will value college graduates who have inquiring minds and possess higher-level thinking skills (Harvey, Moon, Geall, & Bower, 1997; Peter D. Hart Research Associates, 2006).

2. **Higher-level thinking skills are vital for citizens in a democracy.** Authoritarian political systems, such as dictatorships and fascist regimes, suppress critical thought and demand submissive obedience to authority. In contrast, citizens living in a democracy are expected to control their political destiny by choosing (electing) their political leaders; thus, judging and choosing wisely are crucial civic responsibilities in a democratic nation. Citizens living and voting in a democracy must use higher-level reasoning skills, such as balanced and critical thinking, to make wise political choices.

3. **Higher-level thinking is an important safeguard against prejudice, discrimination, and hostility.** Racial, ethnic, and national prejudices often stem from narrow, self-centered, or group-centered thinking (Paul & Elder, 2002). Prejudice often results from oversimplified, dualistic thinking that can lead individuals to categorize other people into either "in" groups (us) or "out" groups (them). This type of dualistic thinking can lead, in turn, to ethnocentrism—the tendency to view one's own racial or ethnic group as the superior "in" group and see other groups as inferior "out" groups. Development of higher-level thinking skills, such as taking multiple perspectives and using balanced thinking, counteracts the type of dualistic, ethnocentric thinking that leads to prejudice, discrimination, and hate crimes.

Learning More through the World Wide Web

Internet-Based Resources for Further Information on Higher-Level Thinking

For additional information related to the ideas discussed in this chapter, we recommend the following Web sites:

Critical Thinking:

www.criticalthinking.org

Creative Thinking:

www.amcreativityassoc.org

Higher-Level Thinking Skills:

www.wcu.edu/ceap/houghton/Learner/think/thinkhigherorder.html

4.1 Self-Assessment of Higher-Level Thinking Characteristics

Listed here are four general characteristics of higher-level thinkers accompanied by a set of traits related to each characteristic. When you read the traits listed beneath each of the general characteristics, place a checkmark next to any trait that you think is true of you.

Characteristics of Higher-Level Thinkers

1. Tolerant and Accepting
   - Keep emotions under control when someone criticizes their viewpoint
   - Do not tune out ideas that conflict with their own
   - Feel comfortable with disagreement
   - Are receptive to hearing different points of view

2. Inquisitive and Open-Minded
   - Are eager to continue learning new things from different people and different experiences
   - Have an inquiring mind that's genuinely curious, inquisitive, and ready to explore new ideas
   - Find differences of opinion and opposing viewpoints interesting and stimulating
   - Attempt to understand why people hold different viewpoints and try to find common ground between them

3. Reflective and Tentative
   - Suspend judgment until all the evidence is in, rather than making snap judgments before knowing the whole story
   - Acknowledge the complexity, ambiguity, and uncertainty associated with certain issues, and are willing to perhaps say, "I need to give this more thought," or "I need more evidence before I can draw a conclusion"
   - Take time to think things through before drawing conclusions, making choices, and reaching decisions
   - Periodically reexamine personal viewpoints to see whether they should be maintained or changed as a result of new experiences and evidence

4. Honest and Courageous
   - Give fair consideration to ideas that others may instantly disapprove of or find distasteful
   - Are willing to express personal viewpoints that may not conform to those of the majority
   - Are willing to change old opinions or beliefs when they are contradicted by new evidence
   - Are willing to acknowledge the limitations or weaknesses of their attitudes and beliefs

Look back at the list and count the number of checkmarks you placed in each of the four general areas:

1. Tolerant and Accepting = _____

2. Inquisitive and Open-Minded = _____

3. Reflective and Tentative = _____

4. Honest and Courageous = _____

For which characteristic did you have (a) the *most* checkmarks, (b) the *least* checkmarks?

What do you think accounts for this difference?

4.2 Demonstrating Higher-Level Thinking in Your Current Courses

Look at the syllabus for three courses you're enrolled in this term and find an assignment or exam that carries the greatest weight (counts the most) toward your final course grade. If you're taking fewer than three courses, you can choose more than one assignment or exam from the same course.

Course	Major Assignment or Test
1.	
2.	
3.	

On the grid that follows, place a checkmark in each box that represents the form of higher-level thinking you think will be required on each of these major assignments or tests. (For a quick review of the major forms of higher-level thinking, see the higher-level thinking definitions on p. 191.)

Major Assignment or Test

	Course 1	Course 2	Course 3
Applied Thinking			
Analysis			
Synthesis			
Multidimensional Thinking			
Inferential Reasoning			
Balanced Thinking			
Critical Thinking			
Creative Thinking			

Choose one box you checked for each course and describe how you would demonstrate that particular form of higher-level thinking on that particular assignment or test. For instance, if you checked a box indicating that you will use multidimensional thinking, describe what perspectives or factors you will take into consideration.

Course 1 exam or assignment: _____

Form of higher-level thinking required:

How I plan to demonstrate this form of thinking:

Course 2 exam or assignment: _____

Form of higher-level thinking required:

How I plan to demonstrate this form of thinking:

Course 3 exam or assignment: _____

Form of higher-level thinking required:

How I plan to demonstrate this form of thinking:

Trick or Treat: Confusing or Challenging Test?

Students in Professor Plato's philosophy course just got their first exam back and they're going over the test together in class. Some students are angry because they feel that Professor Plato deliberately included "trick questions" to confuse them. Professor Plato responds by saying that his test questions were not designed to trick the class but to "challenge them to think."

Reflection and Discussion Questions

1. Why do you think that some students thought that Professor Plato was trying to trick or confuse them?

2. What do you think the professor meant when he told his students that his test questions were designed to "challenge them to think"?

3. On future tests, what might the students do to reduce the likelihood that they will feel tricked again?

4. On future tests, what might Professor Plato do to reduce the likelihood that students will complain about being asked "trick questions"?

CHAPTER 5

Appreciating Diversity

Learning Objectives

Read to answer these key questions:

- What is diversity and why is it important?

- How can an understanding and appreciation of diversity help me to be successful in school and in work?

- What is some vocabulary useful for understanding diversity?

- What are some ideas for communicating across cultures?

- What are some myths and facts about sexual orientation?

- How can I gain an appreciation of diversity?

Our schools, our workplaces, and our nation are becoming more diverse. Gaining an understanding and appreciation of this diversity will enhance your future success. Understanding yourself and having pride in your unique characteristics is the first step in the process. Self-knowledge includes information about your personality, interests, talents, and values. Earlier in this text you had the opportunity to begin this exploration. This chapter challenges you to examine some additional characteristics that make you a unique individual and to take pride in yourself while respecting the differences of others.

Diversity Is Increasing

Another word for diversity is differences. These differences do not make one group inferior or superior. Differences are not deficits: they are just differences. Look around your classroom, your place of employment, or where you do business. You will notice people of a variety of races, ethnic groups, cultures, genders, ages, socioeconomic levels, and sexual orientations. Other differences that add to our uniqueness include religious preference, political affiliation, personality, interests, and values. It is common to take pride in who we are and to look around and find people who share our view of the world. The challenge is to be able to look at the world from the point of view of those who are different from us. These differences provide an opportunity for learning.

Our schools and communities are becoming increasingly diverse. In the United States, one in every five students has a parent born in a foreign country. Nationwide, non-Latino whites make up only 63 percent of the population. The current population includes 16 percent African Americans, 15 percent Latinos, and 5 percent Asians. There is also an increase in people who identify themselves as multiracial. About seven million people or 2.4 percent of the population identify with at least two different racial groups. California, one of the most populous states, is leading the nation in diversity. There is no single group in the majority: 43 percent are Latinos, 36 percent are non-Latino whites, 9 percent are African Americans, and 8 percent are Asian.[1] In New Mexico, Hawaii, and the District of Columbia, non-Latino whites are also in the minority.[2]

In our schools, places of work, and communities, we increasingly study, work, and socialize with people from different ethnic groups. This morning I talked with a student from Mexico and another from France. My classes have students from Mexico, Japan, Argentina, and Iraq. A colleague called on the phone and we spoke in Spanish. He invited me to a Greek café and deli where we ate Greek salad and purchased feta cheese and baklava. This diversity provides different perspectives, and products from other countries enrich our lives. It requires open-mindedness and respect for differences for it all to work.

We also live in a **global economy**. Increased trade among the nations of the world requires an understanding and appreciation of cultural differences. The United States is in the center of the largest free-trade area in the world. In 1994, the North American Free Trade Agreement (NAFTA) created a free-trade area that includes Canada, the United States, and Mexico. This act resulted in a freer flow of goods among these countries and an increase in international business. The success of this international business depends on increased cooperation and problem solving among these nations. Free-trade agreements will probably be expanded to other countries in Latin America in the near future.

Another major step toward the global economy was the creation of a single currency in Europe, the euro, which was successfully launched on January 1, 2002. The purpose of this largest money changeover in history was to establish a system in which people, goods, services, and capital can move freely across national borders. The European countries using the euro have made their economies more competitive by facilitating trade, travel, and investment.

International trade accounts for a quarter of all economic activity in the United States.[3] All we have to do is look around us to see that many of the foods and products we use in our daily lives come from other countries.

Last night Jessica invited friends over for dinner and made stir-fried vegetables with chicken. She used ingredients from Vietnam, Thailand, Italy, Japan and Mexico. These foods were all purchased at her local grocery store. The guests ate dinner on plates made in Malaysia and drank wine from Australia. The next morning, she got up and dressed in a shirt made in the Dominican Republic and pants made in Mexico. She then put on her walking shoes, which were made in Thailand, and listened to Jamaican music on her iPod, which was made in China. For breakfast she ate a banana grown in Honduras and drank coffee from Colombia. She drove to school in a car that was made in Japan.

Global trade brings us many new and inexpensive products and is having a major impact on the economy and careers of the future.

Changes in technology have made an awareness and appreciation of diversity more important. The world is becoming an **electronic village** connected by an array of communication and information technologies: computers, the Internet, communications satellites, cell phones, fax machines, and the myriad of electronic devices that are an integral part of our lives today. These devices make rapid communication possible all over the world and are essential for international business and trade. The Internet is like a vast information superhighway, and each computer is an onramp to the highway. Those who do not have a computer or lack computer skills will be left off the highway and have limited access to information and opportunities.

The increased use of the Internet offers both great opportunities and challenges. The Internet can help to break down barriers between people. When communicating with someone over the Internet, differences such as race, age, religion, or economic status are not obvious. The flow of information and ideas is unrestricted, and people with similar interests can communicate easily with one another. There is great potential for use as well as misuse of the Internet. Chat groups can share information about medical conditions or treatments, but hate groups can also use the Internet to promote their political agendas.

The Internet presents new challenges for communicating, since nonverbal cues are often missing. Looking at a person's face or listening to the tone of voice adds a great deal to communication. A new type of "netiquette" has evolved as a result. For example, using all caps is a form of YELLING! Increasingly words are shortened and changed for ease of communication, resulting in a type of Internet grammar. Understanding websites in other languages is another new challenge.

Journal Entry #1

How will the global economy and the electronic village affect your future career and lifestyle?

Benefits of Diversity

- Gain critical thinking skills
- Pride in self and culture
- Learn from others
- Improve interpersonal skills
- Learn flexibility
- Develop cultural awareness

Why Is Diversity Important?

Our society, schools, and work environments are becoming more diverse. Having an understanding and appreciation of diversity can help you to be successful at school, at work, and in your personal life. Here are some benefits:

- **Gain skills in critical thinking.** Critical thinking requires identifying different viewpoints, finding possible answers, and then constructing your own reasonable view. Critical thinking skills are one of the expected outcomes of higher education. Many of your college assignments are designed to teach these skills. Whether you are writing an essay in an English class, participating in a discussion in a history class, or completing a laboratory experiment, critical thinking skills will help you to complete the task successfully. Critical thinking skills are also helpful in finding good solutions to problems or challenges you might find at work. For example, for a business manager, an important task is helping employees to work together as a team. The critical thinking process results in greater understanding of others and better problem-solving skills. To stay competitive, businesses need to find creative solutions for building better products and providing good customer service. Critical thinking skills help people work together to come up with good ideas to make a business a success.

- **Have pride in yourself and your culture.** Having pride in yourself is the foundation of good mental health and success in life. Sonia Nieto did research on a group of successful students. These students had good grades, enjoyed school, had plans for the future, and described themselves as successful. Nieto found that "one of the most consistent, and least expected, outcomes to emerge from these case studies has been a resoluteness with which young people maintain pride and satisfaction in their culture and the strength they derive from it."[4] Having pride in yourself and your culture is an important part of high self-esteem and can help you to become a better student and worker. Having good self-esteem provides the confidence to accept and care for others. The best schools and workplaces provide an environment where people can value their own culture as well as others. With respect between different cultures, ideas can be freely exchanged and the door is opened to creativity and innovation.

  The world is constantly changing and we must be ready to adapt to new situations. Sometimes it is difficult to balance "fitting in" and maintaining our own cultural identity. Researchers have described a process called **transculturation,** in which a person adapts to a different culture without sacrificing individual cultural identity. One study of Native Americans showed that retention of traditional cultural heritage was an important predictor of success. A Native American student described the process this way: "When we go to school, we live a non-Indian way but we still keep our values. . . . I could put my values aside just long enough to learn what it is I want to learn but that doesn't mean I'm going to forget them. I think that is how strong they are with me."[5] Cultural identity provides strength and empowerment to be successful.

- **Gain the ability to network and learn from others.** In college, you will have the opportunity to learn from your professors and other students who are different from yourself. You may have professors with very different personality styles and teaching styles. Your success will depend on being aware of the differences and finding a way to adapt to the situation. Each student in your classes will also come from a different perspective and have valuable ideas to add to the class.

  It is through networking with other people that most people find jobs. You are likely to find a job through someone you know, such as a college professor, a student in one of your classes, a community member, or a previous employer. Once you have the job, you will gain proficiency by learning from others. The best managers are open to learning from others and help different people to work together as a team. No matter how educated or experienced you become, you can always learn from others. Bill Cosby once told a graduating class at Washington University, "Don't ever think you know more than the person mopping the floor."[6] Every person has a different view of the world and has important ideas to share.

- **Improve interpersonal skills.** A popular Native American proverb is that you cannot understand another person until you have walked a few miles in their moccasins. Being able to understand different perspectives on life will help you to improve your personal relationships. Good interpersonal skills bring joy to our personal relationships and are very valuable in the workplace. The Secretary of Labor's Commission on

Achieving Necessary Skills (SCANS) identifies having good interpersonal skills as one of the five critical competencies needed in the workplace. Workers need to work effectively in teams, teach others, serve customers, exercise leadership, negotiate to arrive at a decision, and work well with cultural diversity.[7] Efficiency and profits in any industry depend on good interpersonal skills and how well workers can provide customer service.

- **Learn to be flexible and adapt to the situation.** These two qualities are necessary for dealing with the rapid change that is taking place in our society today. We learn these qualities by successfully facing personal challenges. If you are a single parent, you have learned to be flexible in managing time and resources. If you served in the military overseas, you have learned to adapt to a different culture. If you are a new college student, you are probably learning how to be independent and manage your own life. Flexibility is a valuable skill in the workplace. Today's employers want workers who can adapt, be flexible, and solve problems.

- **Develop cultural awareness.** Cultural awareness is valuable in your personal life and in the workplace. In your personal life, you can have a wider variety of satisfying personal relationships. You can enjoy people from different cultural backgrounds and travel to different countries.

In a global economy, cultural awareness is increasingly important. Tuning into cultural differences can open up business opportunities. For example, many companies are discovering that the buying power of minorities is significant. They are developing ad campaigns to sell products to Asians, Latinos, African Americans, and other groups.

Companies now understand that cultural awareness is important in international trade. American car manufacturers could not understand why the Chevy Nova was not selling well in Latin America. In Spanish, "No va" means "It doesn't go" or "It doesn't run." Kentucky Fried Chicken found out that "Finger-lickin' good" translates as "Eat your fingers off" in Chinese! Being familiar with the cultures and languages of different countries is necessary for successful international business.

Journal Entry #2

How will an understanding of diversity help you to be successful in school and work?

Vocabulary for Understanding Diversity

Knowing some basic terms will aid in your understanding of diversity.

- **Race.** Race refers to a group of people who are perceived to be physically different because of traits such as facial features, color of skin, and hair.
- **Ethnicity.** Ethnicity refers to a sense of belonging to a particular culture and sharing the group's beliefs, attitudes, skills, ceremonies, and traditions. An ethnic group usually descends from a common group of ancestors, usually from a particular country or geographic area.
- **Ethnocentrism.** Ethnocentrism is the belief that one's own ethnic, religious, or political group is superior to all others.

"I have learned that success is to be measured not so much by the position that one has reached in life as by the obstacles which he has had to overcome while trying to succeed."

Booker T. Washington

- **Culture.** Culture is the behavior, beliefs, and values shared by a group of people. It includes language, morals, and even food preferences. Culture includes everything that we learn from the people around us in our community.

- **Gender, sex.** Gender refers to cultural differences that distinguish males from females. Different cultures raise men and women to act in specified ways. Sex refers to anatomical differences.

- **Sexism.** Sexism is a negative attitude or perception based on sex.

- **Stereotype.** A stereotype is a generalization that expresses conventional or biased ideas about people in a certain group. Stereotypes can lead to discrimination based on these ideas. They cause us to view others in a limited way and reduce our ability to see people as individuals.

- **Prejudice.** A prejudice is a prejudgment of someone or something. Prejudices are often based on stereotypes and reflect a disrespect for others. Sometimes people who are prejudiced are insecure about their own identities.

- **Discrimination.** Discrimination happens when people are denied opportunities because of their differences. Prejudice and stereotype are often involved.

- **Racism.** Racism occurs when one race or ethnic group holds a negative attitude or perception of another group. It is prejudice based on race. Anthropologists generally accept that the human species can be categorized into races based on physical and genetic makeup. These scientists accept the fact that there is no credible evidence that one race is superior to another. People who believe that their own race is superior to another are called racists.

- **Cultural pluralism.** Each group celebrates the customs and traditions of their culture while participating in mainstream society.

- **Genocide.** Genocide is the deliberate and systematic destruction of a racial, political, or cultural group. It can include the destruction of the language, religion, or cultural practices of a group of people.

"Injustice anywhere is a threat to justice everywhere."
Martin Luther King, Jr.

"You must be the change you want to see in the world."
Mahatma Gandhi

Understanding Diversity

There are 6.6 billion people in the world today. Statistics provided by the Population Reference Bureau and the United Nations can give us a better understanding of diversity in the world today. By geographic area, the world's population can be broken down into these percentages:[8]

- 61 Asians
- 14 Africans
- 11 Europeans
- 9 Central and South Americans
- 5 North Americans (Canada and the United States)

If visitors from outer space were to visit the earth and report back about the most common human being found, they would probably describe someone of Asian descent. Statistics also show that approximately 50 percent of the world population suffers from malnutrition and 80 percent live in substandard housing. Moreover, 6 percent of the population living in the United States, Japan, and Germany owns half of the wealth of the world. In addition, continuous wars and fighting among the people of the earth have contributed to human suffering and the flight of many refugees.

As children, we accept the values, assumptions, and stereotypes of our culture. We use our own culture as a filter to understand the world. Because of this limited perception, people often consider their culture to be superior and other cultures to be inferior.[9] The belief that one's own culture, religious, or political group is superior to others is called

ethnocentrism. Native Americans have argued that the celebration of Columbus Day, commemorating the discovery of the New World by Christopher Columbus, is an example of ethnocentrism. In reality, the Native Americans lived here long before Christopher Columbus arrived in 1492.

Ethnocentrism can lead to discrimination, interpersonal conflict, and even wars between different groups of people. In extreme cases, it can even lead to **genocide**, the deliberate and systematic destruction of a racial, political, or cultural group. History is full of examples of genocide. In the United States, Native Americans were massacred and their land was confiscated in violation of treaties. In Mexico and South America, the Spanish conquerors systematically destroyed native populations. During World War II, six million Jews were killed. Pol Pot and the Khmer Rouge killed millions of Cambodians. Unfortunately, genocide continues today in various conflicts around the world.

An understanding of the harmful effects of stereotypes is necessary to improve our understanding and appreciation of diversity. A **stereotype** is an assumption that all members of a group are alike. For example, a tall African American woman in one of my classes was constantly dealing with the assumption that she must be attending college to play basketball. Actually, she was very academically oriented and not athletic at all. It is important to remember that we all have individual differences within groups of the same ethnicity or cultural background.

All of us use stereotypes to understand people different from ourselves. Why does this happen? There are many different reasons:

- It is a fast way to make sense of the world. It requires little thought.
- We tend to look for patterns to help us understand the world.
- We are often unable or unwilling to obtain all the information we need to make fair judgments about other people.
- Stereotypes can result from fear of people who are different. We often learn these fears as children.
- The media promotes stereotypes. Movies, magazines, and advertisements often present stereotypes. These stereotypes are often used as the basis of humor. For example, the media often uses people who are overweight in comedy routines.

The problem with stereotypes is that we do not get to know people as individuals. All members of a culture, ethnic group, or gender are not alike. If we make assumptions about a group, we treat everyone in the group the same. Stereotypes can lead to prejudice and discrimination. For example, a person who is overweight may find it more difficult to find a job because of stereotyping.

Psychologists and sociologists today present the idea of **cultural relativity**, in which different cultures, ethnic groups, genders, and sexual orientations are viewed as different but equally valuable and worthy of respect.[10] These differences between cultures can help us learn new ideas that can enrich our view of the world. They can also promote greater understanding and better relationships among individuals and nations.

Understanding Diversity, Part I

Test what you have learned by selecting the correct answers to the following questions.

1. The belief that one's own ethnic, religious, or political group is superior to all others is called

   a. cultural pluralism.
   b. cultural relativity.
   c. ethnocentrism.

2. The assumption that all members of a group are alike is

   a. discrimination.
   b. stereotype.
   c. prejudice.

3. The deliberate destruction of a racial, cultural, or political group of people is called

   a. genocide.
   b. racism.
   c. ethnocentrism.

4. Most people on the earth are

   a. North Americans.
   b. Europeans.
   c. Asians.

5. Cultural relativity is defined as

   a. the belief that one's own ethnic group is superior.
   b. groups that are viewed as different, but equally valuable.
   c. an ethnic group that descends from a common group of ancestors.

How did you do on the quiz? Check your answers: 1. c, 2. b, 3. a, 4. c, 5. b

Journal Entry # 3

Describe an incidence in which you experienced discrimination. Consider discrimination in a broad context, including ethnicity, culture, language, gender, sexual orientation, weight, height, appearance, personality type, values, politics, religion, age, experience, socioeconomic background, academic skills, or any other factor which could cause discrimination.

A New Look at Diversity: The Human Genome Project

Although the people of the world represent many racial, ethnic, and cultural groups, biologists are taking a new look at diversity by learning about human genes. Genes are composed of segments of DNA that determine the transmission of hereditary traits by controlling the operation of cells. Cells are the basic building blocks of the human body.

The Human Genome Project, a multibillion-dollar and multinational government-sponsored research project to map all human genes, was completed in 2003. This map is a catalog of all the genetic information contained in human cells. They have identified the genes and determined the sequence of the three billion chemical base pairs in human DNA. Although the project is completed, analysis of the data will continue for many years.[11] The human genome is considered a biological treasure chest that will allow scientists to discover how a body grows, ages, stays healthy, or becomes ill. This knowledge is invaluable in discovering new medications and improving health.

Results of the Human Genome Project show that we are all genetically similar while having unique individual differences. One of the interesting findings is that "as scientists have long suspected, though the world's people may look very different on the outside, genetically speaking humans are all 99.9 percent identical."[12] While we are genetically very similar, each individual can be identified by his or her genetic code. With the exception of identical twins, each individual human being is slightly different because of the unique combination of DNA letters inherited from one's parents.

Dr. Craig Venter, head of Celera Genomics Corporation, has stated that "race is a social concept, not a scientific one."[13] While it may be easy to look at people and describe them as Caucasian, African, or Asian, there is little genetic material to distinguish one race from another. Venter says, "We all evolved in the last 100,000 years from the same small number of tribes that migrated out of Africa and colonized the world."[14] Very few genes control traits that distinguish one race from another, such as skin color, eye color, and width of nose. These outward characteristics have been able to change quickly in response to environmental pressures. People who lived near the equator evolved dark skin to protect them from ultraviolet radiation. People who lived farther from the equator evolved pale skins to produce vitamin D from little sunlight. The genes responsible for these outward appearances are in the range of .01 percent of the total. Researchers on the Human Genome Project agree that **there is only one race: the human race**.

The Human Genome Project will be important for understanding the human body and will help us to find ways to prevent or cure illnesses. It may also provide new information for critical thinking about the idea of ethnocentrism and discover some basic ways in which all human beings are similar.

Communicating across Cultures

Human beings communicate through the use of symbols. A symbol is a word that stands for something else. Problems in communication arise when we assume that a symbol has only one meaning and that everyone understands the symbol in the same way. For example, we use the word "dog" to stand for a four-legged animal that barks. However, if I say the word "dog," the picture in my mind probably doesn't match the picture in your mind because there are many varieties of dogs. I might be picturing a Chihuahua while you are picturing a German shepherd. Language becomes even more complex when we have multiple meanings for one symbol. Consider the ways we use the word "dog":

- She is a dog. (She is unattractive.)
- He is a dog. (He is promiscuous.)
- He is a lucky dog. (He is fortunate.)
- It's a dog. (It is worthless.)
- Just dog it. (Just do enough to get by.)
- He went to the dogs. (He was not doing well.)
- He was in the doghouse. (He was in trouble.)
- Let sleeping dogs lie. (Leave the situation alone.)
- My dogs hurt. (My feet hurt.)

- He put on the dog. (He assumed an attitude of wealth or importance.)
- These are the dog days of summer. (These are hot days when people feel lazy.)
- The book is dog-eared. (The corners of the pages are bent.)
- He led a dog's life. (He was not happy.)
- May I have a doggy bag? (May I have a bag for my leftovers?)
- Doggone it! (I am frustrated!)
- I am dog-tired. (I am very tired.)

Imagine how a computer would translate the above sentences. The translations would be incomprehensible, since there are so many variations in meaning depending on the context. The problem of communication becomes even more difficult for those who are learning English. People who speak a different language might not understand the word "dog" at all because they use a different symbol for the object. Even after studying the language, it is easy to misinterpret the meaning of the word "dog." A recent immigrant was horrified when he was offered a hot dog at a ball game. He thought that this was a civilized country and was surprised that we ate dogs!

The symbols we use to stand for objects are arbitrary, complex, and dependent on our culture, language, and frame of reference. As a result, misunderstandings are common. When my son was very young, he was very frightened by noises on the roof of our house. He was afraid that aliens had landed. He said that he was certain there were aliens on the roof and that Dad said he had seen them too. I later found out that his father said that he had seen illegal aliens, or undocumented workers, in our neighborhood. It is strange that in the English language we use the word "alien" to refer to someone from outer space and someone from a different country. The "aliens" in my son's case turned out to be raccoons playing on the roof. The words that we use have a powerful influence on our lives and can make clear communication difficult.

Both verbal and nonverbal symbols have different meaning in different cultures. George Henderson, in his book *Cultural Diversity in the Workplace*,[15] gives the example of the common thumbs-up gesture, which we commonly interpret as "okay." In Japan the same gesture means money. In Ghana and Iran, it is a vulgar gesture similar to raising your middle finger in the United States. Another example is silence. In the United States, if a teacher asks a question and no one responds right away, the situation is uncomfortable. In Native American cultures, the person who remains silent is admired. Many Asian students listen more than they speak. According to a Zen proverb, "He who knows does not speak and he who speaks does not know." Think about how different our communications, especially business and sales techniques, would have to be in order to be effective in different cultures.

Here are some ideas to help improve your communications with people who are culturally different from you or speak a different language:

- Be sensitive to the fact that communication is difficult and that errors in understanding are likely.
- Remember that the message sent is not necessarily the message received.
- Give people time to think and respond. You do not have to fill in the silence right away.
- Check your understanding of the message. Rephrase or repeat the information to make sure it is correct. Ask questions.
- If you feel insulted by the message, remember that it is quite possible that you could be misinterpreting it. (Remember all the meanings for "dog" listed above.)
- If you are having problems communicating with someone who speaks a different language, speak slowly and clearly or use different words. Talking louder will not help.

- Remain calm and treat others with respect. Be patient.
- Find a translator if possible.
- Study a different language. This will help in understanding other cultures and the different ways that other cultures use symbols.
- Before traveling to a different country, read about the culture and learn some basic phrases in the language used. This will help you to enjoy your travel and learn about other cultures. Attempting to speak the language will show others that you care about and respect the culture.
- Sometimes nonverbal communication can help. If you are adventurous or desperate, smile and act out the message. Be aware that nonverbal communication can be misunderstood also.
- Don't forget your sense of humor.

Journal Entry # 4

What advice would you give to a person preparing to visit another country with a very different culture and language?

Understanding Sexual Orientation

Major causes of stereotyping and the resulting prejudice and discrimination are fear and lack of knowledge of those who are different. Prejudice and discrimination against gays and other minorities have sometimes led to hate crimes. For example, in 1998, Matthew Shepard, a gay student at the University of Wyoming, was lured from a bar, beaten, and tied to a log fence, where he was left during cold weather. He died five days later. His murderers received life sentences in prison. At Matthew's funeral, protesters held up signs saying, "God hates fags."[16] The term "faggot," which comes from the Latin word for a bundle of sticks, may refer to the time of the Inquisition when gays were actually burned at the stake along with witches.[17]

Stereotypes about sexual orientation and the resulting discrimination are common in society today and affect a great number of people. One out of four families has a gay family member and it is estimated that up to 10 percent of the population is gay or lesbian. In a class of 30 students, it is likely that three are gay men or lesbians. Many of these people are fearful of identifying themselves as gay because of potential discrimination and lack of acceptance by the general population. Think about these stereotypes as you read the following scenario:

My brother Jake was always a little different; he was not the "typical boy." Growing up he was my best friend. It was as if he were the sister I never had. He was kind and gentle and compassionate toward all creatures. He enjoyed cooking, taking care of children and growing flowers. I remember that my father tried to make a man of him by encouraging him to join in manly activities such as hunting. My father was frustrated because Jake could not kill a deer. Jake looked the deer in the eye and decided that he could not kill such a beautiful creature. I had to agree with him, but my father was disappointed. He was frustrated in all his attempts to make my brother a man and had frequent conflicts with him. At age 16, my brother ran away from home and was "adopted" by a female teacher at our high school. She encouraged my brother to go to college and he moved across the continent, eventually working his way through medical school and becoming a well-known and respected cardiologist and critical care specialist. I was happy for my brother because he could do what he loved best: helping other people. One day my father had a heart attack and Jake returned home and saved my father's life. At this point, my father was finally proud of the man he had become.

I remember having a conversation with my other brothers about whether Jake was gay or not. I acknowledged the possibility, but said that it would be awful if we asked him and it were not true, so we never asked him. He did not look or act gay; he was just different. In fact, my girlfriends were always trying to get a date with him. One day I received a call from my brother. He was saying good-bye because he was dying. He did not want the family to visit; he just wanted to say good-bye, and he died the next day at the age of 43. Against Jake's wishes, my mother and some of my brothers traveled to New York and were shocked to find that Jake was living with a man who was HIV-positive and that Jake had died of AIDS. My father told everyone that Jake died of cancer. I felt an overwhelming sense of sadness at losing my brother and that he never felt comfortable enough to tell us that he was gay. I will always wonder if I should have asked him about being gay and if I possibly could have been more a part of his life. Since I lost my opportunity to do this, I have resolved to gain a better understanding and appreciation of sexual orientation, which is sadly the only thing I can do at this point.

Becoming educated about sexual orientation can help to diminish anti-gay prejudice and help people who are struggling with their sexual identity. Here is a list of myths and facts about gay men and lesbians. The corrected information below is provided by the Parents, Families, and Friends of Lesbians and Gays (PFLAG). This organization provides information on its website, www.pflagla.org. An organization called Rainbow Bridge also provides educational materials on gays and lesbians. Most college campuses have organizations that support gay, lesbian, bisexual, and transgender students. It is common that people disagree with the following facts because of common stereotypes about sexual orientation.

Myths and Facts about Gays and Lesbians

Myth: Only one percent of the world's population is gay, lesbian, or bisexual.

Fact: It is estimated that about 10 percent of the world's population is gay, lesbian, or bisexual.

Myth: Effeminate men and masculine women are always gay.

Fact: Effeminate men and masculine women can be heterosexual. Some gay persons fit this stereotype, but most look and act like individuals from the heterosexual majority.

Myth: Homosexuality is a choice, a preference, or a learned behavior.

Fact: Homosexuality is not something that one chooses to be or learns to be. As children, gay men and lesbians are not taught or influenced by others to be homosexual. Most current research cites genetic or inborn hormonal factors in homosexuality.[18]

Myth: You can always tell from a person's appearance if he or she is gay.

Fact: Most gay men and lesbians look and act like individuals from the heterosexual majority.

Myth: Lesbians and gay men never make good parents.

Fact: Gay men and lesbians can make good parents. Children of gay and lesbian parents are no different in any aspects of psychological, social, or sexual development from children in heterosexual families. These children tend to be more tolerant of differences.

Myth: Gay men and lesbian women are often involved in child abuse.

Fact: Gay men and lesbians are rarely involved in child abuse. In the United States, heterosexual men commit 90 percent of all sexual child abuse. The molesters are most often fathers, stepfathers, grandfathers, uncles, or boyfriends of the mothers.

Myth: The word "homosexual" is preferred over "gay" or "lesbian."

Fact: The term "gay man" or "lesbian" is preferred over the term "homosexual."

Myth: The term "gay" refers only to men.

Fact: The term "gay" refers to both men and women.

Myth: Some cultures do not have gay men and lesbians.

Fact: All cultures have gay men and lesbians.

Myth: Only gay men get AIDS and it is a death sentence.

Fact: AIDS is increasingly a heterosexual disease. Advances in the early detection and treatment of AIDS make it a chronic, controllable disease for most patients.

Myth: Being gay is an emotional or mental disorder.

Fact: The American Psychological Association does not list being gay as an emotional or mental disorder.

Myth: Through psychotherapy, a gay person can be turned into a heterosexual.

Fact: Psychotherapy has not been successful in changing a person's sexual orientation.

Myth: A person is either completely heterosexual or completely homosexual.

Fact: Based on Dr. Alfred Kinsey's research, few people are predominantly heterosexual or homosexual. Most people fall on a continuum between the two extremes. A person on the middle of the continuum between heterosexual and homosexual would be a bisexual. Bisexuals are attracted to both sexes.[19]

Myth: Homosexuality does not exist in nature. It is dysfunctional.

Fact: Research suggests that homosexuality is "natural." It exists among all animals and is frequent among highly developed species.[20]

Myth: Gay people should not be teachers because they will try to convert their students.

Fact: Homosexual seduction is no more common than heterosexual seduction. Most gay teachers fear they will be fired if it is found out that they are gay.[21]

How to Appreciate Diversity

Having an appreciation for diversity enriches all of us. Poet Maya Angelou has described the world as a rich tapestry and stressed that understanding this concept can enrich and improve the world:

"It is time for us to teach young people early on that in diversity there is beauty and strength. We all should know that diversity makes for a rich tapestry, and we must understand that the threads of the tapestry are equal in value, no matter their color; equal in importance, no matter their texture."[22]

Here are some ways to appreciate diversity:

- Educate yourself about other cultures and people who are different from you. Read about or take courses on the literature or history of another culture, or learn another language.

- Explore your own heritage. Learn about the cultures that are part of your family history.
- Value diversity and accept the differences of others.
- View differences as an opportunity for learning.
- Realize that you will make mistakes when dealing with people from other cultural backgrounds. Learn from the mistakes and move on to better understanding.
- Work to understand differences of opinion. You do not have to agree, but respect different points of view.
- Travel to other countries to discover new ideas and cultures.
- Think critically to avoid stereotypes and misconceptions. Treat each person as an individual.
- Avoid judgments based on physical characteristics such as color of skin, age, gender, or weight.
- Put yourself in the other person's place. How would you feel? What barriers would you face?
- Make friends with people from different countries, races, and ethnic groups.
- Find some common ground. We all have basic needs for good health, safety, economic security, and education. We all face personal challenges and interests. We all think, feel, love, and have hope for the future.
- Be responsible for your own behavior. Do not participate in or encourage discrimination.
- Do good deeds. You will be repaid with good feelings.
- Learn from history so that you do not repeat it. Value your own freedom.
- Challenge racial or homophobic remarks or jokes.
- Teach children and young people to value diversity and respect others. It is through them that we can change the world.

Journal Entry #5

Frequently we learn discrimination through our parents, our community, the media, and our environment. What would you teach your children about diversity?

Stages of Ethical Development

"Education is the most powerful weapon which you can use to change the world."

After much study, Harvard University professor William Perry developed the theory that students move through stages of ethical development.[23] Students move through these patterns of thought and eventually achieve effective intercultural communication.

Stage 1: Dualism

In this stage we view the world in terms of black or white, good or bad, "we" versus "they." Role models and authorities determine what is right. The right answers exist for every problem. If we work hard, we can find the correct answers and all will be well. Decisions are often based on common stereotypes.

Stage 2: Multiplicity

At this stage we become aware that there are multiple possibilities and answers. We know that authorities can disagree on what is right and wrong. We defend our position, but acknowledge that on any given issue, everyone has a right to his or her own opinion.

Stage 3: Relativism

As we learn more about our environment and ourselves, we discover that what is right is based on our own values and culture. We weigh the evidence and try to support our opinions based on data and evidence.

Stage 4: Commitment in Relativism

At this stage, we look at our environment and ourselves and make choices. In an uncertain world, we make decisions about careers, politics, and personal relationships based on our individual values. We make certain commitments based on the way we wish to live our lives. We defend our own values but respect the values of others. There is openness to learning new information and changing one's personal point of view. This position allows for the peaceful coexistence of different points of views and perspectives. It is at this point that we become capable of communicating across cultures and appreciating diversity.

QUIZ

Understanding Diversity, Part II

Test what you have learned by selecting the correct answers to the following questions.

1. Results of the Human Genome Project show that humans are

   a. 80 percent identical.
   b. 50 percent identical.
   c. 99.9 percent identical.

2. Problems in communication occur when we assume that

   a. a symbol has only one meaning.
   b. words have many meanings.
   c. it is easy to match the picture in one person's mind to a picture in another person's mind.

3. The thumbs-up gesture

   a. means "okay" in Japan.
   b. is a vulgar gesture in Iran.
   c. is understood in the same way in all cultures.

4. The following statement about sexual orientation is generally accepted as true:

   a. sexual orientation is not something one chooses or can change.
   b. some cultures do not have gay men and lesbians.
   c. homosexuality is a learned behavior.

5. In the last stage of ethical development, commitment in relativism, we

   a. view the world in terms of "good" and "bad."
   b. become aware of multiple possibilities.
   c. defend our own values but respect the values of others.

How did you do on the quiz? Check your answers: 1. c, 2. a, 3. b, 4. a, 5. c

Student Perspectives on Diversity

The following are some student comments on the subject of diversity. Many students have faced incidents of discrimination and hope for a better future.

I am always faced with problems because I'm black or my hair is long or because I am a large man. I wish people could be more sensitive and love me as a person and not judge me based on what I look like.

I am frequently discriminated against because of my religion. I feel really bad when it happens and it hurts a lot.

I have always faced discrimination because of my sexual orientation and will probably continue to experience discrimination in the future. If you are part of a minority, discrimination is inevitable. The key is to not let it drag you down so that you become a second-class citizen. That can be accomplished by taking pride in who you are and then working to fight against discrimination.

I come from Japan. I noticed that people here think their culture is better than any other. I think it's not bad to love your culture, but it is important to be open to other cultures.

There is a story I tell my children about words being nails. When we speak, we pound our nails into the other person's spirit. We can go back and apologize for hurtful words and maybe that removes the nail, but it still leaves a hole in the spirit.

If you constantly hear people say that you are not as good as another, you eventually start to believe it.

I've been discriminated against because I am female and a blonde. When I hear blonde jokes, I've learned to laugh with people most of the time, but it still hurts my feelings.

Discrimination is passed on to the next generation because a child believes what a parent tells them. We need to teach our children tolerance for differences.

Discrimination hurts people's feelings and doesn't allow them to become successful in life because they lose confidence and self-esteem.

Because I am black, salespeople tend to follow me around in the store thinking I am going to steal something. People of different races call me "nigger."

When I was younger, I used to wear thick glasses. People would call me names such as "four eyes," "nerd," "dork," and "geek." I can look back and laugh at this now, but it made me feel inferior. Discrimination is based on ignorance and hate.

Black kids used to mistreat me because I was not as black as them.

Once when I was 10 years old, I was playing in the park. I noticed this Caucasian kid playing on the slide and he was about to fall off the slide. I went over to catch him and the mother ran over to me and told me to take my hands off of him and that she would rather have him fall than to have some "nigger" put her hands on him. I will never forget this incident!

When I was younger, my father frequently made negative comments about women. Because of his prejudice, I felt less worthy of getting equal treatment for equal education and work. Now my father is trying to overcome this mindset, and I plan to graduate from college to earn equal pay with men.

It is sad that humans can be so cruel to one another. I hope someday this will all end and we can live in peace with one another.

By celebrating diversity, all the people of the world could come together and have peace.

Diversity Is Valuable and People Are Important

In 1963, Dr. Martin Luther King, Jr., made a famous speech in which he said, "I have a dream that my four little children will one day live in a nation where they will not be judged by the color of their skin, but by the content of their character." Because of his message of brotherhood and understanding, his birthday is celebrated as a national holiday. Tragically, King was assassinated because of his strong stand against racism. We are still working toward his ideal of brotherly love.

When I ask students to describe what success means to them, they often talk about having a good career, financial stability, owning a home, and having a nice car. Some students mention family and friends and people who are important to them. Understanding diversity and appreciating other people can add to your personal success and enjoyment of life.

To gain perspective on what is important to your success, it is interesting to think about what people will say about you after you die. What will you think is important at the end of your life? If you can ponder this idea, you can gain some insight into how to live your life now. Go to the following website:

http://www.lindaellisonline.com/The_Dash_Poem_Copyright_Linda_Ellis.htm

Read "The Dash" by Linda Ellis.

Learn to understand, respect, and appreciate the different people in your life. Take time to love those who are important to you. Focus on cooperation and teamwork on the job. Don't forget about the people you meet on your road to success; they are important too. Having an understanding and appreciation of diversity will make the world a better place in which to live.

JOURNAL ENTRIES

Appreciating Diversity

Go to http://www.collegesuccess1.com/JournalEntries.htm for Word files of the Journal Entries

Success over the Internet

Visit the *College Success Website* at http://www.collegesuccess1.com/

The *College Success Website* is continually updated with new topics and links to the material presented in this chapter. Topics include:

- Tolerance
- Ways to fight hate
- Diversity and multicultural resources
- Asian-Pacific students
- Latinos
- Women
- Minorities

Contact your instructor if you have any problems accessing the *College Success Website*.

Notes

1. Robert Rosenblatt and Robert Duke, "A New Boom in U.S. Student Population, Census Finds; Count: Enrollment of 49 Million Equals 1970 Record. But Immigration Is a Concern, Especially in California," *Los Angeles Times,* March 23, 2001.

2. Brian Melly, "One in Three Californians is Hispanic; Whites Minority, Census Shows," *Associated Press,* March 29, 2001.

3. David Broder, "Congress Wants to Shape Trade Debate," *San Diego Union Tribune*, November 7, 2001.

4. Sonia Nieto, *Affirming Diversity: The Sociopolitical Context of Multicultural Education* (New York: Longman, 1996), 283.

5. Terry Huffman, "The Transculturation of Native American College Students," in *American Mosaic: Selected Readings on America's Multicultural Heritage,* ed. Young Song and Eugene Kim (Englewood Cliffs, NJ: Prentice-Hall, 1993), 211–19.

6. Richard Bucher, *Diversity Consciousness* (Englewood Cliffs, NJ: Prentice-Hall, 2000), 119.

7. Secretary's Commission of Achieving Necessary Skills (SCANS), U.S. Department of Labor, *Learning a Living: A Blueprint for High Performance*, 1991.

8. World population statistics from the Population Reference Bureau website: http://www.prb.org/pdf07/07WPDS_Eng.pdf, 2008, and the United Nations website: www.un.org/esa/population, 2008.

9. H. Triandis, "Training for Diversity," paper presented at the annual meeting of the American Psychological Association, San Francisco, 1991.

10. Benjamin Lahey, *Psychology: An Introduction* (Dubuque, IA: Brown and Benchmark, 1995), 20. "Human Genome Project Information," U.S. Department of Energy Office of Science, http://www.ornl.gov/sci/techresources/Human_Genome/home.shtml, 2008.

11. "Human Genome Project Information," U.S. Department of Energy, Office of Science.

12. Sue Goetinck Ambrose, "First Look at Genome Data Leaves Scientists in 'Awe'," *San Diego Union Tribune*, February 11, 2001.

13. Natalie Angier, "Do Races Differ? Not Really, Genes Show," *New York Times,* August 22, 2000.

14. Ibid.

15. George Henderson, *Cultural Diversity in the Workplace: Issues and Strategies* (Westport, CT: Praeger, 1994).

16. "Mourners Gather to Honor Gay Murdered in Wyoming," *Bellingham Herald,* October 17, 1998, A8.

17. California Rainbow Bridge pamphlet, 2000.

18. American Psychological Association, http://www.apa.org.pubinfo.html, 2001.

19. Ibid.

20. Ibid.

21. Ibid.

22. Maya Angelou, *Wouldn't Take Nothing for My Journey Now* (New York: Random House, 1993).

23. William G. Perry, "Cognitive and Ethical Growth: The Making of Meaning," in *The Modern American College* by Arthur Chickering and Associates (Hoboken, NJ: Jossey-Bass, 1981), 76–116.

Find Someone Who . . .

Name _____ Date _____

Walk around the classroom and find someone who fits each description. Have the person write his or her name on the appropriate line.

_____ Shares a favorite hobby

_____ Father or mother grew up in a bilingual family

_____ Parents or grandparents were born outside the United States

_____ Speaks a language besides English

_____ Is the first one in the family to attend college

_____ Enjoys the same sports

_____ Knows someone who has died of AIDS

_____ Has a friend or relative who is gay, lesbian, or bisexual

_____ Has a disability they have had to overcome

_____ Is struggling financially to attend college

_____ Has children

_____ Is a single parent

_____ Has your same major

_____ Was born in the same year as yourself

_____ Attended your high school

_____ Moved here from out of state

_____ Has been in the military

_____ Has participated on an athletic team

_____ Can play a musical instrument or sing

_____ Has played in a band

Exploring Stereotypes

Name _____ Date _____

Part 1. We are all familiar with **common stereotypes** of certain groups. Think about how these groups are often portrayed in the media. Quickly complete each statement.

1. All athletes are _____

2. All lawyers are _____

3. All male hairdressers are _____

4. All construction workers are _____

5. All redheads are _____

6. All people with AIDS are _____

7. All people on welfare are _____

8. All young people are _____

9. All old people are _____

10. All men are _____

11. All women are _____

12. All A students are _____

Part 2. Your instructor will ask you to share the above stereotypes with the class. Then discuss these questions.

1. What prejudices result from such stereotypes?

2. What is the source of these prejudices?

3. What harm can come from these prejudices?

Name _____ Date _____

Part 1. Answer the following questions about yourself. You may be asked to share these answers with a group of students in your class.

1. What is your ethnic background?

2. Where were your parents and grandparents born?

3. How much education do your parents have?

4. What languages do you speak?

5. What is your biggest challenge this semester?

6. What is one of your hopes or dreams for the future?

7. What do you enjoy most?

8. What is your most important value and why?

9. What is one thing you are proud of?

10. What is one thing people would not know about you just by looking at you?

11. Have you ever experienced discrimination because of your differences? If so, briefly describe this discrimination.

Part 2. Meet with two other students you do not know. Introduce yourself and share answers to the above questions. Your instructor will ask you to share your answers to the following questions with the class.

List three interesting things you learned about other persons in your group.

1.

2.

3.

Did you change any assumptions you had about persons in your group?

Name _____   Date _____

Everyone has a unique cultural background based on many different factors. Answer these questions to explore your unique culture.

1. Describe where you grew up and the school you attended.

2. What beliefs did you learn from your family?

3. What beliefs did you learn from your teachers? How would your teachers describe you as a student?

4. How has your religious training or lack of religious training affected your beliefs?

5. If you are in a relationship, describe how your partner has affected your beliefs.

6. If you have children, how have your values and beliefs changed?

7. Are the beliefs you grew up with right for you today? Why or why not?

CHAPTER 6

Maintaining a Healthy Lifestyle

Learning Objectives

Read to answer these key questions:

- How long can I expect to live in the new millennium?

- What are the best ideas on nutrition for maintaining optimum health?

- What are the dangers of smoking, alcohol abuse, and other drugs?

- How can I protect others and myself from HIV/AIDS and other sexually transmitted diseases?

- Why is it important to get enough sleep?

- What is stress and how can I deal with it?

- What are some relaxation techniques?

- How can I make positive changes in my life?

etting a college education is an investment in the quality of your life in the future. Enjoying this increased quality of life depends on maintaining your good health. What you do every day affects your future health. The ordinary choices you make, such as what you eat and how much you exercise, avoiding harmful substances, protecting the body, relaxing, getting enough sleep, and thinking positively, will have a big effect on how long you will enjoy good health and reap the benefits of your education.

Life Expectancy

How long can you expect to live in the new millennium? Since life expectancy is increasing, it is possible that you might live to be 100 years old or older. Life expectancy depends on heredity, environment, and lifestyle. Heredity cannot be changed, but environment and lifestyle depend on personal choice. The choices made at a young age can have a major impact on health in later life.

U.S. Life Expectancy

Year	Male	Female
1900	48.2	51.1
1940	60.8	65.2
1950	65.6	71.1
1960	66.6	73.3
1970	67.1	74.7
1980	70.0	77.4
1990	71.8	78.8
2000	74.1	79.5
2007	75.3	80.4

Source: National Center for Health Statistics[1]

Scientists have been studying centenarians around the world to identify the secrets of longevity.[2] It has been found that 90 percent of centenarians remain functionally independent until age 92. From studies of identical twins that were separated at birth and reared apart, it has been determined that 20 to 30 percent of longevity is genetically determined. The most important factor in longevity is lifestyle. One group that has been studied is the Seventh-Day Adventists in Utah. They avoid alcohol, caffeine, and tobacco and live an average of eight years longer than the average American.

Another group that has been studied is centenarians who live in Okinawa, Japan. These centenarians get plenty of physical and mental exercise. Their diet is rich in fruits and vegetables containing fiber and antioxidants that protect against cancer, heart disease, and stroke. Their diets are low in fat and salt, and they eat more soy than any other population on earth. Soy contains flavonoids that protect against cancer. They practice a dietary philosophy called hara hachi bu, which means eating until 80 percent full. Seiryu Toguchi of Okinawa was a centenarian who lived to be 105 years old. Here is a description of a typical day for him:[3]

. . . He wakes at 6 A.M., in the house in which he was born, and opens the shutters. "It's a sign to my neighbors," he says, "that I am still alive." He does stretching exercises along with a radio broadcast, then eats breakfast: whole-grain rice and miso soup with vegetables. He puts in two hours of picking weeds in his 1,000 sq. ft. field. . . . A fellow has to make a living, so Toguchi buys rice and meat with the profits from his produce. At 12:30 Toguchi eats lunch: goya stir fry with egg and tofu. He naps for an hour or so, then spends two more hours in his field. After dinner he plays traditional songs—a favorite is Spring When I Was 19—on the three-stringed sanchin and makes an entry in his diary as he has done every night for the past decade. "This way," he says, "I won't forget my Chinese characters. It's fun. It keeps my mind sharp."

There are almost 100,000 centenarians in the United States and the population is increasing rapidly. Daisy McFadden of the Bronx in New York is a good example of a centenarian who eats sensibly, exercises, and stays mentally active. For breakfast she has oatmeal, cranberry juice, and a banana. For lunch she has a salad with beets, cucumbers, tomatoes, and either chicken or fish. Dinner is a plate of steamed vegetables and lean meat. She does not drink soda, but occasionally indulges in chocolate chip cookies. McFadden enjoys regular exercise walking to the senior center at least three times a week to use a treadmill, bicycle, or rowing machine. To stay mentally active, she reads the newspaper daily and does the crossword puzzles.[4]

The best advice for living a long and healthy life is to eat sensibly, exercise, and find activities that keep you mentally alert.

> "Life expectancy would grow by leaps and bounds if green vegetables smelled as good as bacon."
> Doug Larson

Balance Nutrition and Exercise for Good Health

Balancing good nutrition with exercise contributes to a long and healthy life. A good diet helps you to enjoy life and feel your best. It helps children to grow and develop and to do well in school. Being informed about the basic principles of nutrition can help you to make healthful choices. The federal government has proposed dietary guidelines that take into account age, gender, and level of exercise.[5]

> "We don't stop playing because we grow old, we grow old because we stop playing."
> George Bernard Shaw

Aim for a healthy weight. Maintaining a healthy weight is one of the keys to a long and healthy life. Being overweight increases the risk of high blood pressure, high blood cholesterol, heart disease, stroke, diabetes, cancer, arthritis, and breathing problems. The problem of overweight children and adults is a major health concern today. The best way to lose weight is by establishing patterns of healthy eating and exercise.

Americans are struggling with how to maintain a healthy weight. Some are turning to crash diets that severely restrict calories and food choices. Crash diets are not recommended because the weight loss is temporary and the body can be deprived of important nutrients. Another serious problem is eating disorders such as anorexia, which can lead to serious health problems and even death in severe cases. Symptoms of an eating disorder include a preoccupation with food or body weight, dramatic weight loss, excessive exercise, self-induced vomiting, and abuse of laxatives. Anyone with these symptoms should consult a health care provider.

Body Mass Index

The Body Mass Index (BMI) is a commonly used method of evaluating a person's weight. It is based on the ratio of weight to height. To calculate your BMI, first answer these two questions:

1. What is your height in inches? _____

2. What is your weight in pounds?_____

Calculate your BMI using the following formula:

$$BMI = (705 \times body\ weight) \div (height \times height)$$

Example: A person who is 66 inches tall and weighs 155 pounds:

$$BMI = (705 \times 155) \div (66 \times 66) = 25$$

Calculate your BMI here. To evaluate your weight, locate your BMI in the chart below.

My BMI = (705 × my weight ___) ÷ (my height in inches___ × my height in inches _____) = _____

Body Mass Index Categories[6]

BMI	Weight
Less than 18.5	Underweight
18.5–24.9	Normal weight
25–29.9	Overweight
30 and above	Obese

There are some exceptions to consider when using BMI to evaluate weight:

- Bodybuilders and other athletes may have a higher BMI because muscle weighs more than fat.
- For the elderly, a BMI between 25 and 27 may be healthier and protect against osteoporosis.
- The BMI is not designed to be used with children.

Another way to evaluate your weight is to simply measure around your waist. A measurement of over 35 inches for women or 40 inches for men places a person at greater risk of health problems. If your BMI is over 25 or your waist measurement increases, reduce calories and increase activity.

Here are some suggestions for managing your weight:

- Be physically active.
- Choose healthy foods.
- Choose foods low in fat and sugars.
- Eat sensible portions.
- Lose weight slowly.

Be physically active each day. There are many benefits to regular physical activity:

- Increases your fitness, endurance, and strength
- Maintains healthy bones, muscles, and joints
- Helps in managing weight
- Lowers risk of cardiovascular disease, colon cancer, and Type 2 diabetes
- Promotes psychological well-being
- Reduces depression and anxiety

Two kinds of physical activity are recommended. Aerobic activity speeds up your heart rate and breathing and increases cardiovascular fitness. Strength and flexibility exercises such as lifting weights and stretching help to maintain strong bones. Choose activities that you enjoy and include them in your daily routine. It is important to remain active throughout your life.

New federal guidelines suggest the need for 30 to 60 minutes of moderately intense physical activity each day. These activities could include an hour of walking, slow swimming, leisurely bicycle riding, or golfing without a cart. More intense exercise such as jogging can provide needed exercise in a shorter time.[7]

Use the government-suggested dietary guidelines to guide your food choices. In 2005, the U.S. Department of Agriculture (USDA) revised dietary guidelines to balance what we eat with level of activity.[8] The USDA created a suggested individualized nutrition plan based on age, gender, and level of physical activity. This plan is called MyPyramid Plan and is available online at:

http://www.mypyramid.gov/

This plan helps to guide food choices for optimum good health. The dietary guidelines are represented by a pyramid with a figure climbing stairs to remind us to balance what we eat with physical activity. In the pyramid, the food bands run from top of the pyramid to the base. The different sizes of the bands show the proportion of foods we should eat from each food group. The bands are wider at the base to remind us to eat most of our

"Walking is the best possible exercise. Habituate yourself to walk very far."

Thomas Jefferson

foods without solid fat and added sugars. The MyPyramid Plan divides foods into these categories from left to right: grains, vegetables, fruits, oils, milk, and meat/beans.

MyPyramid.gov
STEPS TO A HEALTHIER YOU

Source: U.S. Department of Agriculture, http://www.mypyramid.gov, 2010.

The grains category includes whole grain bread, cereal, rice, and pasta. It includes any foods made from wheat, rice, oats, cornmeal, barley, or other cereal grains. For example, other foods in the grain category include oatmeal, breakfast cereals, tortillas, and grits. It is important that the word "whole" is on the list of product ingredients. Grains provide fiber and essential nutrients and aid in weight management. It is recommended that we consume at least three or more ounces of grains daily depending on age, gender, and level of physical activity. What counts as an ounce of grains?

- One slice of bread
- One six-inch tortilla
- One-half of a "mini" bagel
- One cup of cereal
- One-half cup of cooked cereal
- One-half cup of cooked rice
- One pancake
- Three cups popcorn
- One-half cup cooked spaghetti

Grain Group
Make half your grains whole

The vegetables category includes a variety of vegetables such as dark green or orange vegetables, dry beans and peas, starchy vegetables such as corn and potatoes, and other vegetables. The amount of vegetable required ranges from one to two and a half cups depending on age, gender, and level of physical activity. What counts as a cup of vegetables?

Vegetable Group
Vary your veggies

- One cup of any raw or cooked vegetable
- One cup of vegetable juice
- Two cups of leafy green vegetables
- One large ear of corn
- One medium potato

The fruits category includes a variety of fresh, frozen, canned, or dried fruits or fruit juices. It is suggested to go easy on fruit juices because of their higher caloric content. Fruits and vegetables provide necessary fiber and protect the body from diseases such as cancer. The daily recommended amount of fruits is one to two cups depending on age, gender, and activity level. What counts as a cup of fruit?

Fruit Group
Focus on fruits

- One small apple
- One large banana
- One large orange
- Eight strawberries
- One cup of grapes
- One cup of 100 percent fruit juice

The oils category is the smallest section of the pyramid, since they contain about 120 calories per tablespoon. The amount of oil consumed needs to be limited to fit in the total daily caloric allowance. Oils are defined as fats that are liquid at room temperature, including olive oil, corn oil, canola oil, and sunflower oil. It is suggested that most fat should come from fish, nuts, and vegetable oils and to limit solid fats such as butter, margarine, or lard. Some foods are naturally high in oils, including nuts, avocados, olives, and some fish. Oils contain essential fatty acids and are the major source of vitamin E in the diet. The recommended amount of oils ranges from three to seven teaspoons depending on age, gender, and activity level. Most Americans get all the oils they need from:

- Nuts
- Fish
- Cooking oil
- Salad dressings

The milk category includes foods made from milk, such as cheeses and yogurt. If the food maintains its calcium content when processed, it remains part of the food group. Foods such as cream cheese, cream, and butter are not included in the group. Milk food choices should be nonfat or low-fat. The daily recommended amount of milk products is two to three cups depending on age, gender, and level of activity. The milk group provides calcium for bone health over a lifetime. What counts as one cup of milk?

Milk Group
Get your calcium-rich foods

- One and a half ounces of hard cheese (cheddar, mozzarella, Swiss)
- One-third cup of shredded cheese

- Two ounces processed American cheese
- Two cups cottage cheese
- One eight-ounce container of yogurt

The meat and beans category includes low-fat or lean meat and poultry. Other examples include eggs, dry beans and peas, nuts and seeds, and fish. This group of foods provides proteins that serve as the basic building blocks of the human body. The daily recommendation is two to six ounces depending on age, gender, and activity level. What is equivalent to an ounce of meat?

Meat & Bean Group
Go lean with protein

- One-quarter cup of dry beans
- One egg
- One tablespoon peanut butter
- One-half ounce of nuts

Under the USDA guidelines, each person has a budget for some discretionary calories. These calories should not be used to replace the essential nutrients, but can provide extra energy for the body. Discretionary calories include added sugars and fats and range from 100 to 300 calories for most people, depending on activity level. Discretionary calories can be used for eating more of the essential foods or eating some foods with higher fat or sugar content. This category includes items such as butter, gravy, sauces, candy, soda, desserts, beer, or wine. Most people exceed their number of discretionary calories, so limit this category, especially if you need to lose weight.

Here are some examples of recommended food consumption based on age, gender, and activity levels. In these examples, 30 to 60 minutes of physical activity are assumed:

	Female Age 6	Female Age 18	Male Age 18	Male Age 50
Grains	5 oz	6 oz	10 oz	8 oz
Vegetables	1.5 cups	2.5 cups	3.5 cups	3 cups
Fruits	1.5 cups	2 cups	2.5 cups	2 cups
Oils	4 tsp	6 tsp	8 tsp	7 tsp
Milk	2 cups	3 cups	3 cups	3 cups
Meat/Beans	4 oz	5.5 oz	7 oz	6.5 oz
Extra Calories from Fat and Sugar	170	265	425	360
Total Calories	1400	2000	2800	2400

Here are some suggestions for making healthy food choices:

- In establishing a pattern of healthy eating, it is recommended that plant foods form the foundation of a good diet. Two-thirds of the dinner plate should be covered with fruits, vegetables, whole grains, and beans. Use meats and dairy products in moderation and use fats and sweets sparingly. This type of diet is helpful in controlling weight as well as reducing your risk of cancer.[9]
- Eat a variety of grains daily, especially whole grains. Whole grains include brown rice, cracked wheat, graham flour, whole-grain corn, oatmeal, popcorn, barley, whole rye, and whole wheat. Whole grains provide vitamins, minerals, and fiber, which helps you to feel full with fewer calories.
- Eat a variety of fruits and vegetables daily. Eating many kinds and colors of fruits and vegetables provides important vitamins and minerals. Enjoy five servings of fruits and vegetables each day with at least two servings of fruit and three servings of vegetables.
- Limit the use of solid fats such as butter, lard, margarines, and partially hydrogenated shortenings. Solid fats raise blood cholesterol and increase your chances of coronary heart disease. Use vegetable oils instead. Aim for a fat intake of no more that 30 percent of your calories.
- Moderate your intake of sugar. Foods containing added sugars have added calories and little nutritional value. The number one source of added sugar is soft drinks. Drink water instead of or in addition to soft drinks. Sweets, candies, pies, cakes, cookies, and fruit drinks are also major sources of added sugars. Eating too many foods with added sugar contributes to weight gain or eating less of the nutritious foods. Added sugar also contributes to tooth decay.
- Choose and prepare foods with less salt. Eating too much salt can increase your chances of having high blood pressure. High salt intake causes the body to secrete calcium, which is necessary for healthy bones. Only small amounts of salt occur naturally in foods. Most salt is added during food processing. Eat fresh fruits and vegetables to avoid eating too much salt.

How to Lose Weight

If you need to lose weight, you are not alone! Increasing numbers of adults in the United States are struggling with being overweight or obese. The Centers for Disease Control report that approximately 33 percent of adults are overweight and another 33 percent are obese.[10] Being overweight is defined as having a BMI between 25 and 29.9. Obesity is defined as having a BMI of 30 or above. For example, a woman who is five feet four inches tall and weighs 180 pounds is considered obese. Maintaining your ideal weight is a matter of balancing calories in from food and beverages with calories expended through physical activity.

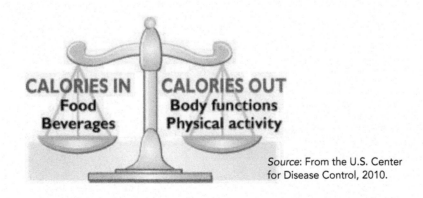

Source: From the U.S. Center for Disease Control, 2010.

Here are some practical suggestions for losing weight if your BMI is over 25 and you are not an athlete:

- Stop drinking sodas. One out of every five calories consumed in the United States is from sodas, and they are the biggest contributors to obesity.[11] Instead of drinking sodas, substitute water or unsweetened tea. Flavor your water with lemons, oranges, limes, strawberries, or mint. Be careful not to substitute sugary fruit juice, coffee, or tea for the sodas, since these drinks are often higher in calories.

- Exercise at least an hour to an hour and a half daily. Exercise is needed to burn the excess calories.

- Use the food pyramid to determine the number of calories needed to maintain your ideal weight. For example, the average 18-year-old female needs 2,000 calories a day. To lose weight, subtract 300 to 500 calories a day from this total.

- Eat five servings of fruits and vegetables a day. Use these fruits and vegetables as snacks.

- To control hunger, eat several small meals of 300 to 400 calories each.

- Make sure to eat breakfast. Eating breakfast helps to provide energy and avoid hunger, which leads to overeating.

- Eat smaller portions. Use a salad plate instead of a dinner plate. When you eat out, save half of your food for another meal.

- Minimize eating out at fast-food restaurants, since it is difficult to make good food choices there.

- If you are sad or anxious, try exercise instead of eating to relieve these symptoms. Practice stress reduction techniques.

Journal Entry #2

There is a saying, "You are what you eat." Based on the food pyramid, how can you improve your nutrition to maintain optimum health?

Nutrition

Test what you have learned by selecting the correct answers to the following questions.

1. If you are not an athlete and your BMI is over 25, it is probably a good idea to:
   a. Severely limit caloric intake.
   b. Go on a diet that limits food choices.
   c. Reduce calories and increase activities.

2. The MyPyramid Plan suggests that we need to balance:
   a. Our eating habits and our lifestyle.
   b. Our desserts and vegetables.
   c. What we eat with our physical activity.

3. In the MyPyramid Plan, an ounce of grain is equivalent to:
   a. Two cups of cooked spaghetti
   b. One cup of cooked rice
   c. One-half cup of cooked cereal

4. In the MyPyramid Plan, the recommended amount of oils consumed in a day is:
   a. 3–7 tablespoons
   b. 3–7 teaspoons
   c. One-half cup

5. In the MyPyramid Plan, the daily recommended amount of foods in the meat and beans category is:
   a. 2–6 ounces
   b. 8–12 ounces
   c. 15–20 ounces

6. For most people, daily discretionary calories range from:
   a. 100–300 calories
   b. 100–600 calories
   c. 500–1000 calories

7. It is suggested that two-thirds of the dinner plate be covered with:
   a. Potatoes
   b. Plant foods such as fruits, vegetables, whole grains, and beans
   c. Meats, fish, or poultry

How did you do on the quiz? Check your answers: 1. c, 2. c, 3. c, 4. b, 5. a, 6. a, 7. b

Avoiding Addictions to Smoking, Alcohol, and Other Drugs

Smoking, abusing alcohol, or using illegal drugs can interfere with your success in college, on the job, and in life. These addictions can cause illness and a shortened life expectancy. Knowledge in these areas will help you make the best choices to maintain your quality of life.

"It's never too late to be what you might have been."

George Elliot

"The greatest wealth is health."

Virgil

Smoking Tobacco: A Leading Cause of Preventable Illness and Death

Smoking is widespread in our society. One in every four adults in the United States smokes, and one in every three teenagers smokes. Tobacco use is the leading cause of preventable illness and death in the United States.[12] One out of every five deaths in the United States is related to smoking. Each year, over 430,000 Americans die too young as a result of smoking-related illnesses.[13] Imagine that three jumbo jets carrying 400 people each crashed every day of the year. This would be similar to the number of people who die each year from smoking-related illnesses.

Smoking is related to a variety of illnesses:

- Smoking damages and irritates the respiratory system. Smoking a package of cigarettes a day is like smearing a cup of tar over the respiratory tract. Smoking causes lung cancer, emphysema, and chronic bronchitis.
- Smoking affects the heart and circulatory system. Smoking causes premature coronary heart disease and several types of blood-vessel diseases.
- Smoking increases the probability of having strokes, which damage the brain and often leave a person with permanent disabilities.
- Smoking affects the eyes and vision. It is speculated that smoking causes vision loss by restricting blood flow to the eyes. Recent studies have connected smoking with macular degeneration, an irreversible form of blindness. Cataracts, or clouding of the lenses of the eyes, are also associated with smoking.
- Smoking irritates the eyes, nose, throat, and gums and can lead to cancer of the mouth, throat, or esophagus.
- Smoking is associated with osteoporosis, the thinning of bones due to mineral loss.
- During pregnancy, smoking damages the developing fetus, causing miscarriages, low birth weight, developmental problems, and impaired lung function at birth.
- Smoking causes premature facial wrinkling due to vasoconstriction of the capillaries of the face.[14]

Why is smoking such a major health problem? It is because smoking is an addiction that is difficult to overcome. Only 20 percent of smokers who decide to quit smoking are successful on a long-term basis.[15] For those who are successful in quitting, tobacco-related health risks are improved over time. Although smoking cessation is difficult, it is worth the investment in improved healthy living. Refraining from smoking, along with a healthy diet and exercise, can increase your life span by as much as 10 years.[16] For help with smoking cessation, visit your physician or college health office. The resources on the College Success website provide helpful hints for giving up smoking.

Alcohol

Each year, many college students die as a result of excessive drinking. Some students drink and drive and die in car accidents. Others die from alcohol poisoning or alcohol-related accidents. Excessive drinking is a factor in poor college performance and high dropout rates. Studies have shown that heavy drinking causes brain damage and interferes with memory.[17] Having some knowledge about alcohol use can help you to make choices to ensure your future quality of life.

Alcohol Abuse Quiz

Read each statement and decide if it is true or false. Place a checkmark in the appropriate column.

True	False	
		Alcohol abuse is the third leading health problem in the United States, behind heart disease and cancer.
		Thirteen percent of people in the United States have a problem with alcohol dependency.
		Alcohol is the most abused drug worldwide.
		Alcohol use or dependency reduces one's lifespan by 10 years.
		Alcohol is involved in 50 percent of all traffic fatalities and homicides.
		Alcohol is involved in two-thirds of college student suicides.
		Alcohol is a major factor in HIV infection.
		Alcohol is involved in 90 percent of college rapes.
		Women are at higher risk than men of serious medical conditions related to alcohol use.
		The age span 18 to 21 is the period of heaviest alcohol consumption for most drinkers in the United States.
		Each year college students spend about $5.5 billion on alcohol, mostly beer.
		College students drink enough beer each year to fill an Olympic-size swimming pool on every campus in the United States.
		Students spend more money on beer than they do on books, soda, coffee, juice, and milk combined.
		Excessive alcohol use leads to memory loss and neurological problems.
		More students drink than use cocaine, marijuana, or cigarettes combined.

How did you do on the quiz? All of the above statements are true. The fact that all of the above statements are true points to the serious nature of alcohol abuse on college campuses and in society in general.[18]

Binge Drinking

Heavy drinking causes students to miss class and fall behind in schoolwork. College students who are considered binge drinkers are at risk of many alcohol-related problems. Binge drinking is simply drinking too much alcohol at one time. In men, binge drinking is defined by researchers as drinking five or more drinks in a row. In women, it is drinking four or more drinks in a row.[19] It takes about one hour to metabolize one drink, so it would take five hours to metabolize five drinks. Researchers estimate that two out of five college students (44 percent) are binge drinkers.[20] Students who are binge drinkers are 21 times more likely to:

- Be hurt or injured
- Drive a car after drinking
- Get in trouble with campus or local police
- Engage in unprotected sex
- Engage in unplanned sexual activity
- Damage property
- Fall behind in schoolwork
- Miss class[21]

It is particularly significant that there is a connection between binge drinking and driving. Among frequent binge drinkers, 62 percent of men and 49 percent of women said that they had driven a car after drinking. About half of the students in this study reported being a passenger in a car in which the driver was high or drunk.[22] A drink is defined as:

- A 12-ounce beer
- A four-ounce glass of wine
- A shot of liquor (1.5 ounces of 80-proof distilled spirits) straight or in a mixed drink

National studies on alcohol consumption in colleges find that students are less likely to participate in binge drinking when they put a high priority on studying, have special interests or hobbies, and participate in volunteer activities. The majority of college students (56 percent nationally) either abstain from drinking or drink in moderation. Students least likely to be binge drinkers are African American, Asian, 24 years or older, or married. Students at highest risk for binge drinking include intercollegiate athletes and members of fraternities and sororities. Students most likely to be binge drinkers are white, male, and under 24 years of age.[23]

Blood Alcohol Content (BAC)

The amount of alcohol in your blood is referred to as blood alcohol content (BAC). It is recorded in milligrams of alcohol per 100 milliliters of blood. For example, a BAC of .10 means that 1/10 of 1 percent or 1/1,000 of your total blood is alcohol. BAC depends on the amount of blood in your body, which varies with your weight, and the amount of alcohol consumed over time. The liver can only process one drink per hour. The rest builds up in the bloodstream. Below are listed the effects of increasing BAC:

.02   Mellow feeling, slight body warmth, less inhibited

.05   Noticeable relaxation, less alert, less self-focused, coordination impairment begins, most people reach this level with one or two drinks

.08   Drunk driving limit, definite impairment in coordination and judgment

.10   Noisy, possible embarrassing behavior, mood swings, reduction in reaction times

.15   Impaired balance and movement, clearly drunk

.30   Many lose consciousness

.40   Most lose consciousness, some die

.50   Breathing stops, many die[24]

The above figures point out some important facts for college students. It does not take many drinks to reach the drunken driving limit. Most people reach the drunken driving limit if they have one to three drinks, depending on weight and time since the last drink. BAC increases if you are lighter weight or if you have just had a drink. As the BAC increases, more serious effects occur. Tragically, each year college students die from alcohol poisoning, which occurs when large quantities of alcohol are consumed in a short period of time. This sometimes occurs during the hazing periods in college fraternities and sororities. Colleges are taking steps to stop hazing on college campuses nationwide.

Increased Risks for Women

Because women absorb and metabolize alcohol differently than men do, they are at greater risk of alcohol-related problems. Women have less body water than men and achieve a higher concentration of alcohol in the blood after drinking the same amount as men. Women are more likely to develop liver damage, brain damage, and heart damage. Some research has suggested that women who are moderate to heavy drinkers are at higher risk for breast cancer.[25]

Besides considering health effects, women need to be concerned about personal safety when alcohol is being used. When alcohol is being consumed, women are at higher risk of becoming the victims of violent crime. Among frequent binge drinkers, women report higher rates of rape and nonconsensual sex.[26]

What Is Moderate Drinking?

If adults choose to drink alcohol, it is recommended that they drink in moderation.[27] Moderation is defined as no more than one drink per day for women or two drinks per day for men. Drinking more than this can increase the risks for car accidents, high blood pressure, stroke, violence, suicide, and certain types of cancer. Women who drink during pregnancy increase the risk of birth defects. Too much alcohol causes social and psychological problems, cirrhosis of the liver, inflammation of the pancreas, and damage to the brain and heart. Heavy drinkers are also at risk for malnutrition, since alcohol contains calories that may be substituted for more nutritional foods.

It has been found that drinking in moderation may lower the risk of coronary heart disease in men over the age of 45 and women over the age of 55. However, there are other factors contributing to a healthy heart, including a healthy diet, exercise, avoidance of smoking, and maintaining a healthy weight.

There are certain people who should not drink:

- Children and adolescents
- Individuals of any age who cannot restrict their drinking to moderate levels
- Women who are pregnant or who are likely to become pregnant
- Individuals who drive or operate machinery that requires skill, attention, or coordination
- Individuals taking over-the-counter or prescription drugs that interact with alcohol

Warning Signs of Alcoholism

Alcoholics Anonymous has published 12 questions to determine if alcohol is a problem in your life. Answer these questions honestly:

1. Have you ever decided to stop drinking for a week or so but could only stop for a couple of days?

2. Do you wish people would mind their own business about your drinking and stop telling you what to do?

3. Have you ever switched from one kind of drink to another in the hope that this would keep you from getting drunk?

4. Have you ever had to have a drink upon awakening during the past year? Do you need a drink to get started or to stop shaking?

5. Do you envy people who can drink without getting into trouble?

6. Have you had problems connected with drinking during the past year?

7. Has your drinking caused problems at home?

8. Do you ever try to get extra drinks at a party because you do not get enough?

9. Do you tell yourself you can stop drinking any time you want to, even though you keep getting drunk when you don't mean to?

10. Have you missed days of work or school because of drinking?

11. Do you ever have blackouts from drinking, when you cannot remember what happened?

12. Have you ever felt that your life would be better if you did not drink?

If you answered yes to four of the above questions, it is likely that you have a problem with alcohol.

Other Drugs

While alcohol is the most commonly used drug, street drugs such as marijuana, cocaine, LSD, methamphetamines, rohypnol (the "date rape drug"), ecstasy, ketamine (a PCP-like anesthetic), and heroin interfere with the accomplishment of life goals. Clark Carr, President of Narconon, describes the following impact of illegal drug usage:

"One of the worst impacts of street drugs is their impact on ambition. Drugs have insidious yet devastating effects upon children and their ability to envision hopes and dreams. Ambition enables a person to learn to enjoy life and to pursue happiness without drugs, but it can be destroyed through drug use. When a person is intoxicated by drugs, important functions are adversely affected, including concentration, recording, and recalling. These tools are essential to learning, and without them education is impaired. Addiction becomes the all-consuming focus of activities aimed at procuring more drugs. Education, careers, relationships, and life itself take a back seat."[28]

People take drugs in order to feel better. However the high from taking drugs is followed by a low that is relieved by taking more drugs, leading to addiction. With increased drug use, the lows get lower and it becomes more difficult to reach a high. Drugs have varying levels of toxicity, but they all stress the body's nervous, digestive, respiratory, circulatory, and reproductive systems. The problem is that drugs can become life-destroying. Anyone contemplating taking drugs should ask these four questions:

1. Are the benefits going to outweigh the liabilities?

2. Will I experience more pleasure than pain, or more pain than pleasure?

3. Will the pleasure be temporary? How will I feel tomorrow?

4. Will the drug do more harm than good?

Answering these questions honestly can help you to make the right choices. An addiction to smoking, alcohol, or illegal drugs can be difficult to control. If you need help with problems caused by drug or alcohol addiction, see your physician or contact your college health office. The *College Success Website* contains useful links to help you to cope with addictive behavior and make some positive changes in your life.

Avoiding Addictions

Test what you have learned by selecting the correct answers to the following questions.

1. The leading cause of preventable death in the United States is

   a. car accidents.
   b. smoking-related illnesses.
   c. obesity.

2. The most abused drug worldwide is

   a. marijuana.
   b. cocaine.
   c. alcohol.

3. Binge drinking for men is defined as

   a. five drinks in a row.
   b. seven drinks in a row.
   c. 10 drinks in a row.

4. Depending on weight and time of last drink, a person generally reaches the drunk driving limit of .08 with

   a. one to three drinks.
   b. three to five drinks.
   c. five to nine drinks.

5. Moderate drinking for women is defined as

   a. one drink per day.
   b. two drinks per day.
   c. three drinks per day.

How did you do on the quiz? Check your answers: 1. b, 2. c, 3. a, 4. a, 5. a

Protecting Yourself from HIV/AIDS and Other Sexually Transmitted Infections

Human immunodeficiency virus (HIV) and acquired immune deficiency syndrome (AIDS) have been described as the worst plague in modern history. AIDS is the fourth leading cause of death in the world. It is estimated that by 2020, the number of people dying from AIDS will be approximately equal to all people killed in wars in the 20th century.[29] New drugs have been developed that inhibit the growth of the virus that leads to AIDS, but there is still no cure for AIDS. These new medications are extending the healthy life of infected patients.[30] Since AIDS continues to be a leading cause of death among Americans ages 25 to 44, knowing how to protect yourself from HIV/AIDS and other sexually transmitted diseases is an important survival skill.[31] The U.S. Centers for Disease Control and Prevention provide some helpful information to minimize your risk of infection.[32]

What is HIV? HIV is the human immunodeficiency virus that causes AIDS. The virus kills the "CD4" cells that help your body fight off infection.

What is AIDS? AIDS is the acquired immunodeficiency syndrome. It is the disease you get when HIV destroys the body's immune system. Normally your immune system helps to fight off illness. When the immune system is destroyed, you can become very sick and die.

How is HIV acquired? HIV is acquired in the following ways:

- It is acquired by having unprotected sex (sex without a condom) with someone who has HIV. The virus can be in an infected person's blood, semen, or vaginal secretions. It can enter the body through tiny cuts or sores on the skin, or the lining of the vagina, penis, rectum, or mouth.
- It is acquired by sharing a needle and syringe to inject drugs or by sharing equipment used to prepare drugs for injection with someone who has HIV.
- HIV can be acquired from a blood transfusion received before 1985. Since 1985, blood is tested for HIV.
- Babies born to women who are HIV-positive can become infected during pregnancy, birth, or breastfeeding.

You cannot get HIV from the following:

- Working with or being around someone who has HIV
- Sweat, tears, spit, clothes, drinking fountains, phones, or toilet seats
- Insect bites or stings
- Donating blood
- A closed-mouth kiss

What are the best ways to protect yourself? Here are some guidelines:

- Don't share needles or syringes for injecting drugs, steroids, or vitamins, or for tattooing or body piercing. Germs from an infected person can stay in the needle and then be injected into the next person using the needle.
- Don't have sex. This is truly "safe sex."
- If you choose to have sex, have sex with only one partner that you know doesn't have HIV and is only having sex with you.
- Use a latex condom every time you have sex. This is referred to as "safer sex."
- Don't share razors or toothbrushes because of the possibility of contact with blood.
- If you are pregnant, get tested for HIV. Drug treatments are available to reduce the chances of your baby being infected with HIV.

How do I know if I have HIV or AIDS? A person can have HIV or AIDS and feel perfectly healthy. The only way to know is to get tested. Most college health offices and your local health department offer confidential testing.

What other infections are spread through sexual activity? There are more than 25 different infections spread through sexual activity. There are 19 million new cases of sexually transmitted infections (STIs) each year, half of them in young people ages 15–24.[33] According to the Centers for Disease Control and Prevention, these infections can "result in severe health consequences, cancer, impaired fertility, premature birth, infant death and disability."[34] The increase in STIs has paralleled the AIDS epidemic. The guidelines for protecting against HIV apply to other STIs as well.

The most common STIs in the United States include chlamydia, gonorrhea, syphilis, genital herpes, human papillomavirus, hepatitis B, trichomoniasis, and bacterial vaginosis. Bacterial infections such as gonorrhea, syphilis, and chlamydia can be cured with antibiotics. Viral infections such as herpes, hepatitis, and genital warts can be treated but not cured. A vaccine has been developed to prevent hepatitis B, and it is recommended that teenagers and college students obtain this vaccination to avoid the serious liver damage that can result from this infection.

Women suffer the most from STIs because they have more frequent and serious complications from them than men do. Many STIs can be passed to the fetus, newborn, or infant before, during, or after birth. Chlamydia and gonorrhea can lead to pelvic inflammatory disease (PID), which can cause chronic pelvic pain, infertility, or potentially fatal ectopic pregnancies. The human papilloma virus (HPV) can increase the risk of cervical cancer in women. A new vaccine for HPV has just become available and is recommended for girls and women ages 11 to 26. It is most effective for girls and women who have not been exposed to HPV and is effective in preventing 70 percent of the cancers caused by HPV.

> "Sleep is a golden chain that ties our health and our bodies together."
> Thomas Dekker

> "A good laugh and a long sleep are the best cures in the doctor's book."
> Irish Proverb

Getting Enough Sleep

College students often miss out on sleep while cramming for exams, enjoying an active social life, and trying to balance work and school. However, getting enough sleep is important for learning. Without enough sleep, long-term memory is impaired and concentration is difficult.[35] If you are sleep-deprived, it is more difficult to read, study and store information in long-term memory.

Getting enough sleep is important for optimal brain function. Nobel Laureate Francis Crick, who studies the brain at the Salk Institute in California, has proposed that the purpose of sleep is to allow the brain to "take out the trash."[36] Sleep gives the brain time to process the day's events, store what is needed, and delete irrelevant material. Sleep is necessary to properly store the experiences of each day in the brain. It is believed that sleeping helps the brain to replenish its energy supplies.[37]

Not getting enough sleep results in a decline in mental performance. Colonel Gregory Belenky of the Walter Reed Army Institute of Research studied the effects of sleeplessness on military personnel.[38] He found that mental performance declined by 25 percent in every 24-hour sleepless period. Another researcher found that being awake for 24 hours causes the same mental impairment as being drunk.[39] After 24 hours of continuous simulated combat, artillery teams lost track of where they were and what they were firing at. During the Persian Gulf War, sleep-deprived soldiers lost a sense of where they were and began firing on their own tanks, destroying two of them. Lack of sleep impairs higher cognitive functions such as critical thinking. It becomes more difficult to make decisions, pay attention to detail, and react to new information. College students who stay up all night studying for exams suffer from the same declines in mental performance.

Depriving yourself of sleep also has negative impacts on your health.[40] Lack of sleep can make you less energetic, increase your irritability, cause depression, and make you accident-prone. It is estimated that sleepy drivers cause about 100,000 car accidents each year. Lack of sleep can harm brain cells, weaken the immune system, and decrease muscle-building growth hormones. Blood levels of the stress hormone cortisol are increased. Sleep deprivation can cause increased stress, memory impairment, risk of illness, and the growth of fat instead of muscle. Researchers are now finding evidence that lack of sleep hastens the aging process.[41]

So, how much sleep do you need? Everyone has different needs for sleep. One way to determine your personal need for sleep is to think about how much sleep you get at the end of a long vacation when you do not have to get up at a certain time. At first you may sleep longer to make up for any sleep deficits. Toward the end of the vacation, you will probably be getting the amount of sleep your body needs for optimum performance. Gregory Belenky recommends, "If you simply want to put one foot in front of the other, five hours will do. But if you want to be doing things where you're required to think, plan, or anticipate, then you probably need eight or eight and a half hours of sleep."[42] It is interesting to note that current research shows that it is not healthy to sleep more than eight hours because too much sleep can alter sleep patterns and lead to sluggishness, fatigue, and other health problems.[43]

Journal Entry #3

Are you getting enough sleep for optimum performance in school and to maintain good health? If not, what is your plan to get more sleep?

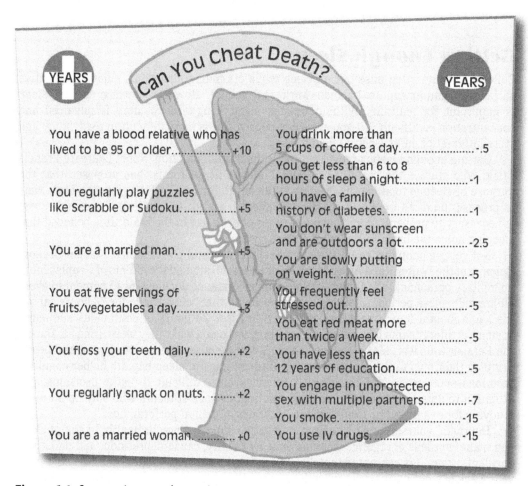

Figure 6.1 Steps to increase longevity.

Stress and Relaxation

One of the major challenges in life is dealing with stress and being able to relax. For college students, it is important to realize that too much stress interferes with memory, concentration, and learning. After graduation, it is important to be able to deal with stress on the job.

What Is Stress?

Imagine that you are a caveman or cavewoman. You come out of your cave and notice that the sun is up and the birds are chirping. You are feeling good and your heart rate is normal. All of a sudden you hear a twig snap. You look to your right and notice a large saber-toothed tiger. You have two choices. You can either fight the tiger or take flight. This is called the "fight or flight" reaction to stress.

The body produces some powerful hormones to help give you the strength to fight or to run away. These hormones increase your heart rate and metabolism to give you quick energy. During the fighting or fleeing, the stress hormones are used up and the body returns to normal. The problem today is that the stresses we face are not saber-toothed tigers and we do little physical fighting or running away. The stress hormones still accumulate, but we no longer use them up.

Is all stress bad? Imagine a world where there is absolutely no stress. While the thought is intriguing, it would probably be very boring. Some stress is positive and essential for well-being. For example, when we run a race, play a game of football, or act in a play, we experience stress, but it provides excitement and motivation. When a teacher announces a test, a little stress can cause the student to study for the test. Hans Selye, a famous researcher on stress, called this positive type of stress "eustress." He even went so far as to suggest, "Without stress, there could be no life."[44]

Hans Selye described negative stress as "distress." Distress has several physical symptoms that are uncomfortable and detract from good health. These symptoms can range from headaches, stomachaches, and sleeplessness to serious health problems such as high blood pressure, heart disease, and stroke. It is helpful to know some relaxation techniques to deal with the distress.

"Slow down and everything you are chasing will come around and catch you."
John De Paola

"Tension is who you think you should be. Relaxation is who you are."
Chinese Proverb

Get Aerobic Exercise

Aerobic exercise is simply exercise that raises your heart rate and exercises your heart. It includes activities such as walking, running, swimming, dancing, and playing sports. It is recommended that people do some type of aerobic exercise three to five times a week. In addition to strengthening the heart, aerobic exercise burns up stress hormones and allows us to relax.

One of the best relaxation techniques is to find some physical activities that you enjoy and participate in them often. It often requires some planning to fit these activities into our busy schedules. It is important to see these activities as a priority and to take time to enjoy them.

Practice Stress-Reducing Thoughts

Much of the stress we experience is a result of the thoughts we have in our heads, specifically, negative self-talk. We experience a situation, we say negative things to ourselves about it, and the result is an emotional reaction that causes stress. This sequence of events is referred to as the ABCs of emotions:

Situation (A) ⟶ Self-statement (B) ⟶ Emotion (C)

For example, Nicole is caught in rush hour traffic. She wonders why traffic is not moving. She watches the light, hoping that she can make it through the intersection before the light changes to red. She gets angry when the car in front of her stops just as the light changes to yellow. She has to wait for another light. She glances at her watch and watches the time go by as she sits in traffic. She thinks about all the things she needs to do at home. She realizes that she needs to stop at the grocery store to get something for dinner. She thinks about getting fast food on the way home but remembers that she has spent too much money this month. Besides, she realizes that the fast food is not good for her diet. Finally she arrives home at 6:04 p.m. She has a headache and feels stressed out.

Here is an analysis of this situation using the ABCs of emotion:

Situation (A) $\longrightarrow$ Self-statement (B) $\longrightarrow$ Emotion (C)

Traffic jam (A) $\longrightarrow$ Negative self-statement (B) $\longrightarrow$ Angry, stressed (C)

Negative self-statements run through Nicole's head as she deals with the traffic jam:

- Why does this always happen to me?
- Why are the cars ahead so slow?
- Stupid drivers! Can't they move any faster?
- I'm always broke.
- I'll never lose weight.

As a result of these statements, Nicole feels angry and stressed out and even has a headache. Let's look at a different way of handling this situation. Diane is also caught in rush hour traffic. She thinks to herself, "Rush hour traffic. Oh, well. Can't do anything about that." She decides to relax. She turns on her favorite radio station and enjoys the music. She notices the trees and plants along the side of the road and notices that spring is coming. She notices a new restaurant along the way and decides to try it out next Saturday night. She starts to think about spring break and how she will spend her vacation time. She anticipates the warm greetings of her family when she arrives home. She arrives home at 6:04 p.m. with a smile on her face. Let's analyze this situation:

Situation (A) $\longrightarrow$ Self-statement (B) $\longrightarrow$ Emotion (C)

Traffic jam (A) $\longrightarrow$ Positive self-statements (B) $\longrightarrow$ Happy (C)

When you are trying to deal with a stressful situation, listen to your self-statements. What are you saying to yourself? If these statements are negative, you will have negative emotions and will be stressed out. Think of some positive, stress-reducing thoughts that you can use in stressful situations. Here are some examples, but you will be better off to think up some of your own:

- That's the way it goes. No use getting upset.
- It's not the end of the world.
- Keep cool.
- It's no big deal.
- Relax.
- Life's too short to let this bother me.
- It's their problem.
- Life's like that.
- Be happy.
- I'll just do the best I can.
- No need to worry.

Take Action to Resolve Your Problems

If you have problems that are causing stress, take action to resolve them. Here are some steps you can take to solve problems and reduce stress:

- Concentrate your efforts on doing something about the problem.
- Seek information on how to solve the problem. This step may involve doing research or speaking to others.

- Make a plan of action.
- Make it a priority to solve the problem.
- Do what needs to be done to solve the problem, one step at a time.

Psychological Hardiness

Psychologists have studied people who are psychologically hardy.[45] These individuals are able to deal with stress in a positive way and avoid the negative consequences of stress. How do they stay healthy in spite of high-powered jobs and constant challenges? People who are stress-resistant have a positive attitude toward life and the challenges it presents. Psychologically hardy individuals have the following qualities:

- They are open to change. They view change as a challenge rather than a threat.
- They have a feeling of involvement in whatever they are doing. They are committed to their occupations and endeavors.
- They have a sense of control over events rather than a feeling of powerlessness. Having a sense of control is essential to good mental health.

Some of the hardiest individuals were those who survived the concentration camps during World War II. In spite of enduring extreme hardships, some found the strength to survive their ordeal and to live well-adapted lives. Scientists studying these survivors discovered that they used several resources for survival. Knowledge and intelligence was one resource. With knowledge and intelligence, these people could see many ways of dealing with the situation and were able to choose the best alternative. These survivors also had a strong sense of identity. They were confident and powerful individuals. Another important resource was a strong social network that gave people the collective strength to survive.

Other Relaxation Techniques

Another way to deal with stress is to practice some physical and mental relaxation techniques. Here are a few suggestions:

- Listen to soothing music. Choose music that has a beat that is slower than your heart rate. Classical or New Age music can be very relaxing.
- Take a few deep breaths.
- Focus on your breathing. If you are thinking about breathing, it is difficult to think about your worries.
- Lie down in a comfortable place and tense and relax your muscles. Start with the muscles in your head and work your way down to your toes. Tense each muscle for five to 10 seconds and then release the tension completely.
- Imagine yourself in a pleasant place. When you are actually in a beautiful place, take the time to make a mental photograph. Memorize each detail and then close your eyes to see if you can still recall the scene. Return to this place in your mind when you feel stressed. Some people visualize the mountains, the beach, the ocean, a mountain stream, waterfalls, a tropical garden, or a desert scene. Choose a scene that works for you.
- Use positive thinking. Look for the good things in life and take the time to appreciate them.
- Maintain a healthy diet and get enough exercise.
- Practice yoga or tai chi.

- Keep things in perspective. Ask yourself, "Will it be important in 10 years?" If so, do something about it. If not, just relax.
- Focus on the positives. What have you learned from dealing with this problem? Has the problem provided an opportunity for personal growth?
- Discuss your feelings with a friend who is a good listener or get professional counseling.
- Keep your sense of humor. Laughter actually reduces the stress hormones.
- Maintain a support network of friends and loved ones.
- Practice meditation. It is a way of calming the mind.
- Get a massage or give one to someone else.

Journal Entry # 4

Comment on your level of stress. What stress management techniques work best for you?

Making Positive Changes in Your Life

You are probably aware of the importance of implementing many of the ideas in this chapter. However, actually making some positive changes is difficult. Dr. James Prochaska has studied the process of change and identifies the six stages: [46]

1. **Precontemplation.** In this stage, a person denies that there is a problem and is not ready to change. If the habit causes difficulties, the person may blame the problems on others, especially those who are pressuring for change. There are two ways to move out of this stage. One way is through an increasing awareness or knowledge of the problem. Another way is through emotional arousal. For example, a person may see another dying of lung cancer and decide that it is time to quit smoking.

2. **Contemplation.** In this stage, a person begins to be aware of a problem and thinks seriously about taking some action. He or she weighs the pros and cons, the benefits and sacrifices, and thinks about the difficulty of change. People can only move to the next stage when they develop the self-confidence to believe that they can make a change. In the example of smoking cessation, at this stage a person would begin to look at the negative consequences of smoking but would consider change difficult.

3. **Preparation.** During this stage, people develop a strategy for change. They realize that change is necessary and desire to make the change. They discuss the change with friends and find the needed resources to make the change. They set an actual date to take action. In our smoking example, a person would start talking with friends and family members about quitting smoking and would set a time to stop smoking.

4. **Action.** This is the "just do it" stage. Without action, the goal cannot be accomplished. This stage requires some commitment. A person trying to quit smoking might just stop smoking "cold turkey" or cut down on daily smoking by a specific amount.

5. **Maintenance.** Once you have reached your goal, maintenance is the next step. This stage is the most difficult one as people struggle with the impulse to return to old patterns. Once a person has stopped smoking, the real test is maintaining the behavior.

6. **Termination.** This is permanent change. It is a time when temptations stop. Many people find it difficult to reach this stage.

Six Stages of Change

1. Precontemplation
2. Contemplation
3. Preparation
4. Action
5. Maintenance
6. Termination

What is important to realize about Prochaska's model is that change is a process and that there will be slip-ups along the way. His research shows that successful changers experience some failures along the way. However, he suggests that action that fails is better than no action at all. His research shows that those who tried to act and failed were more likely to succeed in the future. In one study of 200 people who made New Year's resolutions and were still keeping them two years later, the subjects had an average of 14 lapses before they were successful in keeping their resolutions.

Setbacks in the process of change are natural, and it is important not to give up. The process of change is difficult, but rewarding when you can follow through. When you are successful, you enjoy better health and gain confidence in your ability to make positive changes.

KEYS TO SUCCESS   Live to Be 100

It is possible that you could live to be 100 years old. Of course, if you live to be 100, you will want to be healthy and capable of enjoying your life. Many people are doing this already.

John Glenn, the world's oldest astronaut at age 77, returned from space in 1998. Dr. John Charles joked that "he did pretty good for a 40-year-old guy."[47] He suffered no more bone or muscle loss than the younger astronauts on the mission, and his heart rate was slightly better than those of the younger astronauts. Doctors were so impressed with John Glenn's physical condition that they decided to take better care of their own health. How does John Glenn stay fit? He has taken care of himself over his lifetime. He walks several miles a day, does some light weight training, and eats a balanced diet. He challenges the notion that seniors are frail individuals. Glenn enjoyed the ride and is encouraging NASA to send more senior citizens into orbit.

Sarah "Sadie" Delaney wrote a bestselling novel with her sister Bessie at age 104. It contained their reminiscences of a century of achievement of African American women. They shared memories of slavery, segregation, and racism that they had experienced during their lives. Sadie lived to be 109 years old and Bessie died at age 104. They were from a family of 10 children, all of whom went to college. Their mother was a teacher and taught the children self-discipline, compassion, and confidence. When Bessie and Sadie were

> "Nobody grows old by merely living a number of years. We grow old by deserting our ideals. Years may wrinkle the skin, but to give up enthusiasm wrinkles the soul."
> Samuel Ullman

> "Wrinkles should merely indicate where smiles have been."
> Mark Twain

> "Anyone who stops learning is old, whether at twenty or eighty."
> Henry Ford

asked how they had lived so long, Bessie said, "Honey, we never married; we never had husbands to worry us to death." Sadie added, "Don't get married just because he looks pretty. He's got to have good genes and have some sense."[48]

Mae Laborde became an actress at age 93. She has played the role of Vanna White (40 years in the future), appeared on *MADtv*, and faced down the Grim Reaper in a commercial about the elderly without health insurance. She is always

continued

smiling, has a positive attitude, and is ready to take on the world. She says it is never too late to follow your dreams.

Jerry Bloch at age 81 became the oldest man to climb El Capitan Mountain in Yosemite National Park. He chose the toughest and most challenging route up the mountain because he felt it might be his last mountain-climbing adventure because he was getting older.

Jeanne Calment passed away in 1997 at the age of 122. She was the oldest living person at that time. She was quite active into her old age. She took up fencing at age 85, rode a bicycle at age 100, and produced a rap CD at age 121. During her younger life she engaged in activities such as playing the piano, tennis, roller-skating, bicycling, swimming, hunting, and going to the opera. She was never bored, and remained spirited and mentally sharp until the end. She became known for her wit and humor. One of her sayings was, "I've never had but one wrinkle, and I'm sitting on it."

Since you may live to be 100, take some advice from the experts: exercise to stay physically fit, be careful about whom you marry, stay active, have a positive attitude, and maintain your sense of humor.

Journal Entry #5

Write at least five intention statements about improving your health. Think about nutrition, exercise, avoiding addictions, preventing disease and relaxation, or other factors influencing your health. I intend to . . . .

JOURNAL ENTRIES

Maintaining a Healthy Lifestyle

Go to http://www.collegesuccess1.com/JournalEntries.htm for Word files of the Journal Entries

Success over the Internet

Visit the *College Success Website* at http://www.collegesuccess1.com/

The *College Success Website* is continually updated with new topics and links to the material presented in this chapter. Topics include:

- Health Topics A–Z
- Wellness
- Men and women's health topics
- Resources for smoking cessation
- Pregnancy
- Sexually transmitted diseases
- HIV/AIDS
- Planned Parenthood
- Nutrition
- Fitness
- Addictive behavior (drugs, alcohol, smoking)
- Resources for dealing with addiction to drugs, alcohol, or smoking
- Treatment centers for alcohol and drug problems
- Internet addictions
- Sleep problems
- Stress
- Panic attacks
- Anxiety
- Mental health

Contact your instructor if you have any problems in accessing the *College Success Website*.

Notes

1. U.S. Department of Health and Human Services, Centers for Disease Control and Prevention, National Center for Health Statistics, "Death in the United States, 2007," http://www.cdc.gov/nchs/data/databriefs/db26.htm.

2. Richard Corliss and Michael Lemonick, "How to Live to be 100," *Time*, August 30, 2004.

3. Ibid.

4. Jenna Goudreau, "How to Live to Be 101," MSN Health and Fitness, accessed July 2010, http://health.msn.com.

5. U.S. Department of Agriculture, http://www.mypyramid.gov.

6. U.S. Department of Agriculture, *Body Mass Index and Health*, March 2000.

7. U.S. Department of Agriculture, http://www.mypyramid.gov.

8. Ibid.

9. Associated Press, "Proper Diet Urged to Fight Cancer, Not Supplements," *San Diego Union Tribune*, September 5, 2000.

10. U.S. Centers for Disease Control and Prevention, "Overweight and Obesity,"accessed August 3, 2010, http://www.cdc.gov/obesity/causes/index.html.

11. Marilyn Marchione, "Soda Causes Obesity, Researchers Report," *San Diego Union Tribune*, March 5, 2006.

12. U.S. Department of Health and Human Services, Centers for Disease Control and Prevention, http://www.cdc.gov/tobacco, 2002.

13. Andrew Bridges, "Doctors May Push Smoking Age of 21," *San Diego Union Tribune*, February 21, 2002.

14. Paul H. Brodish, *The Irreversible Health Effects of Cigarette Smoking*, prepared for the American Council on Science and Health, June 1998.

15. Ibid.

16. Gary Fraser and David Shavlik, "Ten Years of Life," *Archives of Internal Medicine* 161, no. 13 (9 July 2001).

17. "Binge Drinking Affects Brain, Memory," http://www.alcoholism.about.com.

18. Samuel Autman, "CSU Panel Urges Offensive against Alcohol Abuse," *San Diego Union Tribune*, May 8, 2001. Lewis Eigan, *Alcohol Practices, Policies and Potentials of American Colleges and Universities*, U.S. Department of Health and Human Services, 1991. National Institute on Alcohol Abuse and Alcoholism, U.S. Department of Health and Human Services, *Are Women More Vulnerable to Alcohol's Effects?*, 1999. Pacific Institute for Research and Evaluation, *Cost of Underage Drinking*, U.S. Department of Justice, 1999. Also from http://www.alcoholism.about.com and http://www.stopcollegebinging.com.

19. Henry Wechsler and Toben Nelson, "Binge Drinking and the American College Student: What's Five Drinks?" *Psychology of Addictive Behaviors* 15, no. 4 (2001): 287–91.

20. Henry Wechsler, *Binge Drinking on America's College Campuses: Findings from the Harvard School of Public Health College Alcohol Study*, 2000.

21. Henry Wechsler, "College Binge Drinking in the 1990s: A Continuing Problem," *Journal of American College Health* 48 (2000): 199–210.

22. Ibid.

23. Henry Wechsler, *Findings from the Harvard School of Public Health College Alcohol Study*, 2000, http://www.hsph.harvard.edu/cas.

24. From http://www.habitsmart.com/bal.html.

25. National Institute on Alcohol Abuse and Alcoholism, U.S. Department of Health and Human Services, Alcohol Alert, No. 46, *Are Women More Vulnerable to Alcohol's Effects?*, 1999.

26. Henry Wechsler, Kuo Lee, and H. Lee, Harvard School of Public Health, 1999.

27. U.S. Department of Agriculture, *Dietary Guidelines for Americans*, 2000.

28. Clark Carr, "There is No Free Ride," *Freedom* (1998).

29. Lawrence Altman, "Peak of AIDS Epidemic Still to Come, U.N. Says," *San Diego Union Tribune*, July 3, 2002.

30. E. J. Mundell, "Hope for AIDS Cure Remains Alive," *WashingtonPost.com*, January 5, 2007.

31. U.S. Centers for Disease Control and Prevention, *Comprehensive HIV Prevention Messages for Young People*, 2002.

32. U.S. Centers for Disease Control and Prevention, National Center for HIV, STD, and TB Prevention, Divisions of HIV/AIDS Prevention, *HIV and AIDS: Are You at Risk?*, 2000.

33. U.S. Centers for Disease Control and Prevention, "Surveillance 2006: Trends in Sexually Transmitted Diseases in the United States 2006," http://cdc.gov/STD/trends2006.htm.

34. Cheryl Clark, "Sex Cops Help Find Those Who Spread Diseases," *San Diego Union Tribune*, March 11, 2002.

35. Darryl E. Owens, "Sleep's Impact on Learning A to Zzzzz," *San Diego Union Tribune*, October 2, 2000.

36. Scott LaFee, "A Chronic Lack of Sleep Can Lead to the Big Sleep," *San Diego Union Tribune*, October 8, 1997.

37. Ronald Kotulak, "Skimping on Sleep May Make You Fat, Clumsy and Haggard," *San Diego Union Tribune*, June 14, 1998.

38. Gregory Belenky, Walter Reed Army Institute of Research, *Sleep, Sleep Deprivation, and Human Performance in Continuous Operations*, 1997.

39. Lindsey Tanner, "AMA Backs 80-hour Workweek Limit for Doctors-in-Training," *San Diego Union Tribune*, June 21, 2002.

40. Ronald Kotulak, "Skimping on Sleep."

41. Nicole Ziegler Dizon, "Aging Men's Flab Tied to a Lack of Deep Sleep," *San Diego Union Tribune*, August 16, 2000.

42. From http://www.thirdage.com/cgi-bin/NewsPrint.cgi, 2002.

43. Francesco Cappuccio, Warwick Medical School, "Researchers Say Lack of Sleep Doubles Risk of Death . . . But So Can Too Much Sleep," http://www2warwick.ac.uk, 2008.

44. From http://www.stress.org, 2002.

45. Maya Pines, "Psychological Hardiness: The Role of Challenge in Health," *Psychology Today*, December 1980.

46. James Prochaska, "What It Takes to Change," *Health Net News*, Fall 1997.

47. Katherine Rizzo, "John Glenn, 77, Handled Space Like a Young Man," *San Diego Union Tribune*, January 29, 2000.

48. Chelsea Carter, "Sarah 'Sadie' Delaney, 109, Wrote Best Seller with her Sister at 104," *San Diego Union Tribune*, 1999.

Name _____   Date _____

Read the following description of Ollie American's diet and analyze it by answering the following questions about food groups, servings, and daily activity.

Ollie American gets up in the morning and heads for school. On the way to school, he stops at a convenience store and grabs a 32-ounce soda and a bag of chips. He sips the soda and eats the chips on the way to school. He feels energized and ready to face the day. Around mid-morning, he starts to feel a little tired and goes to the vending machine during a break in class. He buys a can of soda and a candy bar to last him through the morning. At lunch, Ollie American is starving, so he and his friends head for a local fast-food place. Ollie orders a large hamburger with everything on it, a large order of fries, and a soda.

After class, Ollie heads for home. For relaxation, he spends a couple of hours playing a video game. Since this is Monday evening football night, Ollie is having some friends over to watch the game. The group puts their money together to order several large pepperoni pizzas. They decide to stop at the store on the way home to purchase some beer and chips to go with the pizza. During the game, Ollie has about half of a large pizza, a half-bag of chips, and four cans of beer.

Ollie has noticed that he is starting to gain weight. He is six feet tall and weighs 230 pounds.

1. What is Ollie's body mass index (BMI)?

   BMI = (705 × body weight) ÷ by (height × height)

2. According to Ollie's BMI, is he considered obese?

3. Ollie is eating many foods that belong in the discretionary calories category (high in sugar or fat). What foods are contributing to Ollie's weight gain?

4. Use the government-suggested dietary guidelines to analyze Ollie's diet. This exercise assumes that Ollie is a male, 21 years old, and does not exercise regularly.

Food Groups	Recommended	List Actual Food Choices
Grains	8 ounce equivalents (1 ounce equivalent is about 1 slice of bread, I cup dry cereal, or ½ cup rice or pasta)	How many ounces?
Vegetables	3 cups (Includes dark green, orange, starchy, dry beans and peas, and other veggies)	How many cups?
Fruits	2 cups	How many cups?
Oils	7 teaspoons	How many teaspoons?
Milk	3 cups (1½ ounces of cheese = 1 cup milk, a large pizza contains 16 ounces of cheese)	How many cups?
Meat and Beans	6.5 ounces (1 ounce equivalent is 1 ounce of meat, poultry or fish, 1 tablespoon peanut butter, ½ ounce nuts, ¼ ounce dry beans or peas)	How many ounces?
Discretionary Calories	360 calories	List foods high in fat or sugar.

5. What suggestions would you make to help Ollie choose a more healthy diet and lose weight?

Name _____ Date _____

Use the following worksheet to analyze your diet. This plan is based on 2,000 calories. Go to www.mypyramid.gov to find your individualized recommendations.

Food Groups	Recommended	List Actual Food Choices
Grains	6 ounce equivalents (1 ounce equivalent is about 1 slice of bread, I cup dry cereal, or ½ cup rice or pasta)	How many ounces?
Vegetables	2½ cups (Includes dark green, orange, starchy, dry beans and peas and other veggies)	How many cups?
Fruits	2 cups	How many cups?
Oils	6 teaspoons	How many teaspoons?
Milk	3 cups (1½ ounces of cheese = 1 cup milk, a large pizza contains 16 ounces of cheese)	How many cups?
Meat and Beans	5.5 ounces (1 ounce equivalent is 1 ounce of meat, poultry or fish, 1 tablespoon peanut butter, ½ ounce nuts, ¼ ounce dry beans or peas)	How many ounces?
Discretionary Calories	100–300 calories	List foods high in fat or sugar.

1. How much do you exercise daily outside of your daily routine?

2. Compare your results to the recommended dietary guidelines. What did you discover?

3. What changes will you make in your exercise routine and diet in the future?

Name _____ Date _____

Go to www.livingto100.com and use the Living to 100 Life Expectancy Calculator to assess your health habits.

What are your good health habits?

What are some areas you need to improve?

Based on the above list, write three intention statements for maintaining good health in the future.

1.

2.

3.

Name _____ Date _____

The following story is based on a news article about road rage. As you read the article, think about Mr. Road Rage and the negative thoughts he was thinking. What stress-reducing thoughts could have been used to avoid these tragic results? Then answer the questions below. You may want to do this as a group exercise with some of your classmates.

> Mr. Road Rage, who shot a man as a result of a traffic-related altercation, was sentenced to 19 years in prison today. He was a quiet man with no previous criminal record. People at his place of work, where he was employed as a computer programmer, were surprised to learn what had happened. Mr. Road Rage was not a violent man. He had even tried to get out of the Navy as a conscientious objector because he hated violence.

> What happened? Mr. Rage was on the way home from work when some teenagers on bicycles cut right in front of him. Mr. Rage almost hit them. He was so angry that he stopped to talk with the teenagers. They began to call each other names and exchange obscene gestures. One of the teenagers became so angry with Mr. Rage that he threw his bicycle at Mr. Rage's car, making a small dent. The teenagers quickly left the scene. Mr. Rage continued to his apartment complex where he saw one of the teenagers involved in the altercation. He went to his apartment and got an old gun and decided that he would make a citizen's arrest of the teenager. The teenager resisted; and during the scuffle that ensued, the gun went off and the teenager was killed.

During Mr. Rage's murder trial, one of his colleagues at work said that Mr. Rage's behavior was completely out of character. He never imagined that such an incident could occur.

1. List the negative thoughts that might have been going through Mr. Rage's head during this incident.

2. What stress-reducing thoughts could Mr. Rage have used to avoid this situation?

3. Make a list of stress-reducing thoughts that you can use in stressful situations.

What Is Your Stress Index?*

Name _____   Date _____

Do you frequently: Yes   No

1. Neglect your diet?   _____   _____

2. Try to do everything yourself?   _____   _____

3. Blow up easily?   _____   _____

4. Seek unrealistic goals?   _____   _____

5. Fail to see the humor in situations others find funny?   _____   _____

6. Act rude?   _____   _____

7. Make a big deal out of everything?   _____   _____

8. Look to other people to make things happen?   _____   _____

9. Have difficulty making decisions?   _____   _____

10. Complain you are disorganized?   _____   _____

11. Avoid people whose ideas are different from your own?   _____   _____

12. Keep everything inside?   _____   _____

13. Neglect exercise?   _____   _____

14. Have only a few supportive relationships?   _____   _____

15. Use psychoactive drugs, such as sleeping pills and tranquilizers, without   _____   _____
    physician approval?

16. Get too little rest?   _____   _____

17. Get angry when you are kept waiting?   _____   _____

18. Ignore stress symptoms?   _____   _____

19. Procrastinate?   _____   _____

20. Think there is only one right way to do something?   _____   _____

21. Fail to build in relaxation time?   _____   _____

22. Gossip?   _____   _____

23. Race through the day?   _____   _____

24. Spend a lot of time lamenting the past?   _____   _____

25. Fail to get a break from noise and crowds?   _____   _____

*From Andrew Slaby, *Sixty Ways to Make Stress Work for You*.

Score 1 for each yes answer and 0 for each no. Total score: _____

1–6   There are a few hassles in your life. Make sure, though, that you aren't trying so hard to avoid problems that you shy away from challenges.

7–13   You've got your life in pretty good control. Work on the choices and habits that could still be causing some unnecessary stress in your life.

14–20   You're approaching the danger zone. You may well be suffering stress-related symptoms and your relationships could be strained. Think carefully about choices you've made and take relaxation breaks each day.

Above 20 Emergency! You must stop now, rethink how you are living, change your attitudes, and pay scrupulous attention to your diet, exercise, and relaxation programs.

CHAPTER 7

Taking Notes, Writing, and Speaking

Learning Objectives

Read to answer these key questions:

- Why is it important to take notes?

- What are some good listening techniques?

- What are some tips for taking good lecture notes?

- What are some note-taking systems?

- What is the best way to review my notes for the test?

- What is power writing?

- How can I make a good speech?

Knowing how to listen and take good notes can make your college life easier and may help you in your future career as well. Professionals in many occupations take notes as a way of recording key ideas for later use. Whether you become a journalist, attorney, architect, engineer, or other professional, listening and taking good notes can help you to get ahead in your career.

Good writing and speaking skills are important to your success in college and in your career. In college, you will be asked to write term papers and complete other writing assignments. The writing skills you learn in college will be used later in jobs involving high responsibility and good pay; on the job, you will write reports, memos, and proposals. In college, you will probably take a speech class and give oral reports in other classes; on the job, you will present your ideas orally to your colleagues and business associates.

Why Take Notes?

The most important reason for taking notes is to remember important material for tests or for future use in your career. If you just attend class without taking notes, you will forget most of the material by the next day.

How does taking notes enhance memory?

- In college, the lecture is a way of supplementing the written material in the textbook. Without good notes, an important part of the course is missing. Note taking provides material to rehearse or recite, so that it can be stored in long-term memory.
- When you take notes and impose your own organization on them, the notes become more personally meaningful. If they are meaningful, they are easier to remember.
- Taking notes helps you to make new connections. New material is remembered by connecting it to what you already know.
- For kinesthetic and tactile learners, the physical act of writing the material is helpful in learning and remembering it.
- For visual learners, notes provide a visual map of the material to be learned.
- For auditory learners, taking notes is a way to listen carefully and record information to be stored in the memory.
- Note taking helps students to concentrate, maintain focus, and stay awake.
- Attending the lectures and taking notes helps you to understand what the professor thinks is important and to know what to study for the exam.

The College Lecture

You will experience many different types of lectures while in college. At larger universities, many of the beginning-level courses are taught in large lecture halls with 300 people or more. More advanced courses tend to have fewer students. In large lecture situations, it is not always possible or appropriate to ask questions. Under these circumstances, the large lecture is often supplemented by smaller discussion sessions where you can ask questions and review the lecture material. Although attendance may not be checked, it is important to attend both the lectures and the discussion sessions.

A formal college lecture is divided into four parts. Understanding these parts will help you to be a good listener and take good notes.

1. **Introduction.** The professor uses the introduction to set the stage and to introduce the topic of the lecture. Often an overview or outline of the lecture is presented. Use the introduction as a way to begin thinking about the organization of your notes and the key ideas you will need to write down.

2. **Thesis.** The thesis is the key idea in the lecture. In a one-hour lecture, there is usually one thesis statement. Listen carefully for the thesis statement and write it down in your notes. Review the thesis statement and related ideas for the exam.

3. **Body.** The body of the lecture usually consists of five or six main ideas with discussion and clarification of each idea. As a note taker, your job is to identify the main ideas, write them in your notes, and put in enough of the explanation or examples to understand the key ideas.

4. **Conclusion.** In the conclusion, the professor summarizes the key points of the lecture and sometimes asks for questions. Use the conclusion as an opportunity to check your understanding of the lecture and to ask questions to clarify the key points.

> "Education is not a problem. It is an opportunity."
> Lyndon B. Johnson

How to Be a Good Listener

Effective note taking begins with good listening. What is good listening? Sometimes students confuse listening with hearing. Hearing is done with the ears. Listening is a more active process done with the ears and the brain engaged. Good listening requires attention and concentration. Practice these ideas for good listening:

- **Be physically ready.** It is difficult to listen to a lecture if you are tired, hungry, or ill. Get enough sleep so that you can stay awake. Eat a balanced diet without too much caffeine or sugar. Take care of your health and participate in an exercise program so that you feel your best.

- **Prepare a mental framework.** Look at the course syllabus to become familiar with the topic of the lecture. Use your textbook to read, or at least survey, the material to be covered in the lecture. If you are familiar with the key concepts from the textbook, you will be able to understand the lecture and know what to write down in your notes. If the material is in your book, there is no need to write it down in your notes.

  The more complex the topic, the more important it is for you to read the text first. If you go to the lecture and have no idea what is being discussed, you may be overwhelmed and find it difficult to take notes on material that is totally new to you. Remember that it is easier to remember material if you can connect it to material you already know.

- **Find a good place to sit.** Arrive early to get a good seat. The best seats in the classroom are in the front and center of the room. If you were buying concert tickets, these would be the best and most expensive seats. Find a seat that will help you to hear and focus on the speaker. You may need to find a seat away from your friends to avoid distractions.

- **Have a positive mental attitude.** Convince yourself that the speaker has something important to say and be open to new ideas. This may require you to focus on your goals and to look past some distractions. Maybe the lecturer doesn't have the best speaking voice or you don't like his or her appearance. Focus on what you can learn from the professor rather than outward appearances.

- **Listen actively to identify the main points.** As you are listening to the lecture, ask yourself, "What is the main idea?" In your own words, write the main points down in your notes. Do not try to write down everything the professor says. This will be impossible and unnecessary. Imagine that your mind is a filter and you are actively sorting through the material to find the key ideas and write them down in your notes. Try to identify the key points that will be on the test and write them in your notes.

- **Stay awake and engaged in learning.** The best way to stay awake and focused is to listen actively and take notes. Have a mental debate with the professor. Listen for the main points and the logical connection between ideas. The physical act of writing the notes will help to keep you awake.

Tips for Good Note Taking

Here are some suggestions for taking good notes:

1. Attend all of the lectures. Because many professors do not take attendance, students are often tempted to miss class. If you do not attend the lectures, however, you will not know what the professor thinks is important and what to study for the test. There will be important points covered in the lectures that are not in the book.

2. Have the proper materials. A three-ring notebook and notebook paper are recommended. Organize notes chronologically and include any handouts given in class. You can have a small notebook for each class or a single large notebook with dividers for each class. Just take the notebook paper to class and later file it in your notebook at home. Use your laptop as an alternative to a paper notebook.

3. Begin your notes by writing the date of the lecture, so you can keep your notes in order.

4. Write notes on the front side only of each piece of paper. This will allow you to spread the pages out and see the big picture or pattern in the lectures when you are reviewing.

5. Write notes neatly and legibly so you can read and review them easily.

6. Do not waste time recopying or typing your notes. Your time would be better spent reviewing your notes.

7. As a general rule, do not rely on a tape recorder for taking notes. With a tape recorder, you will have to listen to the lecture again on tape. For a semester course, this would be about 45 hours of tape! It is much faster to review carefully written notes.

8. Copy down everything written on the board and the main points from PowerPoint or other visual presentations. If it is important enough for the professor to write on the board, it is important enough to be on the test.

9. Use key words and phrases in your notes. Leave out unimportant words and don't worry about grammar.

10. Use abbreviations as long as you can read them. Entire sentences or paragraphs are not necessary and you may not have time to write them.

11. Don't loan your whole notebook to someone else because you may not get it back. If you want to share your notes, make copies.

12. If the professor talks too fast, listen carefully for the key ideas and write them down. Leave spaces in your notes to fill in later. You may be able to find the information in the text or get the information from another student.

13. Explore new uses of technology for note taking. Students are taking notes and sharing them on Facebook and GradeGuru, for example.

QUIZ

Listening and Note Taking

Test what you have learned by selecting the correct answers to the following questions.

1. When taking notes on a college lecture, it is most important to
   a. write down everything you hear.
   b. write down the main ideas and enough explanation to understand them.
   c. write down names, dates, places, and numbers.

2. To be a good listener,
   a. read or skim over the material before you attend the lecture.
   b. attend the lecture first and then read the text.
   c. remember that listening is more important than note taking.

3. To stay awake during the lecture,
   a. drink lots of coffee.
   b. sit near your friends so you can make some comments on the lecture.
   c. listen actively by taking notes.

4. Since attendance is not always checked in college classes,
   a. it is not necessary to attend class if you read the textbook.
   b. it is acceptable to miss lectures as long as you show up for the exams.
   c. it is up to you to attend every class.

5. When taking notes, be sure to
   a. use complete sentences and good grammar.
   b. write down whatever is written on the board or the visual presentations.
   c. write the notes quickly without worrying about neatness.

How did you do on the quiz? Check your answers: 1. b, 2. a, 3. c, 4. c, 5. b

Journal Entry #1

Write one paragraph giving advice to a new student about taking notes in college. Use any of these questions to guide your thinking:

• Why is note taking necessary in college?
• How can you be a good listener?
• What are some tips for taking good notes?
• What are some ideas that don't work?

Note-Taking Systems

There are several systems for taking notes. How you take notes will depend on your learning style and the lecturer's speaking style. Experiment with these systems and use what works best for you.

The Cornell Format

The Cornell format is an efficient method of taking notes and reviewing them. It appeals to students who are logical, orderly, and organized and have lectures that fit into this pattern. The Cornell format is especially helpful for thinking about key points as you review your notes.

Step 1: Prepare. To use the Cornell format, you will need a three-ring notebook with looseleaf paper. Draw or fold a vertical line 2½ inches from the left side of the paper. This is the recall column that can be used to write key ideas when reviewing. Use the remaining section of the paper for your notes. Write the date and title of the lecture at the top of the page.

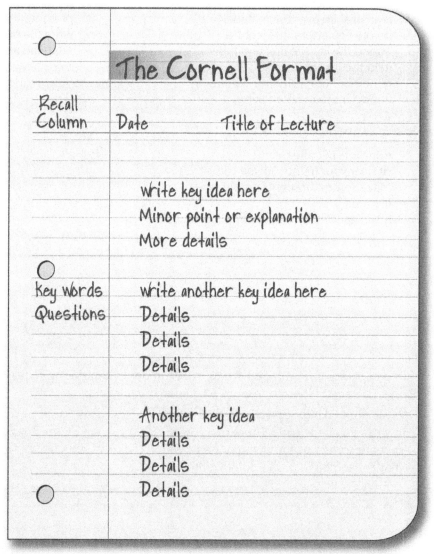

Figure 7.1 The Cornell format is an efficient way of organizing notes and reviewing them.

Step 2: Take notes. Use the large area to the right of the recall column to take notes. Listen for key ideas and write them just to the right of the recall column line, as in the diagram above. Indent your notes for minor points and illustrative details. Then skip a space and write the next key idea. Don't worry about using numbers or letters as in an outline format. Just use the indentations and spacing to highlight and separate key ideas. Use short phrases, key words, and abbreviations. Complete sentences are not necessary, but write legibly so you can read your notes later.

Step 3: Use the recall column for review. Read over your notes and write down key words or ideas from the lecture in the recall column. Ask yourself, "What is this about?" Cover up the notes on the right-hand side and recite the key ideas of the lecture. Another variation is to write questions in the margin. Find the key ideas and then write possible exam questions in the recall column. Cover your notes and see if you can answer the questions.

The Outline Method

If the lecture is well organized, some students just take notes in outline format. Sometimes lecturers will show their outline as they speak.

- Use Roman numerals to label main topics. Then use capital letters for main ideas and Arabic numerals for related details or examples.
- You can make a free-form outline using just indentation to separate main ideas and supporting details.
- Leave spaces to fill in material later.
- Use a highlighter to review your notes as soon as possible after the lecture.

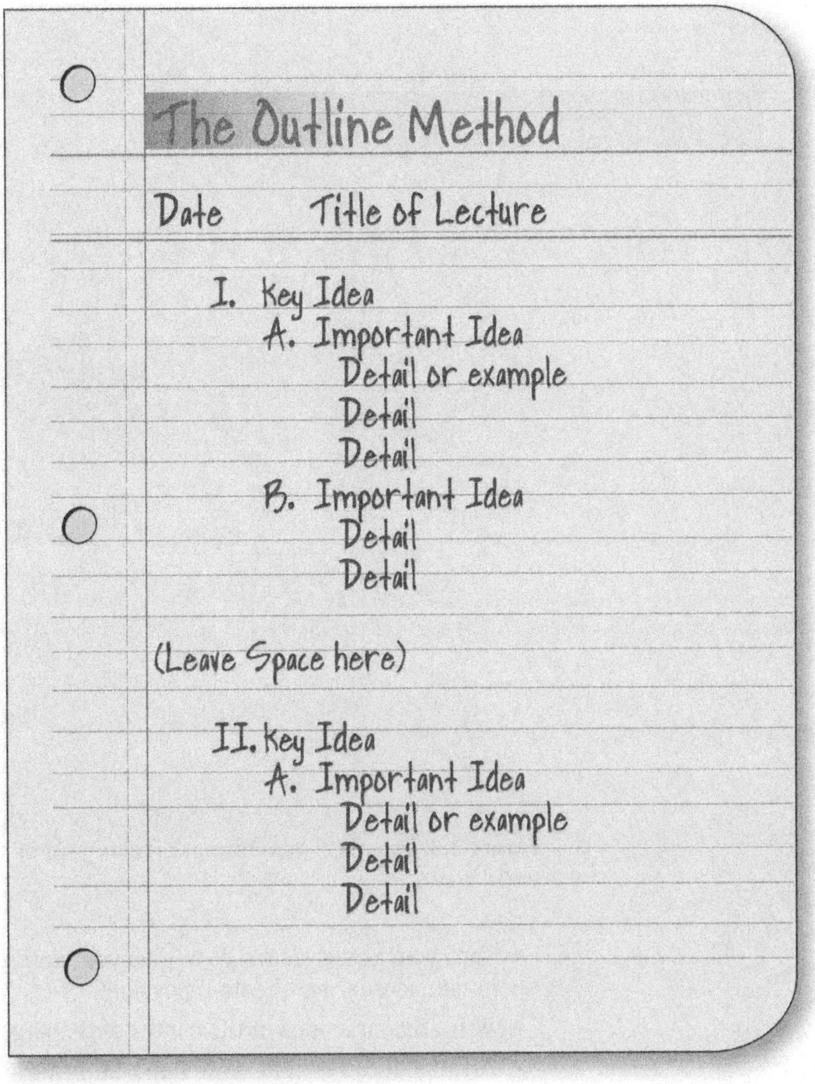

Figure 7.2 If a lecture is well organized, the outline format of taking notes works well.

The Mind Map

A mind map shows the relationship between ideas in a visual way. It is much easier to remember items that are organized and linked together in a personally meaningful way. As a result, recall and review is quicker and more effective. Mind maps have appeal to visual learners and those who do not want to be limited by a set structure, as in the outline formats. They can also be used for lectures that are not highly structured. Here are some suggestions for using the mind-mapping technique:

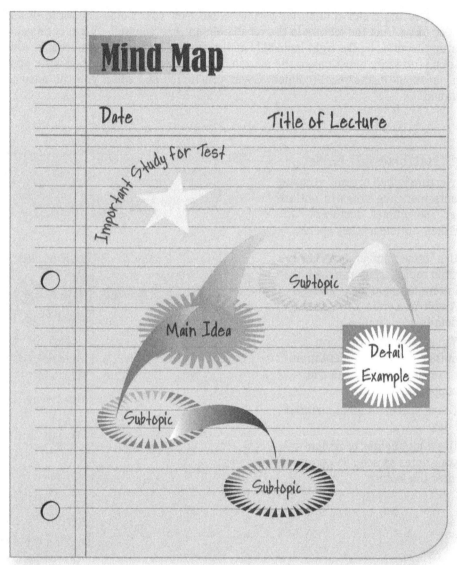

Figure 7.3 The mind map format of taking notes shows the relationship between ideas in a visual way.

- Turn your paper sideways to give you more space. Use standard-size notebook paper or consider larger sheets if possible.
- Write the main idea in the center of the page and circle it.
- Arrange ideas so that more important ideas are closer to the center and less important ideas are farther out.
- Show the relationship of the minor points to the main ideas using lines, circles, boxes, charts, and other visual devices. Here is where you can use your creativity and imagination to make a visual picture of the key ideas in the lecture.

- Use symbols and drawings.
- Use different colors to separate main ideas.
- When the lecturer moves to another main idea, start a new mind map.
- When you are done with the lecture, quickly review your mind maps. Add any written material that will be helpful in understanding the map later.
- A mind map can also be used as:
  - a review tool for remembering and relating the key ideas in the textbook;
  - a preparation tool for essay exams in which remembering main ideas and relationships is important; and
  - the first step in organizing ideas for a term paper.

Improving Note-Taking Efficiency

Improve note-taking efficiency by listening for key words that signal the main ideas and supporting details. Learn to write faster by using telegraphic sentences, abbreviations, and symbols.

Signal Words

Signal words are clues to understanding the structure and content of a lecture. Recognizing signal words can help you identify key ideas and organize them in your notes. The table on the following page lists some common signal words and their meaning.

Telegraphic Sentences

Telegraphic sentences are short, abbreviated sentences used in note taking. They are very similar to the text messages sent on a cell phone. There are four rules for telegraphic sentences:

1. Write key words only.
2. Omit unnecessary words (*a, an, the*).
3. Ignore rules of grammar.
4. Use abbreviations and symbols.

Here is an example of a small part of a lecture followed by a student's telegraphic notes:

Heavy drinking of alcoholic beverages causes students to miss class and to fall behind in schoolwork. College students who are considered binge drinkers are at risk for many alcohol-related problems. Binge drinking is simply drinking too much alcohol at one time. Binge drinking is defined by researchers as drinking five or more drinks in a row for men or four or more drinks in a row for women. Researchers estimate that two out of five college students (40 percent) are binge drinkers.

Binge drinking—too much alcohol at one time
    Men = 5 in row
    Women = 4
    2 out of 5 (40%) college students binge

Signal Words

Type	Examples	Meaning
Main idea words	And most important A major development The basic concept is Remember that The main idea is We will focus on The key is	Introduce the key points that need to be written in your notes.
Example words	To illustrate For example For instance	Clarify and illustrate the main ideas in the lecture. Write these examples in your notes after the main idea. If multiple examples are given, write down the ones you have time for or the ones that you understand the best.
Addition words	In addition Also Furthermore	Add more important information. Write these points down in your notes.
Enumeration words	The five steps First, second, third Next	Signal a list. Write down the list in your notes and number the items.
Time words	Before, after Formerly Subsequently Prior Meanwhile	Signal the order of events. Write down the events in the correct order in your notes.
Cause and effect words	Therefore As a result If . . ., then	Signal important concepts that might be on the exam. When you hear these words, label them "cause" and "effect" in your notes and review these ideas for the exam.
Definition words	In other words It simply means That is In essence	Provide the meanings of words or simplify complex ideas. Write these definitions or clarifications in your notes.
Swivel words	However Nevertheless Yes, but Still	Provide exceptions, qualifications, or further clarification. Write down qualifying comments in your notes.
Compare and contrast words	Similarly Likewise In contrast	Present similarities or differences. Write these similarities and differences in your notes and label them.
Summary words	In conclusion To sum up In a nutshell	Restate the important ideas of the lecture. Write the summaries in your notes.
Test words	This is important. Remember this. You'll see this again. You might want to study this for the test.	Provide a clue that the material will be on the test. Write these down in your notes and mark them in a way that stands out. Put a star or asterisk next to these items or highlight them. Each professor has his or her own test clue words.

Abbreviations

If you have time, write out words in their entirety for ease of reading. If you are short on time, use any abbreviation as long as you can read it. Here are some ideas:

1. Use the first syllable of the word.

democracy	dem
education	ed
politics	pol
different	diff
moderate	mod
characteristic	char
develop	dev

2. Use just enough of the word so that you can recognize it.

republican	repub
prescription	prescrip
introduction	intro
intelligence	intell
association	assoc

3. Abbreviate or write out the word the first time, then use an acronym. For example, for the United States Department of Agriculture, abbreviate it as "US Dept of Ag" and then write it as USDA in subsequent references. Other examples:

short-term memory	STM
as soon as possible	ASAP

4. Omit vowels.

background	bkgrnd
problem	prblm
government	gvt

5. Use g in place of ing.

checking	ckg
decreasing	decrg

6. Write your notes in text message format.

Symbols

Use common symbols or invent your own to speed up the note-taking process.

Common Symbols Used in Note Taking

Symbol	Meaning	Symbol	Meaning
&	and	B4	before
w	with	BC	because
wo	without	esp	especially
wi	within	diff	difference
<	less than	min	minimum
>	more than	gov	government
@	at	ex	example
/	per	↑	increasing
2	to, two, too	↓	decreasing
∴	therefore	=	equal
vs	versus, against	≠	not equal

How to Review Your Notes

Immediate review. Review your notes as soon as possible after the lecture. The most effective review is done immediately or at least within 20 minutes. If you wait until the next day to review, you may already have forgotten much of the information. During the immediate review, fill in any missing or incomplete information. Say the important points to yourself. This begins the process of rehearsal for storing the information in long-term memory.

There are various methods for review depending on your note-taking system:

- For the Cornell format, use the recall column to write in key words or questions. Cover your notes and see if you can recall the main ideas. Place checkmarks by the items you have mastered. Don't worry about mastering all the key points from the beginning. With each review, it will be easier to remember the information.
- For the outline format, use a highlighter to mark the key ideas as you repeat them silently to yourself.
- For mind maps, look over the information and think about the key ideas and their relationships. Fill in additional information or clarification. Highlight important points or relationships with color.

Intermediate review. Set up some time each week for short reviews of your notes and the key points in your textbook from previous weeks. Quickly look over the notes and recite the key points in your mind. These intermediate reviews will help you to master the material and avoid test anxiety.

Test review. Complete a major review as part of your test preparation strategy. As you look through your notes, turn the key ideas into possible test questions and answer them.

Final review. The final review occurs after you have received the results of your test. Ask yourself these questions:

- What percentage of the test questions came from the lecture notes?
- Were you prepared for the exam? Is so, congratulate yourself on a job well done. If not, how can you improve next time?
- Were your notes adequate? If not, what needs to be added or changed?

QUIZ

Note-Taking Efficiency

Test what you have learned by selecting the correct answers to the following questions.

1. Recognizing signal words will help you to
   a. know when the lecture is about to end.
   b. identify the key ideas and organize them in your notes.
   c. know when to pay attention.

2. When taking notes, be sure to
   a. write your notes in complete sentences.
   b. use correct grammar.
   c. use telegraphic sentences.

3. The best time to review your notes is
   a. as soon as possible after the lecture.
   b. within 24 hours.
   c. within one week.

4. Using abbreviations in note taking is
   a. not a good idea.
   b. a good idea as long as you can read them.
   c. makes review difficult.

5. To avoid test anxiety,
   a. review your notes just before the test.
   b. review your notes the week before the test.
   c. review your notes periodically throughout the semester.

How did you do on the quiz? Check your answers: 1. b, 2. c, 3. a, 4. b, 5. c

Journal Entry #2

Write five intention statements about improving your note-taking skills. Consider your note-taking system, how to take notes more efficiently, and the best way to review your notes. I intend to . . .

Power Writing

Effective writing will help you in school, on the job, and in your personal life. Good writing will help you to create quality term papers. The writing skills that you learn in college will be used later in jobs involving high responsibility and good pay. You can become an excellent writer by learning about the steps in POWER writing: prepare, organize, write, edit, and revise.

Power Writing

- Prepare
- Organize
- Write
- Edit
- Revise

Prepare

Plan your time. The first step in writing is to plan your time so that the project can be completed by the due date. Picture this scene: It is the day that the term paper is due. A few students proudly hand in their term papers and are ready to celebrate their accomplishments. Many of the students in the class are absent, and some will never return to the class. Some of the students look as though they haven't slept the night before. They look stressed and weary. At the front of the class is a line of students wanting to talk with the instructor. The instructor has heard it all before:

- I had my paper all completed and my printer jammed.
- My hard drive crashed and I lost my paper.
- I was driving to school and my paper flew off my motorcycle.
- I had the flu.
- My children were sick.
- I had to take my dog to the vet.
- My dog ate my paper.
- My car broke down and I could not get to the library.
- My grandmother died and I had to go to the funeral.
- My roommate accidentally took my backpack to school.
- I spilled salad dressing on my paper, so I put it in the microwave to dry it out and the writing disappeared!

To avoid being in this uncomfortable and stressful situation, plan ahead. Plan to complete your project at least one week ahead of time so that you can deal with life's emergencies. Life does not always go as planned. You or your children may get sick, or your dog may do strange things to your homework. Your computer may malfunction, leading you to believe it senses stress and malfunctions just to frustrate you even more.

To avoid stress and do your best work, start with the date that the project is due and then think about the steps needed to finish. Write these dates on your calendar or on your list of things to do. Consider all these components:

Project due date:

To do	By when?
1. Brainstorm ideas.	_____
2. Choose a topic.	_____
3. Gather information.	_____
4. Write a thesis statement.	_____
5. Write an outline.	_____
6. Write the introduction.	_____

> "The most valuable of all education is the ability to make yourself do the thing you have to do, when it has to be done, whether you like it or not."
>
> Aldous Huxley

7. Write the first draft. _____

8. Prepare the bibliography. _____

9. Edit. _____

10. Revise. _____

11. Print and assemble. _____

Prepare

- Plan your time
- Find space and time
- Choose general topic
- Gather information
- Write thesis statement

Find a space and time. Find a space where you can work. Gather the materials that you will need to write. Generally, writing is best done in longer blocks of time. Determine when you will work on your paper and write the time on your schedule. Start right away to avoid panic later.

Choose a general topic. This task will be easy if your topic is already clearly defined by your instructor or your boss at work. Make sure that you have a clear idea of what is required, such as length, format, purpose, and method of citing references and topic. Many times the choice of a topic is left to you. Begin by doing some brainstorming. Think about topics that interest you. Write them down. You may want to focus your attention on brainstorming ideas for five or 10 minutes, and then put the project aside and come back to it later. Once you have started the process of thinking about the ideas, your mind will continue to work and you may have some creative inspiration. If inspiration does not come, repeat the brainstorming process.

Gather information. Go to your college library and use the Internet to gather your information. As you begin, you can see what is available, what is interesting to you, and what the current thinking is on your topic. Note the major topics of interest that might be useful to you. Once you have found some interesting material, you will feel motivated to continue your project. As you find information relevant to your topic, make sure to write down the sources of your information to use in your bibliography. The bibliography contains information about where you found your material. Write down the author, the title of the publication, the publisher, and the place and date of publication. For Internet resources, list the address of the website and the date accessed.

Write the thesis statement. The thesis statement is the key idea in your paper. It provides a direction for you to follow. It is the first step in organizing your work. To write a thesis statement, review the material you have gathered and then ask these questions:

- What is the most important idea?
- What question would I like to ask about it?
- What is my answer?

For example, if I decide to write a paper for my health class on the harmful effects of smoking, I would look at current references on the topic. I might become interested in how the tobacco companies misled the public on the dangers of smoking. I would think about my thesis statement and answer the questions stated above.

- **What is the most important idea?** Smoking is harmful to your health.
- **What question would I like to ask about it?** Did the tobacco companies mislead the public about the health hazards of smoking?
- **What is my answer?** The tobacco companies misled the public about the hazards of smoking in order to protect their business interests.
- **My thesis statement:** Tobacco companies knew that smoking was hazardous to health, but to protect their business interests, they deliberately misled the public.

The thesis statement helps to narrow the topic and provide direction for the paper. I can now focus on reference material related to my topic: research on health effects of smoking, congressional testimony relating to regulation of the tobacco industry, and how advertising influences people to smoke.

Organize

Organize

• List related topics
• Arrange in logical order
• Have an organizational structure

At this point you have many ideas about what to include in your paper, and you have a central focus, your thesis statement. Start to organize your paper by listing the topics that are related to your thesis statement. Here is a list of topics related to my thesis statement about smoking:

- Tobacco companies' awareness that nicotine is addictive
- Minimizing health hazards in tobacco advertisements
- How advertisements encourage people to smoke
- Money earned by the tobacco industry
- Health problems caused by smoking
- Statistics on numbers of people who have health problems or die from smoking
- Regulation of the tobacco industry
- Advertisements aimed at children

Think about the topics and arrange them in logical order. Use an outline, a mind map, a flowchart, or a drawing to think about how you will organize the important topics. Keep in mind that you will need an introduction, a body, and a conclusion. Having an organizational structure will make it easier for you to write because you will not need to wonder what comes next.

Write

Write the First Sentence
Begin with the main idea.

Write the Introduction

Write

• First sentence
• Introduction
• Body
• Conclusion
• References

This is the road map for the rest of the paper. The introduction includes your thesis statement and establishes the foundation of the paper. It introduces topics that will be discussed in the body of the paper. The introduction should include some interesting points that provide a "hook" to motivate the audience to read your paper. For example, for a paper on the hazards of smoking, you might begin with statistics on how many people suffer from smoking-related illnesses and premature death. Note the large profits earned by the tobacco industry. Then introduce other topics: deception, advertisements, and regulation. The introduction provides a guide or outline of what will follow in the paper.

Write the Body of the Paper
The body of the paper is divided into paragraphs that discuss the topics that you have introduced. As you write each paragraph, include the main idea and then explain it and give examples. Here are some good tips for writing:

1. Good writing reflects clear thinking. Think about what you want to say and write about it so the reader can understand your point of view.
2. Use clear and concise language. Avoid using too many words or scholarly-sounding words that might get in the way of understanding.

3. Don't assume that the audience knows what you are writing about. Provide complete information.

4. Provide examples, stories, and quotes to support your main points. Include your own ideas and experiences.

5. Beware of plagiarism. Plagiarism is copying the work of others without giving them credit. It is illegal and can cause you to receive a failing grade on your project or even get you into legal trouble. Faculty regularly uses software programs that identify plagiarized material in student papers. You can avoid plagiarism by using quotation marks around an author's words and providing a reference indicating where you found the material. Another way to avoid plagiarism is by carefully reading your source material while using critical thinking to evaluate it. Then look away from the source and write about the ideas in your own words, including your critical thinking about the subject. Don't forget to include a reference for the source material in your bibliography.

Write the Conclusion

The conclusion summarizes the topics in the paper and presents your point of view. It makes reference to the introduction and answers the question posed in your thesis statement. It often makes the reader think about the significance of your point and the implications for the future. Make your conclusion interesting and powerful.

Include References

No college paper is complete without references. References may be given in footnotes, endnotes, a list of works cited, or a bibliography. You can use your computer to insert these references. There are various styles for citing references depending on your subject area. There are computer programs that put your information into the correct style. Ask your instructor which style to use for your particular class or project. Three frequently used styles for citing references are APA, Chicago, and MLA.

1. The American Psychological Association (APA) style is used in psychology and other behavioral sciences. Consult the *Publication Manual of the American Psychological Association*, 6th ed. (Washington, DC: American Psychological Association, 2010). You can find this source online at www.apastyle.org.

2. Chicago style is used by many professional writers in a variety of fields. Consult the *Chicago Manual of Style*, 16th ed. (Chicago: University of Chicago Press, 2010). You can find this source online at www.chicagomanualofstyle.org/home.html.

3. The Modern Language Association (MLA) style is used in English, classical languages, and the humanities. Consult the *MLA Handbook for Writers of Research Papers*, 7th ed. (New York: Modern Language Association, 2009). This source is available online at www.mla.org/style.

Each of these styles uses a different format for listing sources, but all include the same information. Make sure you write down this information as you collect your reference material. If you forget this step, it is very time-consuming and difficult to find later.

- Author's name
- Title of the book or article
- Journal name
- Publisher
- City where book was published
- Publication date
- Page number (and volume and issue numbers, if available)

Here are some examples of citations in the APA style:

- **Book.** Include author, date of publication, title, city of publication, and publisher.

  Fralick, M. (2011). *College and career success* (5th ed.). Dubuque, IA: Kendall Hunt.

- **Journal article.** Include author, date, title, name of journal, volume and issue numbers, pages.

  Fralick, M. (1993). College success: A study of positive and negative attrition. *Community College Review, 20*(5), 29–36.

- **Website.** Include author, date listed or updated, document title or name of website, URL or website address, and date accessed. Include as many of the above items as possible. Methods of citing information from the Internet are still evolving.

  Fralick, M. (2011, January). *Note taking*. Retrieved January 2011 from College Success 1 at http://www.collegesuccess1.com/

Save Your Work

As soon as you have written the first paragraph, save it on your computer. Save your work in two places: on your hard drive and on a flash drive or external hard drive. At the end of each section, save your work again to both of these places. When you are finished, print your work and save a paper copy. Then, if your hard drive crashes, you will still have your work at another location. If your file becomes corrupted, you will still have the paper copy. Following these procedures can save you a lot of headaches. Any writer can tell you stories of lost work because of computer problems, lightning storms, power outages, and other unpredictable events.

Put It Away for a While

> "All things are difficult before they are easy."
> John Norley

The last step in writing the first draft is easy. Put it away for a while and come back to it later. In this way, you can relax and gain some perspective on your work. You will be able to take a more objective look at your work to begin the process of editing and revising.

Writer's Block

Many people who are anxious about writing experience "writer's block." You have writer's block if you find yourself staring at that blank piece of paper or computer screen not knowing how to begin or what to write. Here are some tips for avoiding writer's block.

Tips to Overcome Writer's Block

1. Write freely
2. Use brainstorming
3. Realize it's a first draft
4. Read reference materials
5. Break up assignment
6. Find a good place to write
7. Beware of procrastination

- **Write freely.** Just write anything about your topic that comes to mind. Don't worry about organization or perfection at this point. Don't censure your ideas. You can always go back to organize and edit later. Free-writing helps you to overcome one of the main causes of writer's block: you think it has to be perfect from the beginning. This expectation of perfection causes anxiety. You freeze up and become unable to write. Perhaps you have past memories of writing where the teacher made many corrections on your paper. Maybe you lack confidence in your writing skills. The only way you will become a better writer is to keep writing and perfecting your writing skills, so to start the writing process, just write what comes to mind. Don't worry how great it is. You can fix it later. Just begin.

- **Use brainstorming if you get stuck.** For five minutes, focus your attention on the topic and write whatever comes to mind. You don't even need to write full sentences; just jot down ideas. If you are really stuck, try working on a different topic or take a break and come back to it later.

- **Realize that it is only the first draft.** It is not the finished product and it does not have to be perfect. Just write some ideas on paper; you can revise them later.

- **Read through your reference materials.** The ideas you find can get your mind working. Also, reading can make you a better writer.
- **Break the assignment up into small parts.** If you find writing difficult, write for five minutes at a time. Do this consistently and you can get used to writing and can complete your paper.
- **Find a good place for writing.** If you are an introvert, look for a quiet place for concentration. If you are an extrovert, go to a restaurant or coffee shop and start your writing.
- **Beware of procrastination.** The more you put off writing, the more anxious you will become and the more difficult the task will be. Make a schedule and stick to it.

Edit and Revise

The editing and revising stage allows you to take a critical look at what you have written. It takes some courage to do this step. Once people see their ideas in writing, they become attached to them. With careful editing and revising, you can turn in your best work and be proud of your accomplishments. Here are some tips for editing and revising:

1. **Read your paper as if you were the audience.** Pretend that you are the instructor or another person reading your paper. Does every sentence make sense? Did you say what you meant to say? Read what you have written, and the result will be a more effective paper.

2. **Read paragraph by paragraph.** Does each paragraph have a main idea and supporting details? Do the paragraphs fit logically together? Use the cut-and-paste feature on your computer to move sentences and paragraphs around if needed.

3. **Check your grammar and spelling.** Use the spell check and grammar check on your computer. These tools are helpful, but they are not thorough enough. The spell check will pick up only misspelled words. It will skip words that are spelled correctly but not the intended word—for example, if you use "of" instead of "on" or "their" instead of "there." To find such errors, you need to read your paper after doing a spell check.

4. **Check for language that is biased in terms of gender, disability, or ethnic group.** Use words that are gender neutral. If a book or paper uses only the pronoun "he" or "she," half of the population is left out. You can often avoid sexist language by using the plural forms of nouns:

(singular) The successful student knows *his* values and sets goals for the future.

(plural) Successful students know *their* values and set goals for the future.

After all, we are trying to make the world a better place, with opportunity for all. Here are some examples of biased language and better alternatives.

Biased Language	*Better Alternatives*
policeman	police officer
chairman	chair
fireman	firefighter
draftsman	drafter
mankind	humanity
manmade	handcrafted
housewife	homemaker
crippled and disabled persons	persons with disabilities

Tips for Editing and Revising

1. Read your paper objectively
2. Read paragraph by paragraph
3. Check grammar and spelling
4. Check for biased language
5. Have someone else read your paper
6. Review the introduction and conclusion
7. Prepare final copy
8. Prepare title page

5. **Have someone else read your paper.** Ask your reader to check for clarity and meaning. After you have read your paper many times, you do not really see it anymore. If you need assistance in writing, colleges offer tutoring or writing labs where you can get help with editing and revising.

6. **Review your introduction and conclusion.** They should be clear, interesting, and concise. The introduction and conclusion are the most powerful parts of your paper.

7. **Prepare the final copy.** Check your instructor's instructions on the format required. If there are no instructions, use the following format:

   - Use double-spacing.
   - Use 10- or 12-point font.
   - Use one-inch margins on all sides.
   - Use a three-inch top margin on the first page.
   - Single-space footnotes and endnotes.
   - Number your pages.

8. **Prepare the title page.** Center the title of your paper and place it one third of the page from the top. On the bottom third of the page, center your name, the professor's name, the name of the class, and the date.

Final Steps

Make sure you follow instructions about using a folder or cover for your paper. Generally professors dislike bulky folders or notebooks because they are difficult to carry. Imagine your professor trying to carry 50 notebooks to his or her office! Unless asked to do so, do not use plastic page protectors. Professors like to write comments on papers, and it is extremely difficult to write on papers with page protectors.

Turning your paper in on time is very important. Some professors do not accept late papers. Others subtract points if your paper is late. Put your paper in the car or someplace where you will have to see it before you go to class. **Then reward yourself for a job well done!**

Journal Entry #3

Write five intention statements about improving your writing. While thinking about your statements, consider the steps of POWER writing: prepare, organize, write, edit, and revise. Do you need to work on problems such as writer's block or getting your writing done on time? I intend to . . .

"Let us think of education as the means of developing our greatest abilities, because in each of us there is a private hope and dream which, fulfilled, can be translated into greater benefit for everyone and greater strength for our nation."
John F. Kennedy

Effective Public Speaking

You may need to take a speech class in order to graduate from college, and many of your classes will require oral presentations. Being a good speaker can contribute to your success on the job as well. A study done at Stanford University showed that one of the top predictors of success in professional positions was the ability to be a good public speaker.[1] You will need to present information to your boss, your colleagues, and your customers or clients.

Learn to Relax

Whenever I tell students that they will need to take a speech class or make an oral presentation, I see a look of panic on their faces. Good preparation can help you to feel confident about your oral presentation. Professional speaker Lilly Walters believes that you can deal with 75 percent of your anxiety by being well prepared.[2] You can deal with the remaining 25 percent by using some relaxation techniques.

- If you are anxious, admit to yourself that you are anxious. If it is appropriate, as in a beginning speech class, you can even admit to the audience that you are anxious. Once you have admitted that you are anxious, visualize yourself confidently making the speech.
- You do not have to be perfect; it is okay to make mistakes. Making mistakes just shows you are human like the rest of us.
- If you are anxious before your speech, take three to five deep breaths. Breathe in slowly and hold your breath for five seconds, and then breathe out slowly. Focus your mind on your breathing rather than your speech.
- Use positive self-talk to help you to relax. Instead of saying to yourself, "I will look like a fool up there giving the speech," tell yourself, "I can do this" or "It will be okay."
- Once you start speaking, anxiety will generally decline.
- With experience, you will gain confidence in your speaking ability and will be able to relax more easily.

Preparing and Delivering Your Speech

Write the Beginning of the Speech

The beginning includes a statement of your objective and what your speech will be about. It should prepare the audience for what comes next. You can begin your speech with a personal experience, a quote, a news article, or a joke. Jokes can be effective, but they are risky. Try out your joke with your friends to make sure that it is funny. Do not tell jokes that put down other people or groups.

Write the Main Body of the Speech

The main body of the speech consists of four or five main points. Just as in your term paper, state your main points and then provide details, examples, or stories that illustrate them. As you present the main points of your speech, consider your audience. Your speech will be different depending on whether it is made to a group of high school students, your college classmates, or a group of professionals. You can add interest to your speech by using props, pictures, charts, PowerPoint, music, or video clips. College students today are increasingly using PowerPoint software to make classroom presentations. If you are planning to enter a professional career, learning how to make PowerPoint presentations will be an asset.

Write the Conclusion

In your conclusion, summarize and review the key points of your speech. The conclusion is like the icing on a cake. It should be strong, persuasive, and interesting. Invest some time in your ending statement. It can be a call to action, a recommendation for the future, a quote, or a story.

Practice Your Speech

Practice your speech until you feel comfortable with it. Prepare a memory system or notes to help you deliver your speech. You will want to make eye contact with your audience, which is difficult if you are trying to read your speech. A memory system useful for delivering speeches is the loci system. Visualize a house, for example: the entryway is the introduction, and each room represents a main point in the speech. Visualize walking into each room and what you will say in each room. Each room can have items that remind you of what you are going to say. At the conclusion, you say good-bye at the door. Another technique is to prepare brief notes or outlines on index cards or sheets of paper. When you are practicing your speech, time it to see how long it is. Keep your speech within the time allowed. Most people tend to speak longer than necessary.

Review the Setup

If you are using props, make sure that you have them ready. If you are using equipment, make sure it is available and in working condition. Make arrangements in advance for the equipment you need and, if possible, check to see that it is running properly right before your presentation.

Deliver the Speech

Wear clothes that make you feel comfortable, but not out of place. Remember to smile and make eye contact with members of the audience. Take a few deep breaths if you are nervous. You will probably be less nervous once you begin. If you make a mistake, keep your sense of humor. I recall the famous chef Julia Child doing a live television production on how to cook a turkey. As she took the turkey out of the oven, it slipped and landed on the floor right in front of the television cameras. She calmly picked it up and said, "And remember that you are the only one that really knows what goes on in the kitchen." It was one of the shows that made her famous.

QUIZ

Writing and Speaking

Test what you have learned by selecting the correct answers to the following questions.

1. To make sure to get your paper done on time,
   a. have someone remind you of the deadline.
   b. write the due date on your calendar and the date for completion of each step.
   c. write your paper just before the due date to increase motivation.

2. The thesis statement is the
   a. most important sentence in each paragraph.
   b. key idea in the paper.
   c. summary of the paper.

3. If you have writer's block, it is helpful to
   a. delay writing your paper until you feel relaxed.
   b. make sure that your writing is perfect from the beginning.
   c. begin with brainstorming or free writing.

4. No college paper is complete without
   a. the references.
   b. a professional-looking cover.
   c. printing on quality paper.

5. You can deal with most of your anxiety about public speaking by
   a. striving for perfection.
   b. visualizing your anxiety.
   c. being well prepared.

How did you do on the quiz? Check your answers: 1. b, 2. b, 3. c, 4. a, 5. c

Write one paragraph giving advice to a new college student on how to make a speech. Use any of these questions to guide your thinking:

- What are some ways to deal with anxiety about public speaking?
- How can you make your speech interesting?
- What are some steps in preparing a speech?
- What are some ideas that don't work?

KEYS TO SUCCESS   Be Selective

Psychologist and philosopher William James said, "The essence of genius is knowing what to overlook."[3] This saying has a variety of meanings. In reading, note taking, marking a college textbook, and writing, it is important to be able to pick out the main points first and then identify the supporting details. Imagine you are trying to put together a jigsaw puzzle. You bought the puzzle at a garage sale and all the pieces are there, but the lid to the box with the picture of the puzzle is missing. It will be very difficult, if not impossible, to put this puzzle together. Reading, note taking, marking, and writing are very much like putting a puzzle together. First you will need an understanding of the main ideas (the big picture) and then you can focus on the details.

How can you get the overall picture? When reading, you can get the overall picture by skimming the text. As you skim the text, you get a general outline of what the chapter contains and what you will learn. In note taking, actively listen for the main ideas and write them down in your notes. In marking your text, try to pick out about 20 percent of the most important material and underline or highlight it. In writing, think about what is most important, write your thesis statement, and then provide the supporting details. To select what is most important, be courageous, think, and analyze.

Does this mean that you should forget about the details? No, you will need to know some details too. The supporting details help you to understand and assess the value of the main idea. They help you to understand the relationship between ideas. Being selective means getting the general idea first, and then the details will make sense to you and you will be able to remember them. The main ideas are like scaffolding or a net that holds the details in some kind of framework so you can remember them. If you focus on the details first, you will have no framework or point of reference for remembering them.

Experiment with the idea of being selective in your personal life. If your schedule is impossibly busy, be selective and choose to do the most important or most valuable activities. This takes some thinking and courage too. If your desk drawer is stuffed with odds and ends and you can never find what you are looking for, take everything out and only put back what you need. Recycle, give away, or throw away surplus items around the house. You can take steps toward being a genius by being selective and taking steps to simplify and organize your life and your work.

Journal Entry #5

How can being selective help you achieve success in college and in life? Use any of these questions to guide your thinking:

- How can being selective help you to be a better note taker, writer, or speaker?
- How can being selective help you to manage your time and your life?
- What is the meaning of this quote by William James: "The essence of genius is knowing what to overlook?"

JOURNAL ENTRIES

Taking Notes, Writing, and Speaking

Go to http://www.collegesuccess1.com/JournalEntries.htm for Word files of the Journal Entries

Success over the Internet

Visit the *College Success Website* at http://www.collegesuccess1.com/

The *College Success Website* is continually updated with new topics and links to the material presented in this chapter. Topics include:

- Note taking
- Mind maps
- Memory and note taking
- Telegraphic sentences
- Signal words
- Listening to lectures
- Grammar and style
- Quotes to use in speeches and papers
- The virtual public speaking assistant
- Researching, organizing, and delivering a speech
- Best speeches in history

Contact your instructor if you have any problems accessing the *College Success Website.*

Notes

1. T. Allesandra and P. Hunsaker, *Communicating at Work* (New York: Fireside, 1993), 169.

2. Lilly Walters, *Secrets of Successful Speakers: How You Can Motivate, Captivate, and Persuade* (New York: McGraw-Hill, 1993), 203.

3. Quoted in Rob Gilbert, ed., *Bits and Pieces*, August 12, 1999, 15.

Note-Taking Checklist

Name _____ Date _____

Place a checkmark next to the note-taking skills you have now.

_____ I attend every (or almost every) lecture in all my classes.

_____ I check the syllabus to find out what is being covered before I go to class.

_____ I read or at least skim through the reading assignment before attending the lecture.

_____ I attend lectures with a positive attitude about learning as much as possible.

_____ I am well rested so that I can focus on the lecture.

_____ I eat a light, nutritious meal before going to class.

_____ I sit in a location where I can see and hear easily.

_____ I have a laptop or a three-ring binder, looseleaf paper, and a pen for taking notes.

_____ I avoid external distractions (friends, sitting by the door).

_____ I am alert and able to concentrate on the lecture.

_____ I have a system for taking notes that works for me.

_____ I am able to determine the key ideas of the lecture and write them down in my notes.

_____ I can identify signal words that help to understand key points and organize my notes.

_____ I can write quickly using telegraphic sentences, abbreviations, and symbols.

_____ If I don't understand something in the lecture, I ask a question and get help.

_____ I write down everything written on the board or on visual materials used in the class.

_____ I review my notes immediately after class.

_____ I have intermediate review sessions to review previous notes.

_____ I use my notes to predict questions for the exam.

_____ I have clear and complete notes that help me to prepare adequately for exams.

Evaluate Your Note-Taking Skills

Name _____ Date _____

Use the note-taking checklist on the previous page to answer these questions.

1. Look at the items that you checked. What are your strengths in note taking?

2. What are some areas that you need to improve?

3. Write at least three intention statements about improving your listening and note-taking skills.

Assess Your College Writing Skills

Name _____ Date _____

Read the following statements and rate how true they are for you at the present time. Use the following scale:

5 Definitely true
4 Mostly true
3 Somewhat true
2 Seldom true
1 Never true

_____ I am generally confident in my writing skills.

_____ I have a system for reminding myself of due dates for writing projects.

_____ I start writing projects early so that I am not stressed by finishing them at the last minute.

_____ I have the proper materials and a space to write comfortably.

_____ I know how to use the library and the Internet to gather information for a term paper.

_____ I can write a thesis statement for a term paper.

_____ I know how to organize a term paper.

_____ I know how to write the introduction, body, and conclusion of a paper.

_____ I can cite references in the appropriate style for my subject.

_____ I know where to find information about citing material in APA, MLA, or Chicago style.

_____ I know what plagiarism is and know how to avoid it.

_____ I can deal with "writer's block" and get started on my writing project.

_____ I know how to edit and revise a paper.

_____ I know where I can get help with my writing.

_____ **Total**

60–70   You have excellent writing skills, but can always learn new ideas.

50–59   You have good writing skills, but there is room for improvement.

Below 50 You need to improve writing skills. The skills presented in this chapter will help. Consider taking a writing class early in your college studies.

Thinking about Writing

Name _____ Date _____

List 10 suggestions from this chapter that could help you improve your writing skills.

1.

2.

3.

4.

5.

6.

7.

8.

9.

10.

Name _____ Date _____

John is a new college student who needs help with college success skills. Using what you have learned in this chapter, give John some advice on how to take notes in class. This exercise can be done individually or as a group exercise in class.

John is a new college student who has just graduated from high school. He is not sure what he wants to do with his life, but his parents want him to go to college. He misses the first class in Psychology 101 because he thinks nothing important happens on the first day. On the second day of class, John walks into class and finds some friends from high school. He takes a seat near them and starts a lively conversation. He has no books, paper, or pencil.

The lecture is on the biological foundations of behavior. The topic is new for John and he is unfamiliar with the terms and concepts used in the lecture. He notices that the professor is wearing a tie that he must have purchased in 1970 and has an irritating habit of scratching his head. In addition, he is boring and speaks in a dull and monotonous way. John finds it difficult to concentrate. He becomes sleepy and starts to doze off during the lecture. At the end of the lecture, John realizes that he is going to have problems with psychology. For the next class, John brings a tape recorder and records the class. Again he finds it difficult to stay awake during the lecture. He works late at night and has scheduled this class for 8:00 in the morning.

What are the five most important suggestions you could make to help John take notes and be successful in this class?

1.

2.

3.

4.

5.

CHAPTER 8

Planning Your Career and Education

Learning Objectives

Read to answer these key questions:

- What are some employment trends for the future?

- What are work skills necessary for success in the twenty-first century?

- How do I research a career?

- How do I plan my education?

- How can I make good decisions about my future?

- How can I obtain my ideal job?

- What is a dangerous opportunity?

t is always easier to get where you are going if you have a road map or a plan. To start the journey, it is helpful to know about yourself, including your personality, interests, talents, and values. Once you have this picture, you will need to know about the world of work and job trends that will affect your future employment opportunities. Next, you will need to make decisions about which road to follow. Then, you will need to plan your education to reach your destination. Finally, you will need some job-seeking skills such as writing a resume and preparing for a successful interview.

Employment Trends

The world is changing quickly, and these changes will affect your future career. To assure your future career success, you will need to become aware of career trends and observe how they change over time so that you can adjust your career plans accordingly. For example, recently a school was established for training bank tellers. The school quickly went out of business and the students demanded their money back because they were not able to get jobs. A careful observer of career trends would have noticed that bank tellers are being replaced by automatic teller machines (ATMs) and would not have started a school for training bank tellers. Students observant of career trends would not have paid money for the training. It is probably a good idea for bank tellers to look ahead and plan a new career direction.

How can you find out about career trends that may affect you in the future? Become a careful observer by reading about current events. Good sources of information include:

- Your local newspaper, especially the business section
- News programs
- Current magazines
- Government statistics and publications
- The Internet

When thinking about future trends, use your critical thinking skills. Sometimes trends change quickly or interact in different ways. For example, since we are using email to a great extent today, it might seem that mail carriers would not be as much in demand in the future. However, since people are buying more goods over the Internet, there has been an increased demand for mail carriers and other delivery services. Develop the habit of looking at what is happening to see if you can identify trends that may affect your future.

Usually trends get started as a way to meet the following needs:[1]

- To save money
- To reduce cost
- To do things faster
- To make things easier to use
- To improve safety and reliability
- To lessen the impact on the environment

The following are some trends to watch that may affect your future career. As you read about each trend, think about how it could affect you.

Baby Boomers, Generation X, and the Millennial Generation

About every 20 years, sociologists begin to describe a new generation with similar characteristics based on shared historical experiences. Each generation has different opportunities and challenges in the workplace.

The Baby Boomers were born following World War II between 1946 and 1964. Four out of every 10 adults today are in this Baby Boom Generation.[2] Because there are so many aging Baby Boomers, the average age of Americans is increasing. Life expectancy is also increasing. By 2015 the projected life expectancy will be 76.4 for men and 81.4 for women.[3] In the new millennium, many more people will live to be 100 years old or more! Think about the implications of an older population. Older people need such things as health care, recreation, travel, and financial planning. Occupations related to these needs are likely to be in demand now and in the future.

Those born between 1965 and 1977 are often referred to as Generation X. They are sometimes called the "baby bust" generation because fewer babies were born during this period than in the previous generations. There is much in the media about this generation having to pay higher taxes and Social Security payments to support the large number of aging Baby Boomers. Some say that this generation will not enjoy the prosperity of the Baby Boomers. Those who left college in the early nineties faced a recession and the worst job market since World War II.[4] Many left college in debt and returned home to live with their parents. Because of a lack of employment opportunities, many in this generation became entrepreneurs, starting new companies at a faster rate than previous generations.

Jane Bryant Quinn notes that in spite of economic challenges, Generation Xers have a lot going for them:[5]

- They have record-high levels of education, which correlate with higher income and lower unemployment.
- There is a demand for more skilled workers, so employers are more willing to train employees. Anthony Carnevale, chairman of the National Commission for Employment Policy, "sees a big demand for 'high-school plus'—a high school diploma plus technical school or junior college."
- Generation Xers are computer literate, and those who use computers on the job earn 10 to 15 percent more than those who don't.
- This group often has a good work ethic valued by employers. However, they value a balanced lifestyle with time for outside interests and family.
- As Baby Boomers retire, more job opportunities are created for this group.
- Unlike the Baby Boomers, this generation was born into a more integrated and more diverse society. They are better able than previous generations to adapt to diversity in society and the workplace.

Many of today's college students are part of the Millennial Generation, born between 1977 and 1995. This generation is sometimes called Generation Y or the Echo Boomers, since they are the children of the Baby Boomers.[6] This new generation of approximately 60 million is three times larger than Generation X and will eventually exceed the number of Baby Boomers. In this decade, they will become the largest teen population in U.S. history. As the Millennials reach college age, they will attend college in increasing numbers. In the next 10 years, college enrollments will increase by approximately 300,000 students per year. Colleges will find it difficult to accommodate rapidly increasing numbers of students, and as a result, the Millennial Generation will face increasingly competitive college admissions criteria.

Millennials are more ethnically diverse than previous generations with 34 percent ethnic minorities. One in four lives with a single parent; three in four have working mothers. Most of them started using computers before they were five years old. Marketing researchers describe this new generation as "technologically adept, info-savvy, a cyber-generation, the clickeratti."[7] They are the connected generation, accustomed to cell phones, chatting on the Internet, and listening to downloaded music.

Young people in the Millennial Generation share a different historical perspective from the Baby Boom Generation. Baby Boomers remember the Vietnam War and the assassinations of President John F. Kennedy and Martin Luther King. For Millennials, school shootings such as Columbine and acts of terrorism such as the Oklahoma City bombing and the 9–11 attack on New York City stand out as important events. The Millennial Generation will see their main problems as dealing with violence, easy access to weapons, and the threat of terrorism.

Neil Howe and William Strauss paint a very positive picture of this new generation in their book *Millennials Rising: The Next Great Generation*:

- Millennials will rebel by tearing down old institutions that do not work and building new and better institutions. The authors predict that this will be the can-do generation filled with technology planners, community shapers, institution builders, and world leaders.
- Surveys show that this generation describes themselves as happy, confident, and positive.
- They are cooperative team players.
- They generally accept authority and respect their parents' values.
- They follow rules. The rates of homicides, violent crime, abortion, and teen pregnancy are decreasing rapidly.
- The use of alcohol, drugs, and tobacco is decreasing.
- Millennials have a fascination with and mastery of new technology.
- Their most important values are individuality and uniqueness.[8]

It is predicted that the world of work for the Millennials will be dramatically different. Previous generations anticipated having a lifetime career. By the year 2020, many jobs will probably be short-term contracts. This arrangement will provide cost savings and efficiency for employers and flexibility for employees to start or stop work to take vacations, train for new jobs, or meet family responsibilities. One in five people will be self-employed. Retirement will be postponed as people look forward to living longer and healthier lives.[9]

Journal Entry #1

Describe your generation (Baby Boomer, Generation X, or New Millennial). What are your best qualities and challenges?

Moving from Goods to Services and Technology

Human society has moved through several stages. The first stage, about 20,000 years ago, was the hunting and gathering stage. During this time, society depended on the natural environment for food and other resources. When natural resources were depleted, the community moved to another area. The second stage, some 10,000 years ago, was the agricultural stage. Human beings learned to domesticate animals and cultivate crops. This allowed people to stay in one place and develop more permanent villages. About 200 years ago, industrial societies came into being by harnessing power sources to produce goods on a large scale.

Today in the United States, we are evolving into a service, technology, and information society. Fewer people are working in agriculture and manufacturing. Futurists John Naisbitt et al. note that we are moving toward a service economy based on high technology, rapid communications, biotechnology for use in agriculture and medicine, health care, and sales of merchandise.[10] Service areas with increasing numbers of jobs include health care and social assistance; professional, scientific, and technical services; educational services; administrative and support services; waste management and remediation services; accommodation and food services; government; retail trade; transportation and warehousing, finance and insurance; arts, entertainment, and recreation; wholesale trade; real estate, rental, and leasing; and information and management.

Increased Opportunities in Health Care

If you are interested in science and technology along with helping other people, there are many career opportunities in health care. It is estimated that by 2018, there will be an increase of four million new jobs in health care, which will account for 26 percent of all new jobs.[11] This trend is being driven by an aging population, increased longevity, health care reform, and new developments in the pharmaceutical and medical fields. Because of increased health care costs, many of the jobs done by doctors, nurses, dentists, or physical therapists are now being done by physician's assistants, medical assistants, dental assistants, physical therapy aides, and home health aides. Health care workers will increasingly use technology to do their work. For example, a new occupation is nursing informatics, which combines traditional nursing skills with computer and information science.

Increased Need for Education

In the past, the life pattern for many people was to graduate from school, go to work, and eventually retire. Because of the rapid changes in technology and society today, workers will need additional training and education over a lifetime. Education will take place in a variety of forms: community college courses, training on the job, private training sessions, and learning on your own. Those who do not keep up with the new technology will find that their skills quickly become obsolete. Those who do keep up will find their skills in demand.

As we transition from manufacturing to service and technical careers, education beyond high school will become increasingly important. According to the Bureau of Labor

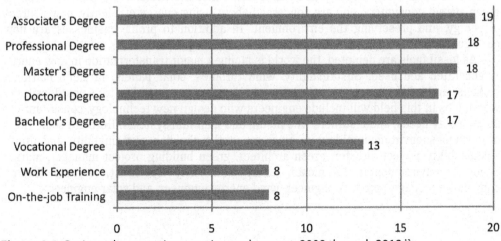

Figure 8.1 Projected percent increase in employment, 2008 through 2018.[13]

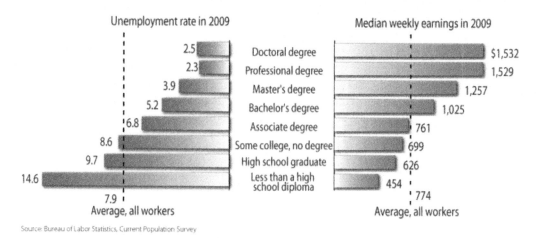

Figure 8.2 Education pays, unemployment rate and median weekly earnings, 2009.[14]

Statistics, occupations that require a postsecondary degree will account for nearly half of all new jobs from 2008 to 2018, with the fastest growth in jobs requiring an associate's degree or higher. In addition, higher education will result in higher earnings and lower unemployment.[12]

Young people who do not continue their education are likely to be stuck in lower-paying jobs, while those who continue their education will have higher-paying jobs. Author Joyce Lain Kennedy believes that the middle class is becoming an endangered species.[15] She states that many jobs traditionally held by the middle class have been "dumbed down," making them so simple that anyone can do them. These jobs pay very little and offer no benefits, no employment stability, and little opportunity for advancement. Young people often hold these jobs in their teens and twenties.

At the other end of the job continuum are jobs requiring a college education or training beyond high school. These high-end jobs often require technical or computer skills. These are the jobs that pay better and offer benefits. It seems that we are becoming a nation of haves and have-nots who are separated by their education and technical skills.

Going Green!

Have you purchased organic products or an energy-efficient light bulb, appliance, or car? If so, you are part of a new environmental movement that is gaining impetus in the U.S., the rise of social responsibility and the citizen consumer. Businesses that are seen as green attract consumers who are concerned about using energy efficiently, new sources of energy, and preserving the environment. In addition to profit, businesses are now concerned about the planet and working conditions for people.

As fossil fuels are depleted, the world is facing a major transformation in how energy is generated and used. Sustainability, wind turbines, solar panels, farmer's markets, biofuels, and wind energy are just some of the ways to transition to a post-fossil-fuel world. Jobs in this field will include engineers who design new technology, consultants to audit energy needs, and installers who install and maintain systems. Here are some titles of green jobs: environmental lawyer, environmental technician, sustainability consultant, sustainability project director, green architect, green building project manager, marine biologist, environmental technician, energy efficiency specialist, organic farmer, compliance manager, product engineer, wind energy engineer, and solar engineer.

A Diverse Workforce

The workforce in the United States is becoming increasingly more diverse. Diversity includes many demographic variables such as ethnicity, religion, gender, national origin, disability, sexual orientation, age, education, geographic origin, and skill characteristics. Having an appreciation for diversity is important in maintaining a work environment that is open and allows for individual differences. Increasing diversity provides opportunities for many different kinds of individuals and makes it important to be able to have good working relationships with all kinds of people.

The U.S. Bureau of Labor Statistics has described some trends that will affect the workplace by 2018.[16]

- Whites are expected to make up a decreasing share of the labor force, while Blacks, Asians, and all other groups will increase their share. Persons of Hispanic origin will increase their share of the labor force from 14.3 to 17.6 percent, reflecting a 33.1 percent growth.
- The number of women in the labor force will grow at a slightly faster rate than the number of men. The male labor force is projected to grow by 7.5 percent, as compared with 9.0 percent for the female labor force.
- The number of workers in younger age groups will decline, while workers in the 55 years and older group will increase, reflecting the increase of aging Baby Boomers.
- Total employment is expected to increase by 10 percent from 2008 to 2018. Changes in consumer demand and advances in technology will continue to change the structure of the economy, with decreasing jobs in manufacturing and increasing numbers of jobs in service and technology.

E-Commerce Is Changing the Way We Do Business

E-commerce, the purchasing of goods, services, and information over the Internet, is a new technology that has revolutionized the way business is done in the 21st century. More people are using e-commerce because of convenience, selection, and the ease of shopping for goods at the best price. Online sales are a growing part of the market, increasing 10 to 20 percent a year for the last several years. In 2010, online shopping accounted for 7 percent of all sales, and 42 percent of retail sales were influenced by online marketing.[17] This growth in e-commerce will have implications for education and business. More colleges are offering courses in e-commerce and incorporating e-commerce topics into traditional business offerings. There are more career opportunities in e-commerce and related fields such as computer graphics, web design, online marketing, and package delivery services.

The Microprocessor

The microprocessor is a silicon chip containing transistors that determine the capability of a computer. In the past 20 years, the power of the microprocessor has increased more than one million times. In the next 20 years, the power will increase a million times again.[18] Because of the increased power of the microprocessor, it will be used in new ways and with new devices. Consider the "smart home" of the future:

As you reach the front door, you are welcomed by a flat screen, rather than a doorbell. You can use this screen to ring the doorbell, talk to the person inside the home or leave a message, which can be accessed by telephone or e-mail.

If you're the homeowner, walk through the door and the curtains go up, letting light in, and the entire house is soon subtly illuminated. The hi-fi will access its database to play your favorite music, and the air-conditioning will be preset to the temperature you prefer.

As you move to the kitchen, you take the ingredients for your lunch—say, flour, a piece of fish and a few stalks of broccoli—to a networked table. This will activate a system that will immediately offer you a range of appropriate recipes. Your smart microwave will fix the dish for you, consulting the recipe you prefer, via the Internet.[19]

The microprocessor is increasingly available to all and for less cost. The personal computer would have occupied an entire building 35 years ago. Today we have access to powerful computers and mobile devices that will play an ever greater role in our daily lives.

It's remarkable how we now take all that power for granted. Using a basic home PC costing less than $1,000, you can balance your household budget, do your taxes, write letters to friends and fax or e-mail them over the Internet, listen to CDs or the radio, watch the news, consult a doctor, play games, book a vacation, view a house, buy a book or a car. The list is endless.[20]

New Advances in Technology and Communication

There has been a recent rapid increase in the development of cell phones and other mobile devices, as well as the use of social media, which will continue to have a major impact on career opportunities. Those who can keep up with the current technology will find increasing career and business opportunities. Graduates will become more marketable if they combine traditional career areas with technology such as social media. For example, students in a marketing degree program will be more in demand if they can use Facebook, LinkedIn, or Twitter to market products.

The Bureau of Labor Statistics reports that two million technology-related jobs will be created by 2018. Jobs in computer systems design and related services are expected to increase by 34 percent by 2018. Jobs that will grow faster than the average include computer-network administrators, data-communications analysts, and Web developers. Some new fields include data-loss prevention, online security, and risk management. Computer science degrees are especially marketable when combined with traditional majors such as finance, accounting, or marketing.[21]

Because we are living in the Information Age, information and technology workers are now the largest group of workers in the United States. Careers in information technology include the design, development, and support of computer software, hardware, and networks. Some newer jobs in this area include animation for video games, films, and videos as well as setting up websites and Internet security. There are also good opportunities for network programmers who can program a group of computers to work together. Because computer use has increased greatly, it is expected that computer-related jobs will expand by 40 percent or more in the next decade.[22]

In the future, computers will continue to become more powerful, mobile, and connected. It is predicted that by 2018, microprocessors will be replaced by optical computers that function at the speed of light. Technology will be embedded in products used for entertainment as well as for home and business use. It is predicted that in the future, the desktop computer as we know it will cease to exist. Instead of a home computer, we will have computerized homes with sensors that monitor energy use and smart appliances with computer chips. Gestures, touch, and voice communication will rapidly replace computer keyboards. The Nintendo Wii™ and the iPhone are current examples. Computers will move from homes and offices into human bodies. Microchips may be embedded in human bodies to monitor health conditions and to deliver medical care. Some futurists forecast a time when computer chips will be embedded in the brain and connected to the Internet. Of course, computer security will become increasingly important with these new advances.[23]

Radiation and laser technologies will provide new technical careers in the future. It has been said that lasers will be as important to the 21st century as electricity was for the 20th century. New uses for lasers are being found in medicine, energy, industry, computers, communications, entertainment, and outer space. The use of lasers is creating new jobs and causing others to become obsolete. For example, many welders are being replaced by laser technicians, who have significantly higher earnings. New jobs will open for people who purchase, install, and maintain lasers.

Careers in fiber optics and telecommunications are among the top new emerging fields in the 21st century. Fiber optics are thin glass fibers that transmit light. This new technology may soon make copper wire obsolete. One of the most important uses of fiber optics is to speed up delivery of data over the Internet and to improve telecommunications. It is also widely used in medical instruments, including laser surgery.

Another interesting development to watch is artificial intelligence software, which enables computers to recognize patterns, improve from experience, make inferences, and approximate human thought. Scientists at the MIT Artificial Intelligence Lab have developed a robot named Cog. Here is a description of Cog and its capabilities:

We have given it a multitude of sensors to "feel" and learn what it is like to be touched and spoken to. Cog's ability to make eye contact and reach out to moving objects is also meant to motivate people to interact with it. These features have taught Cog, among other things, to distinguish a human face from inanimate objects (this puts its development at about a 3-month-old's). It can also listen to music and keep rhythm by tapping on a drum (something a 5-year-old can do). One of the most startling moments in Cog's development came when it was learning to touch things. At one point, Cog began to touch and discover its own body. It looked so eerie and human, I was stunned.[24]

Beware of Outsourcing

To reduce costs and improve profits, many jobs in technology, manufacturing, and service are being outsourced to countries such as India, China, and Taiwan, where well-educated, English-speaking workers are being used to do these jobs. For example, programmers in India can produce software at only 10 percent of the cost of these services in the United States. Jobs that are currently being outsourced include accounting, payroll clerks, customer service, data entry, assembly line workers, industrial and production engineers, machine operators, computer-assisted design (CAD) technicians, purchasing managers, textile workers, software developers, and technical support. It is a good idea to consider this trend in choosing your future career and major. Jobs that are most likely to be outsourced are: [25]

- Repetitive jobs, such as accounting,
- Well-defined jobs, such as customer service,
- Small manageable projects, such as software development,
- Jobs in which proximity to the customer is not important, such as technical support.

Jobs that are least likely to be outsourced include:

- Jobs with ambiguity, such as top management jobs,
- Unpredictable jobs, such as troubleshooters,
- Jobs that require understanding of the culture, such as marketing,
- Jobs that require close proximity to the customer, such as auto repair,
- Jobs requiring a high degree of innovation and creativity, such as product design,
- Jobs in entertainment, music, art, and design.

To protect yourself from outsourcing:

- Strive to be the best in the field.
- Be creative and innovative.
- Avoid repetitive jobs that do not require proximity to the customer.
- Choose a career where the demand is so high that it won't matter if some are outsourced.
- Consider a job in the skilled trades; carpenters, plumbers, electricians, hair stylists, construction workers, auto mechanics, and dental hygienists will always be in demand.

New Advances in Biology

Future historians may describe the 21st century as the biology century because of all the developments in this area. If you are interested in biology, it can lead to good careers in the future. One of the most important developments is the Human Genome Project, which has identified the genes in human DNA, the carrier of genetic material. The research done on the human genome has been an impetus for development in some new careers in biotechnology and biomedical technology. Watch the news for future developments that will affect how we all live and work.

Biotechnology will become increasingly important as a way to combat disease, develop new surgical procedures and devices, increase food production, reduce pollution, improve recycling, and provide new tools for law enforcement. Biotechnology includes genomic profiling, biomedical engineering, new pharmaceuticals, genetic engineering, and DNA identification. One of the most promising outcomes of biotechnology will be the production of new pharmaceuticals. About 90 percent of all drugs ever invented have been developed since 1975, and about 6,000 new drugs are waiting for regulatory approval.[26] In the future, biotechnology may be used to find cures for diabetes, arthritis, Alzheimer's disease, and heart disease.

The field of biomedical engineering, which involves developing and testing health care innovations, is expected to grow by 72 percent by 2018.[27] Biomedical technology is the field in which bionic implants are being developed for the human body. Scientists are working on the development of artificial limbs and organs including eyes, ears, hearts, and kidneys. A promising new development in this field is brain and computer interfaces. Scientists recently implanted a computer chip into the brain of a quadriplegic, enabling him to control a computer and television with his mind.[28] Biotechnology also develops new diagnostic test equipment and surgical tools.

Increase in Entrepreneurship

An important trend for the new millennium is the increase in entrepreneurship, which means starting your own business. For the Baby Boom Generation, it was expected that one would have a job for life. Because of rapid changes in society and the world of work, Millennials can expect to have as many as 10 different jobs over a lifetime.[29] A growing number of entrepreneurs operate their small businesses from home, taking advantage of telecommuting and the Internet to communicate with customers. While being an entrepreneur has some risks involved, there are many benefits, such as flexible scheduling, being your own boss, taking charge of your own destiny, and greater potential for future income if your company is successful. You won't have to worry about being outsourced, either.

The Effect of Terrorism and Need for Security

Fear of terrorism has changed attitudes that will affect career trends for years to come. Terrorist attacks have created an atmosphere of uncertainty that has had a negative effect on the economy and has increased unemployment. For example, the airline industry is struggling financially as people hesitate to fly to their vacation destinations. People are choosing to stay in the safety of their homes, offices, cars, and gated communities. Since people are spending more time at home, they spend more money making their homes comfortable. Faith Popcorn, who is famous for predicting future trends, has called this phenomenon "cocooning," which is "our desire to build ourselves strong and cozy nests where we can retreat from the world, enjoying ourselves in safety and comfort."[30] As a result, construction, home remodeling, and sales of entertainment systems are increasing.

Another result of terrorism is the shift toward occupations that provide value to society and in which people can search for personal satisfaction.[31] More people volunteer their time to help others, and are considering careers in education, social work, and medical occupations. When people are forced to relocate because of unemployment, they are considering moving to smaller towns that have a sense of community and a feeling of safety.

As the world population continues to grow, there is continued conflict over resources and ideologies and an increased need for security and safety. Law enforcement, intelligence, forensics, international relations, foreign affairs, and security administration careers will be in demand.

Nontraditional Workers

Unlike traditional workers, nontraditional workers do not have full-time, year-round jobs with health and retirement benefits. Employers are moving toward using nontraditional workers, including multiple job holders, contingent and part-time workers, independent contractors, and temporary workers. Nearly four out of five employers use nontraditional workers to help them become more efficient, prevent layoffs, and access workers with special skills. There are advantages and disadvantages to this arrangement. Nontraditional workers have no benefits and risk unemployment. However, this arrangement can provide workers with a flexible work schedule in which they work during some periods and pursue other interests or gain new skills when not working.

Journal Entry #2

Do a quick review of the career trends presented in this chapter:

- Moving from the production of goods to service and technology
- Increased opportunities in health care occupations
- Increased need for education
- New green careers
- Increasing diversity in the workplace
- Increased e-commerce and entrepreneurship
- New developments in technology, communication, and biology
- The effect of terrorism and the need for security
- Nontraditional workers

Write one paragraph about how any of these trends might affect your future.

Top Jobs for the Future[32]

Based on current career trends, here are some jobs that should be in high demand for the next 10 years.

Field of Employment	Job Titles
Business	Marketing Manager, Security and Financial Service, Internet Marketing Specialist, Advertising Executive, Buyer, Sales Person, Real Estate Agent, Business Development Manager, Marketing Researcher, Recruiter
Education	Teacher, Teacher's Aide, Adult Education Instructor, Math and Science Teacher
Entertainment	Dancer, Producer, Director, Actor, Content Creator, Musician, Artist, Commercial Artist, Writer, Technical Writer, Newspaper Reporter, News Anchor Person
Health	Emergency Medical Technician, Surgeon, Chiropractor, Dental Hygienist, Registered Nurse, Medical Assistant, Therapist, Respiratory Therapist, Home Health Aide, Primary Care Physician, Medical Lab Technician, Radiology Technician, Physical Therapist, Dental Assistant, Nurse's Aide
Information Technology	Computer Systems Analyst, Computer Engineer, Web Specialist, Network Support Technician, Java Programmer, Information Technology Manager, Web Developer, Database Administrator, Network Engineer
Law/Law Enforcement	Correction Officer, Law Officer, Anti-Terrorist Specialist, Security Guard, Tax/Estate Attorney, Intellectual Property Attorney
Services	Veterinarian, Social Worker, Hair Stylist, Telephone Repair Technician, Aircraft Mechanic, Guidance Counselor, Occupational Therapist, Child Care Assistant, Baker, Landscape Architect, Pest Controller, Chef, Caterer, Food Server
Sports	Athlete, Coach, Umpire, Physical Trainer
Technology	Electrical Engineer, Biological Scientist, Electronic Technician, CAD Operator, Product Designer, Sales Engineer, Applications Engineer, Product Marketing Engineer, Technical Support Manager, Product Development Manager
Trades	Carpenter, Plumber, Electrician
Travel/Transportation	Package Delivery Person, Flight Attendant, Hotel/Restaurant Manager, Taxi Driver, Chauffeur, Driver

Career Trends of the Future

Test what you have learned by selecting the correct answers to the following questions:

1. Most students in college today are in
   a. the Baby Boom Generation.
   b. Generation X.
   c. the Millennial Generation.

2. Use of the Internet will result in
   a. increased e-commerce.
   b. increased use of conventional stores.
   c. decreased mail delivery.

3. The largest group of workers in the United States is in
   a. manufacturing.
   b. information technology.
   c. agriculture.

4. Jobs unlikely to be outsourced include
   a. jobs that require close proximity to the customer.
   b. computer programming jobs.
   c. customer service jobs.

5. Future historians will describe the 21st century as the
   a. art and entertainment century.
   b. biology century.
   c. industrial development century.

How did you do on the quiz? Check your answers: 1. c, 2. a, 3. b, 4. a, 5. b

Work Skills for the 21st Century

Because of rapid changes in technology, college students of today may be preparing for jobs that do not exist right now. After graduation, many college students find employment that is not even related to their college majors. One researcher found that 48 percent of college graduates find employment in fields not related to their college majors.[33] More important than one's college major are the general skills learned in college that prepare students for the future.

To define skills needed in the future workplace, the U.S. Secretary of Labor created the Secretary's Commission on Achieving Necessary Skills (SCANS). Based on interviews with employers and educators, the members of the commission outlined foundation skills and workplace competencies needed to succeed in the workplace in the 21st century.[34] The following skills apply to all occupations in all fields and will help you to become a successful employee, regardless of your major. As you read through these skills, think about your competency in these areas.

Foundation Skills
Basic Skills

- Reading
- Writing
- Basic arithmetic
- Higher-level mathematics
- Listening
- Speaking

Thinking Skills

- Creative thinking
- Decision making
- Problem solving
- Mental visualization
- Knowing how to learn
- Reasoning

Personal Qualities

- Responsibility
- Self-esteem
- Sociability
- Self-management
- Integrity/honesty

Workplace Competencies

Resources

- **Time.** Selects relevant goals, sets priorities, and follows schedules.
- **Money.** Uses budgets, keeps records, and makes adjustments.
- **Materials and facilities.** Acquires, stores, and distributes materials, supplies, parts, equipment, space, or final products.
- **Human resources.** Assesses knowledge and skills, distributes work, evaluates performance, and provides feedback.

Interpersonal

- **Participates as a member of a team.** Works cooperatively with others and contributes to group efforts.
- **Teaches others.** Helps others learn needed skills.
- **Serves clients/customers.** Works and communicates with clients and customers to satisfy their expectations.
- **Exercises leadership.** Communicates, encourages, persuades, and convinces others; responsibly challenges procedures, policies, or authority.
- **Negotiates to arrive at a decision.** Works toward an agreement involving resources or diverging interests.
- **Works with cultural diversity.** Works well with men and women and with people from a variety of ethnic, social, or educational backgrounds.

Information

- **Acquires and evaluates information.** Identifies the need for information, obtains information, and evaluates it.
- **Organizes and maintains information.** Organizes, processes, and maintains written or computerized records.
- **Uses computers to process information.** Employs computers to acquire, organize, analyze, and communicate information.

Systems

- **Understands systems.** Knows how social, organizational, and technological systems work and operates efficiently within them.
- **Monitors and corrects performance.** Distinguishes trends, predicts impacts of actions on systems operations, and takes action to correct performance.
- **Improves and designs systems.** Develops new systems to improve products or services.

Technology

- **Selects technology.** Judges which procedures, tools, or machines, including computers, will produce the desired results.
- **Applies technology to tasks.** Understands the proper procedures for using machines and computers.
- **Maintains and troubleshoots technology.** Prevents, identifies, or solves problems with machines, computers, and other technologies.

Because the workplace is changing, these skills may be more important than the background acquired through a college major. Work to develop these skills and you will be prepared for whatever lies ahead.

How to Research Your Career

After you have assessed your personality, interests, values, and talents, the next step is to learn about the world of work. If you can match your interests to the world of work, you can find work that is interesting and you can excel in it. To learn about the world of work, you will need to research possible careers. This includes reading career descriptions and investigating career outlooks, salaries, and educational requirements.

"The supreme accomplishment is to blur the line between work and play."

Arnold Toynbee

Career Descriptions

The career description tells you about the nature of the work, working conditions, employment, training, qualifications, advancement, job outlook, earnings, and related occupations. The two best sources of job descriptions are the *Occupational Outlook Handbook* and *Occupational Outlook Quarterly*. The *Handbook*, published by the Bureau of Labor Statistics, is like an encyclopedia of careers. You can search alphabetically by career or by career cluster.

The *Occupational Outlook Quarterly* is a periodical with up-to-date articles on new and emerging occupations, training opportunities, salary trends, and new studies from the Bureau of Labor Statistics. You can find these resources in a public or school library, at a college career center, or on the *College Success Website* at http://www.collegesuccess1.com/Links9Career.htm.

"Starting out to make money is the greatest mistake in life. Do what you feel you have a flair for doing, and if you are good enough at it, the money will come."

Greer Garson

Career Outlook

It is especially important to know about the career outlook of an occupation you are considering. Career outlook includes salary and availability of employment. How much does the occupation pay? Will the occupation exist in the future, and will there be employment opportunities? Of course, you will want to prepare yourself for careers that pay well and have future employment opportunities.

You can find information about career outlooks in the sources listed above, current periodicals, and materials from the Bureau of Labor Statistics. The following table, for example, lists the fastest-growing occupations, occupations with the highest salaries, and occupations with the largest job growth. Information from the Bureau of Labor Statistics is also available online.

Employment Projections 2008–2018[35]

10 Fastest-Growing Occupations	10 Industries with the Largest Wage and Salary Employment Growth	10 Occupations with the Largest Numerical Job Growth
Biomedical engineers	Management, scientific, technical	Registered nurses
Network systems and data communications analysts	Physicians	Home health aides
Home health aides	Computer systems design and related	Customer service representatives
Personal and home care aides	General merchandise stores	Food preparation workers
Financial examiners	Employment services	Personal and home care aides
Medical scientists	Local government	Retail salespersons
Physician assistants	Home health care services	Office clerks
Skin care specialists	Services for elderly and disabled	Accountants and auditors
Biochemists and biophysicists	Nursing care facilities	Nursing aides, orderlies
Athletic trainers	Full-service restaurants	Postsecondary teachers

"Think not of yourself as the architect of your career but as the sculptor. Expect to have a lot of hard hammering, chiseling, scraping and polishing."

B.C. Forbes

Planning Your Education

Once you have assessed your personal characteristics and researched your career options, it is important to plan your education. If you have a plan, you will be able to finish your education more quickly and avoid taking unnecessary classes. You can begin work on your educational plan by following the steps below. After you have done some work on your plan, visit your college counselor or advisor to make sure that your plan is appropriate.

Steps in Planning Your Education

_____ 1. **Take your college entrance or assessment tests before you apply to colleges.** Most colleges require the Scholastic Aptitude Test (SAT) or their own local placement tests in order for you to be admitted. You can find information about these tests at your high school or college counseling center or online at http://www.ets.org/ or http://cbweb1.collegeboard.org/index.html. If you are attending a community college, check the college website, admissions office, or counseling office to see what placement exams are required.

_____ 2. **Take English the first semester, and continue each semester until your English requirement is complete.** English courses provide the foundation for further college study. Your SAT or college placement test will determine what level of English you need to take. As a general rule, community colleges require one semester of college-level English. Four-year colleges and universities generally require two semesters or three quarters of college-level English. If your placement scores are low, you may be required to take review courses first.

_____ 3. **Start your math classes early, preferably in the first semester or quarter.** Many high-paying careers require a long series of math classes, particularly those in the sciences, engineering, and business. If you delay taking math courses until later, you may limit your career options and extend your time in college.

_____ 4. **Take the required general education courses.** Find out what your college requires for general education and put these classes on your plan. You will find this information in the college catalog. Be careful to select the correct general education plan. At community colleges, there are different plans for transfer and associate's degree students. At a university, there may be different plans for different colleges within the university. Check with a college counselor or advisor to make sure you have the correct plan.

_____ 5. **Prepare for your major.** Consult your college catalog to see what courses are required for your major. If you are undecided on a major, take the general education courses and start working on a decision about your major. If you are interested in the sciences or engineering, start work on math in the first semester. Start on your major requirements as soon as possible so that you do not delay your graduation.

_____ 6. **Check prerequisites.** A prerequisite is a course that is required before taking a higher-level course. The college catalog lists courses offered and includes prerequisites. Most colleges will not let you register for a course for which you do not have the prerequisite. It is also difficult to succeed in an advanced course without taking the prerequisite first.

_____ 7. **Make an educational plan.** The educational plan includes all the courses you will need to graduate. Again, use the college catalog as your guide.

_____ 8. **Check your plan.** See your college counselor or advisor to check your plan. He or she can save you from taking classes that you do not need and help you to graduate in the minimum amount of time.

Journal Entry #3

How can you match your talents to the world of work? Consider these factors while thinking about your answer: being aware of your strengths, researching careers, planning your education.

Making Good Decisions

Knowing how to make a good decision about your career and important life events is very important to your future, as this short poem by J. Wooden sums up:

> *There is a choice you have to make,*
> *In everything you do.*
> *And you must always keep in mind,*
> *The choice you make, makes you.*[36]

Sometimes people end up in a career because they simply seized an opportunity for employment. A good job becomes available and they happen to be in the right place at the right time. Sometimes people end up in a career because it is familiar to them, because it is a job held by a member of the family or a friend in the community. Sometimes people end up in a career because of economic necessity. The job pays well and they need the money. These careers are the result of chance circumstances. Sometimes they turn out well, and sometimes they turn out miserably.

Whether you are male or female, married or single, you will spend a great deal of your life working. By doing some careful thinking and planning about your career, you can improve your chances of success and happiness. Use the following steps to do some careful decision making about your career. Although you are the person who needs to make the decision about a career, you can get help from your college career center or your college counselor or advisor.

Steps in Making a Career Decision

1. **Begin with self-assessment.**
   - What is your personality type?
   - What are your interests?
   - What are your talents, gifts, and strengths?
   - What is your learning style?
   - What are your values?
   - What lifestyle do you prefer?

2. **Explore your options.**
   - What careers match your personal characteristics?

3. **Research your career options.**
   - Read the job description.
   - Investigate the career outlook.

- What is the salary?

- What training and education is required?

- Speak with an advisor, counselor, or person involved in the career that interests you.

- Choose a career or general career area that matches your personal characteristics.

4. **Plan your education to match your career goal.**

- Try out courses in your area of interest.

- Start your general education if you need more time to decide on a major.

- Try an internship or part-time job in your area of interest.

5. **Make a commitment to take action and follow through with your plan.**

6. **Evaluate.**

- Do you like the courses you are taking?

- Are you doing well in the courses?

- Continue research if necessary.

7. **Refine your plan.**

- Make your plan more specific to aim for a particular career.

- Select the college major that is best for you.

8. **Change your plan if it is not working.**

- Go back to the self-assessment step.

> "Find a job you like and add five days to every week."
>
> H. Jackson Browne

The Decision-Making Process

- **Dependent decisions.** Different kinds of decisions are appropriate in different situations. When you make a dependent decision, you depend on someone else to make the decision for you. The dependent decision was probably the first kind of decision that you ever made. When your parents told you what to do as a child, you were making a dependent decision. As an adult, you make a dependent decision when your doctor tells you what medication to take for an illness or when your stockbroker tells you what stock you should purchase. Dependent decisions are easy to make and require little thought. Making a dependent decision saves time and energy.

  The dependent decision, however, has some disadvantages. You may not like the outcome of the decision. The medication that your doctor prescribes may have unpleasant side effects. The stock that you purchased may go down in value. When students ask a counselor to recommend a major or a career, they are making a dependent decision. When the decision does not work, they blame the counselor. Even if the dependent decision does have good results, you may become dependent on others to continue making decisions for you. Dependent decisions do work in certain situations, but they do not give you as much control over your own life.

- **Intuitive decisions.** Intuitive decisions are based on intuition or a gut feeling about what is the best course of action. Intuitive decisions can be made quickly and are useful in dealing with emergencies. If I see a car heading on a collision path toward me, I have to swerve quickly to the right or left. I do not have time to ask someone else what to do or think much about the alternatives. Another example of an intuitive decision is in gambling. If I am trying to decide whether to bet a dollar on red or black, I rely on my gut feeling to make a choice. Intuitive decisions may work out or they may not. You could make a mistake and swerve the wrong way as the car approaches or you could lose your money in gambling.

- **Planful decisions.** For important decisions, it is advantageous to use what is called a planful decision. The planful decision is made after carefully weighing the consequences and the pros and cons of the different alternatives. The planful decision-making strategy is particularly useful for such decisions as:
    - What will be my major?
    - What career should I choose?
    - Whom should I marry?

Types of Decisions
- Dependent
- Intuitive
- Planful

The steps in a planful decision-making process:

1. **State the problem.** When we become aware of a problem, the first step is to state the problem in the simplest way possible. Just stating the problem will help you to clarify the issues.

2. **Consider your values.** What is important to you? What are your hopes and dreams? By keeping your values in mind, you are more likely to make a decision that will make you happy.

3. **What are your talents?** What special skills do you have? How can you make a decision that utilizes these skills?

4. **Gather information.** What information can you find that would be helpful in solving the problem? Look for ideas. Ask other people. Do some research. Gathering information can give you insight into alternatives or possible solutions to the problem.

5. **Generate alternatives.** Based on the information you have gathered, identify some possible solutions to the problem.

6. **Evaluate the pros and cons of each alternative.** List the alternatives and think about the pros and cons of each one. In thinking about the pros and cons, consider your values and talents as well as your future goals.

7. **Select the best alternative.** Choose the alternative that is the best match for your values and helps you to achieve your goals.

8. **Take action.** You put your decision into practice when you take some action on it. Get started!

The Resume and Job Interview

After investing your time in achieving a college education, you will need some additional skills to get a job. Having a good resume and knowing how to successfully interview for a job will help you to obtain your dream job.

Your Resume

A resume is a snapshot of your education and experience. It is generally one page in length. You will need a resume to apply for scholarships or part-time jobs, or find a position after you graduate. Start with a file of information you can use to create your resume. Keep your resume on file in your computer or on your flash drive so that you can revise it as needed. A resume includes the following:

- Contact information: your name, address, telephone number, and email address
- A brief statement of your career objective

- A summary of your education:
  - Names and locations of schools
  - Dates of attendance
  - Diplomas or degrees received
- A summary of your work and/or volunteer experience
- If you have little directly related work experience, a list of courses you have taken that would help the employer understand your skills for employment
- Special skills, honors, awards, or achievements
- References (people who can recommend you for a job or scholarship)

Your resume is important in establishing a good first impression. There is no one best way to write a resume. Whatever form you choose, write clearly and be brief, neat, and honest. If your resume is too lengthy or difficult to read, it may wind up in the trash can. Adjust your resume to match the job for which you are applying. This is easy to do if you have your resume stored on your computer. Update your resume regularly.

Ask for a letter of reference from your current supervisor at work or someone in a position to recommend you, such as a college professor or community member. Ask the person to address the letter "To Whom It May Concern" so that you can use the letter many times. The person recommending you should comment on your work habits, skills, and personal qualities. If you wait until you graduate to obtain letters of reference, potential recommenders may no longer be there or may not remember who you are. Always ask if you can use a person's name as a reference. When you are applying for a job and references are requested, phone the people who have agreed to recommend you and let them know to expect a call.

Print your resume so that it looks professional. Use a good-quality white, tan, or gray paper.

You will probably need to post your resume online to apply for some scholarships and job opportunities. Having your resume on the computer will make this task easier.

The Cover Letter

When you respond to job announcements, you will send a cover letter with your resume attached. Address your letter to a specific person at the company or organization and spell the name correctly. You can call the personnel office to obtain this information. The purpose of the cover letter is to state your interest in the job, highlight your qualifications, and get the employer to read your resume and call you for an interview. The cover letter should be brief and to the point. Include the following items:

- State the job you are interested in and how you heard about the opening.
- Briefly state how your education and experience would be assets to the company.
- Ask for an interview and tell the employer how you can be contacted.
- Attach your resume.
- Your cover letter is the first contact you have with the employer. Make it neat and free from errors.
- Use spell check and grammar check, read it over again, and have someone else check it for you.

"Many of life's failures are people who do not realize how close they were to success when they gave up."

Thomas Edison

The Job Interview

Knowing how to be successful in an interview will help you to get the job that you want. Here are some ideas for being prepared and making a good impression.

- **Learn about the job.** Before the interview, it is important to research both the company and the job. This research will help you in two ways: you will know if the job is really the one you want, and you will have information that will help you to succeed at the interview. If you have taken the time to learn about the company before the interview, you will make a good impression and show that you are really interested in the job. Here are some ways that you can find this information:

  - Your college or public library may have a profile describing the company and the products it produces. This profile may include the size of the company and the company mission or philosophy.

  - Do you know someone who works for the company? Do any members of your family, friends, or teachers know someone who works for the company? If so, you can find out valuable information about the company.

  - The personnel office often has informational brochures that describe the employer.

  - Visit the company website on the Internet.

- **Understand the criteria used in an interview.** The interviewer represents the company and is looking for the best person to fill the job. It is your job to show the interviewer that you will do a good job. Of course you are interested in salary and benefits, but in order to get hired you must first convince the interviewer that you have something to offer the company. Focus on what you can offer the company based on your education and experience and what you have learned about the company. You may be able to obtain information on salary and benefits from the personnel office before the interview.

  Interviewers look for candidates who show the enthusiasm and commitment necessary to do a good job. They are interested in hiring someone who can work as part of a team. Think about your education and experience and be prepared to describe your skills and give examples of how you have been successful on the job. Give a realistic and honest description of your work.

- **Make a good impression.** Here are some suggestions for making a good impression:

  - Dress appropriately for the interview. Look at how the employees of the company dress and then dress a little better. Of course, your attire will vary with the type of job you are seeking. You will dress differently if you are interviewing for a position as manager of a surf shop or an entry-level job in an engineering firm. Wear a conservative dark-colored or neutral suit for most professional positions. Do not wear too much jewelry, and hide excess body piercings (unless you are applying at a piercing shop). Cover any tattoos if they are not appropriate for the workplace.

  - Relax during the interview. You can relax by preparing in advance. Research the company, practice interview questions, and visualize yourself in the interview room feeling confident about the interview.

  - When you enter the interview room, smile, introduce yourself, and shake hands with the interviewer. If your hands are cold and clammy, go to the restroom before the interview and run warm water over your hands or rub them together.

  - Maintain eye contact with the interviewer and sit up straight. Poor posture or leaning back in your chair could be seen as a lack of confidence or interest in the job.

- **Anticipate the interview questions.** Listen carefully to the interview questions. Ask for clarification of any question you do not understand. Answer the questions concisely and honestly. It helps to anticipate the questions that are likely to be asked and think about your answers in advance. Generally, be prepared to talk about yourself, your

Tips for a Successful Job Interview

- Learn about job
- Understand criteria of interview
- Make a good impression
- Anticipate interview questions
- Send thank-you note

Making a Good Impression

- Dress appropriately
- Relax
- Prepare in advance
- Smile
- Shake hands
- Introduce yourself
- Maintain eye contact
- Sit up straight

goals, and your reasons for applying for the job. Following are some questions that are typically asked in interviews and some suggestions for answering them:

1. **What can you tell us about yourself?** Think about the job requirements, and remember that the interviewer is looking for someone who will do a good job for the company. Talk about your education and experience as they relate to the job. You can put in interesting facts about your life and your hobbies, but keep your answers brief. This question is generally an icebreaker that helps the interviewer get a general picture of you and help you relax.

2. **Why do you want this job? Why should I hire you?** Think about the research you did on this company and several ways that you could benefit the company. A good answer might be, "I have always been good at technical skills and engineering. I am interested in putting these technical skills into practice in your company." A not-so-good answer would be, "I'm interested in making a lot of money and need health insurance."

3. **Why are you leaving your present job?** Instead of saying that the boss was horrible and the working conditions were intolerable (even if this was the case), think of some positive reasons for leaving, such as:

   - I am looking for a job that provides challenge and an opportunity for growth.

   - I received my degree and am looking for a job where I can use my education.

   - I had a part-time job to help me through school. I have graduated and am looking for a career.

   - I moved (or the company downsized or went out of business).

   Be careful about discussing problems on your previous job. The interviewers might assume that you were the cause of the problems or that you could not get along with other people.

4. **What are your strengths and weaknesses?** Think about your strengths in relation to the job requirements, and be prepared to talk about them during the interview. When asked about your weaknesses, smile and try to turn them into strengths. For example, if you are an introvert, you might say that you are quiet and like to concentrate on your work, but you make an effort to communicate with others on the job. If you are an extrovert, say that you enjoy talking and working with others, but you are good at time management and get the job done on time. If you are a perfectionist, say that you like to do an excellent job, but you know the importance of meeting deadlines, so you do the best you can in the time available.

5. **Tell us about a difficulty or problem that you solved on the job.** Think about some problem that you successfully solved on the job and describe how you did it. Focus on what you accomplished. If the problem was one that dealt with other people, do not focus on blaming or complaining. Focus on your desire to work things out and work well with everyone.

> **Tips for Answering Questions**
>
> - Listen carefully
> - Ask for clarification
> - Answer concisely and honestly

6. **Tell us about one of your achievements on the job.** Give examples of projects you have done on the job that have turned out well and projects that gave you a sense of pride and accomplishment.

7. **What do you like best about your work? What do you like least?** Think about these questions in advance and use the question about what you like best to highlight your skills for the job. For the question about what you like the least, be honest but express your willingness to do the job that is required.

8. **Are there any questions that you would like to ask?** Based on your research on the company, think of some specific questions that show your interest in the company. A good question might be, "Tell me about your company's plans for the future." A not-so-good question would be, "How much vacation do I get?"

9. **Write a thank-you note.** After the interview, write a thank-you note and express your interest in the job. It makes a good impression and causes the interviewer to think about you again.

Journal Entry #4

A friend is looking for a job. What advice would you give him or her about the resume and job interview?

KEYS TO SUCCESS — Life Is a Dangerous Opportunity

Even though we may do our best in planning our career and education, life does not always turn out as planned. Unexpected events happen, putting our life in crisis. The crisis might be loss of employment, divorce, illness, or death of a loved one. How we deal with the crisis events in our lives can have a great impact on our current well-being and the future.

The Chinese word for crisis has two characters: one character represents danger and the other represents opportunity. Every crisis has the danger of loss of something important and the resulting emotions of frustration, sorrow, and grief. But every crisis also has an opportunity. Sometimes it is difficult to see the opportunity because we are overwhelmed by the danger. A crisis, however, can provide an impetus for change and growth. A crisis forces us to look inside ourselves to find capabilities that have always been there, although we did not know it. If life goes too smoothly, there is no motivation to change. If we get too comfortable, we stop growing. There is no testing of our capabilities. We stay in the same patterns.

To find the opportunity in a crisis, focus on what is possible in the situation. Every adversity has the seed of a greater benefit or possibility. Expect things to work out well. Expect success. To deal with negative emotions, consider that feelings are not simply a result of what happens to us, but of our interpretation of events. If we focus on the danger, we cannot see the possibilities.

As a practical application, consider the example of someone who has just lost a job. John had worked as a construction worker for nearly 10 years when he injured his back. His doctor told him that he would no longer be able to do physical labor. John was 30 years old and had two children and large house and truck payments. He was having difficulty finding a job that paid as well as his construction job, and was suffering from many negative emotions resulting from his loss of employment.

John decided that he would have to use his brain rather than his back. As soon as he was up and moving, he started taking some general education courses at the local college. He assessed his skills and identified his strengths. He was a good father and communicated well with his children. He had wanted to go to college, but got married early and started to work in construction instead. John decided that he would really enjoy being a marriage and family counselor. It would mean getting a bachelor's and a master's degree, which would take five or more years.

John began to search for a way to accomplish this new goal. He first tackled the financial problems. He investigated vocational rehabilitation, veteran's benefits, financial aid, and scholarships. He sold his house and his truck. His wife took a part-time job. He worked out a careful budget. He began to work toward his new goal with a high degree of motivation and self-satisfaction. He had found a new opportunity.

At times in life, you may face a crisis or setback which causes an unexpected change in plans. If you think positively about the situation, you can think of some new opportunities for the future. This situation is called a dangerous opportunity. Describe a dangerous opportunity you have faced in your life. What were the dangers and what opportunities did you find?

JOURNAL ENTRIES

Planning Your Career and Education

> "Life is not about waiting for the storms to pass . . . it's about learning how to dance in the rain."
> Vivian Greene

Go to http://www.collegesuccess1.com/JournalEntries.htm for Word files of the Journal Entries

Success over the Internet

Visit the *College Success Website* at http://www.collegesuccess1.com/

The *College Success Website* is continually updated with new topics and links to the material presented in this chapter. Topics include:

- Future trends
- Planning your major
- Job descriptions
- Career outlooks
- Career information
- Salary
- Interests
- Self-assessment
- Exploring careers
- Hot jobs for the future
- Profiles of successful people
- Resume writing
- Interviewing
- The personal side of work
- Using the Internet for a job search
- Job openings
- Decision making
- How to write a resume and cover letter
- How to post your resume online

Contact your instructor if you have any problems in accessing the *College Success Website*.

Notes

1. Michael T. Robinson, "Top Jobs for the Future," from www.careerplanner.com, 2004.

2. Gail Sheehy, *New Passages* (New York: Random House, 1995), 34.

3. U.S. National Center for Health Statistics, National Vital Statistics Reports (NVSR), *Deaths: Final Data for 2006*, Vol. 57, No. 14, April 17, 2009.

4. Jeff Giles, "Generalization X," *Newsweek,* June 6, 1994.

5. Jane Bryant Quinn, "The Luck of the Xers, Comeback Kids: Young People Will Live Better Than They Think," *Newsweek,* 6 June 1994, 66–67.

6. Ellen Neuborne, http://www.businessweek.com, 1999.

7. Claudia Smith Brison, http://www.thestate.com, 14 July 2002.

8. Neil Howe and William Strauss, *Millennials Rising: The Next Great Generation* (New York: Vintage Books, 2000).

9. Neuborne, www.businessweek.com, 1999.

10. John Naisbitt, Patricia Aburdeen, and Walter Kiechel III, "How We Will Work in the Year 2000," *Fortune,* 17 May 1993, 41–52.

11. U.S. Bureau of Labor Statistics, *Occupational Outlook Handbook,* 2010–11 Edition, "Overview of the 2008–18 Projections," accessed from http://data.bls.gov

12. Ibid.

13. Ibid.

14. Ibid.

15. Joyce Lain Kennedy, *Joyce Lain Kennedy's Career Book* (Chicago, IL: VGM Career Horizons, 1993), 32.

16. U.S. Bureau of Labor Statistics, "Overview of the 2008–18 Projections."

17. *The Wall Street Journal*, "E-Commerce Growth Slows, But Still Out-Paces Retail," accessed March 2010, http://blogs.wsj.com

18. Bill Gates, "Microprocessors Upgraded the Way We Live," *USA Today,* 22 June 1999.

19. From "The Microsoft Future According to Bill Gates," accessed from http://www.ameinfo.com/33384.html, 2004.

20. Bill Gates, *Business @ the Speed of Thought: Using a Digital Nervous System* (Warner, 1999). Excerpts available at www.speed-of-thought.com.

21. U.S. Bureau of Labor Statistics, "Overview of the 2008–18 Projections."

22. "Tomorrow's Best Careers," from http://www.future-trends.com, 2004.

23. Dan Tynan, "The Next 25 Years in Tech," www.pcworld.com, January 30, 2008.

24. Anne Foerst, "A New Breed of 'Replicants' Is Redefining What It Means to Be Human," *Forbes ASAP,* 1999.

25. Michael T. Robinson, "Offshoring of America's Top Jobs," from http://www.careerplanner.com, 2004.

26. "Tomorrow's Best Careers," from http://www.future-trends.com, 2004.

27. U.S. Bureau of Labor Statistics, "Overview of the 2008–18 Projections."

28. Roxanne Khamsi, "Paralyzed Man Sends E-Mail by Thought," *News @ Nature.Com,* October 13, 2004.

29. Judith Kautz, "Entrepreneurship Beyond 2000," from www.smallbusinessnotes.com, 2004.

30. Faith Popcorn and Lys Marigold, *Clicking: 16 Trends to Future Fit Your Life, Your Work, and Your Business* (New York: HarperCollins, 1996).

31. James E. Challenger, "Career Pros: Terrorism's Legacy," from www.jobjournal.com, 2003.

32. Michael T. Robinson, "Top Jobs for the Future," CareerPlanner.com, 2008.

33. T. J. Grites, "Being 'Undecided' Could Be the Best Decision They Could Make," *School Counselor* 29 (1981): 41–46.

34. Secretary's Commission on Achieving Necessary Skills (SCANS), *Learning a Living: A Blueprint for High Performance* (Washington, DC: U.S. Department of Labor, 1991).

35. U.S. Bureau of Labor Statistics, "Overview of the 2008–18 Projections."

36. Quoted in Rob Gilbert, ed., *Bits and Pieces,* 7 October 1999.

Walton College Information

Computer-Assisted Career Exploration Programs

TypeFocus

The purpose of TypeFocus is to help you make wise career choices by learning about your personality type and what it means to you. TypeFocus is also a free service to students and can be located at the Walton College Career Center website.

SIGI Plus

This computer program is designed to help you identify your interests, skills, and values, find careers that match your personal preferences, and prepare for an occupation. There are eight sections from which to gather information related to careers, and you can use them in any order.

Discover

This computer program can also help you organize your interests and experiences into probable careers. There are nine sections that cover topics, ranging from self-assessments and job characteristics, to identifying training and finding financial planning.

State-Specific Career Information

Information relating to your state, or the state where you will work after graduation, can be used to match your interests and abilities with specific occupations. Current information is provided about occupations in different areas of the specific state, including working conditions, hiring requirements, and job outlook. For example, the Georgia Career Information Services (GCIS), which is updated every year, provides information about specific fields of study, financial aid, military careers, and other colleges throughout the United States.

Walton College Guide for Career Success

Freshman/Sophomore

Get involved in Leadership Walton
Visit with the Career Center
Explore career areas
Collect information
Visit campus Career Center
Research careers in the library and online for orientation on programs and services
Talk with parents, friends, professors, and a career counselor about your career ideas
Develop a resume

List five career options for your intended majors
Select electives to test career ideas
Complete career assessments
Confirm major
Explore experiential options to test career skills, interests and ideas, abilities, career-related hobbies, personality style, and career values
Attend career fairs

Junior/Senior

Increase experience
Implement career plan
Apply for intern/co-op assignment
Attend training sessions
Develop list of targeted employers
Send out graduate school applications
Attend career fairs
Network, network, network

Leadership Walton

The mission of Leadership Walton is to offer a unique program with a blend of academic, leadership, and career development opportunities specifically designed to guide the student toward lifelong professional success. This program fills the gap between academic pursuits and workforce preparation. Leadership Walton is a program offered by the Sam M. Walton College of Business Career Development Center in partnership with Undergraduate Programs. To accomplish this goal, the program is designed to incorporate required and optional academic coursework, career development programming, and leadership development opportunities blended in a defined course of progression that ensures that well-rounded opportunities for student development and preparedness.

Sample Cover Letter

Always sign letters

If a resume or other enclosure is used, note in the letter

Use complete title and address

Applicant's Address
Applicant's Phone Number
Date of Letter

Employer's Name and Title
and Address

If possible, address it to a particular person by name

Salutation:

Opening Paragraph: State why you are writing, name the position or type of work for which you are applying, and mention how you heard of the opening or organization.

Make the addressee want to read your resume

Middle Paragraph(s): Explain why you are interested in working for this employer, and specify your reasons for desiring this type of work. If you have had relevant work experience or related education, be sure to point it out; but do not reiterate your entire resume. Emphasize skills or abilities you have that relate to the job for which you are applying. Be sure to do this in a confident manner, and remember that the reader will view your letter of application as an example of your writing skills.

Be personable and enthusiastic

Final Paragraph: The closing paragraph is the most important. We suggest a persistent, businesslike closing statement, which puts you in control of the response. For example: "I will call you on (date) to discuss this career opportunity with (name of organization)." Indicate your desire for a personal interview. You may suggest alternative dates/times or advise of your flexibility as to time/place, especially if you will be in the city on a certain date and would like to set up an interview. Or, if the company will be recruiting in you area, or if additional information or references are desired, say you are willing to accommodate the company's schedule and requests.

Be brief but specific; your resume contains details

Top and bottom margins should be equal

Sincerely,

Your Name typed

enclosure

Sample Resume for a Recent College Graduate

Lisa Arkansas   123 Arkansas Street, Apartment 2 · Fayetteville, Arkansas 72702 · 479-555-0022 · email@uark.edu

Summary of Qualifications

Results-oriented, detailed professional with comprehensive retail marketing experience. Skilled customer relations, project management, sales analysis, and inventory management. Recently awarded for exceeding sales goals.

Education

University of Arkansas, Sam M. Walton College of Business   **Fayetteville, Arkansas**
Bachelor of Science in Business Administration   *expected May 2013*
- Major: Marketing, Minor: Finance
- Walton College Honors Program, GPA 3.5

Northwest Technical Institute   **Rogers, Arkansas**
General Coursework, GPA 3.1   *August 2007 - May 2008*

Experience

Wal-Mart Stores, Inc.   **Bentonville, Arkansas**
Merchandising Internship   *Summer 2007*
- Responsible for the Open-to-Buy log throughout the summer
- Ordered approximately $3,000,000 worth of women's apparel for Houston convention
- One of only 12 students nationwide to be selected for merchandising internship
- Created new juniors summer modular display for use in Wal-Mart Stores, Inc.

The Buckle   **Fayetteville, Arkansas**
Sales Associate   *July 2006 - February 2007*
- Provided excellent customer service to all patrons
- Managed cash receivables
- Created and organized clothing displays for fall and winter apparel lines
- Consistent top sales associate

Bentonville Parks and Recreation   **Bentonville, Arkansas**
Referee and Umpire   *May 2005 - April 2006*
- Monitored K-8 baseball and basketball games
- Assisted other park staff in ensuring child safety
- Communicated and responded to parents' and children's needs

Computer Skills
- Microsoft Word, Excel, and PowerPoint
- Retail Link
- Adobe Photoshop and PageMaker
- FTP programs
- Proficient in IBM and Macintosh applications

Leadership Experience
- Leadership Walton member, *Fall 2009 - Present*
- Church Mission Trip: Assisted in building houses in Honduras, *June 2007*
- Race for the Cure, *April 2005*

Resume Worksheet for Your Ideal Career

Name _____ Date _____

Use this worksheet to prepare a resume similar to the sample on the previous page. Assume that you have graduated from college and are applying for your ideal career.

1. What is the specific job title of your ideal job?

2. What are two or three qualifications you possess that would especially qualify you for this job? These qualifications can be listed under Highlights on your resume.

3. List your degree or degrees, major, and dates of completion.

4. List five courses you will take to prepare for your ideal career. For each course, list some key components that would catch the interest of your potential employer. Use a college catalog to complete this section.

5. List the skills you would need in each of these areas.

Computer skills:

Technical or other job-related skills:

Personal skills related to your job objective:

6. List employment that would prepare you for your ideal job. Consider internships or part-time employment.

7. What are your interests?

8. What special achievements or awards do you have?

Name _____ Date _____

Answer the following questions to prepare for the interview for your ideal job. If you do not know what your ideal job is, pretend that you are interviewing for any professional job. You may want to practice these questions with a classmate.

1. What can you tell us about yourself?

2. Why are you leaving your present job?

3. What are your strengths and weaknesses?

4. Tell us about a difficulty or problem that you solved on the job.

5. Tell us about one of your achievements on the job.

6. What do you like best about your work? What do you like least?

7. Are there any questions that you would like to ask?

Rate Your Skills for Success in the Workplace

Name _____ Date _____

Read each statement relating to skills needed for success in the workplace. Use the following scale to rate your competencies:

5 = Excellent   **4** = Very good   **3** = Average   **2** = Needs improvement   **1** = Need to develop

_____ **1.** I have good reading skills. I can locate information I need to read and understand and interpret it. I can pick out the main idea and judge the accuracy of the information.

_____ **2.** I have good writing skills. I can communicate thoughts, ideas, and information in writing. I know how to edit and revise my writing and use correct spelling, punctuation, and grammar.

_____ **3.** I am good at arithmetic. I can perform basic computations using whole numbers and percentages. I can make reasonable estimates without a calculator and can read tables, graphs, and charts.

_____ **4.** I am good at mathematics. I can use a variety of mathematical techniques including statistics to predict the occurrence of events.

_____ **5.** I am good at speaking. I can organize my ideas and participate in discussions and group presentations. I speak clearly and am a good listener. I ask questions to obtain feedback when needed.

_____ **6.** I am a creative thinker. I can come up with new ideas and unusual connections. I can imagine new possibilities and combine ideas in new ways.

_____ **7.** I make good decisions. I can specify goals and constraints, generate alternatives, consider risks, and evaluate alternatives.

_____ **8.** I am good at solving problems. I can see when a problem exists, identify the reasons for the problem, and devise a plan of action for solving the problem.

_____ **9.** I am good at mental visualization. I can see things in my mind's eye. Examples include building a project from a blueprint or imagining the taste of a recipe from reading it.

_____ **10.** I know how to learn. I am aware of my learning style and can use learning strategies to obtain new knowledge.

_____ **11.** I am good at reasoning. I can use logic to draw conclusions and apply rules and principles to new situations.

_____ **12.** I am a responsible person. I work toward accomplishing goals, set high standards, and pay attention to details. I usually accomplish tasks on time.

_____ **13.** I have high self-esteem. I believe in my self-worth and maintain a positive view of myself.

_____ **14.** I am sociable, understanding, friendly, adaptable, polite, and relate well to others.

_____ **15.** I am good at self-management. I know my background, skills, and abilities and set realistic goals for myself. I monitor my progress toward completing my goals and complete them.

_____ **16.** I practice integrity and honesty. I recognize when I am faced with a decision that involves ethics and choose ethical behavior.

_____ **17.** I am good at managing my time. I set goals, prioritize, and follow schedules to complete tasks on time.

_____ **18.** I manage money well. I know how to use and prepare a budget and keep records, making adjustments when necessary.

_____ **19.** I can manage material and resources. I can store and distribute materials, supplies, parts, equipment, space, or products.

_____ **20.** I can participate as a member of a team. I can work cooperatively with others and contribute to group efforts.

_____ **21.** I can teach others. I can help others to learn needed knowledge and skills.

_____ **22.** I can exercise leadership. I know how to communicate, encourage, persuade, and motivate individuals.

_____ **23.** I am a good negotiator. I can work toward an agreement and resolve divergent interests.

_____ **24.** I can work with men and women from a variety of ethnic, social, or educational backgrounds.

_____ **25.** I can acquire and evaluate information. I can identify a need for information and find the information I need.

_____ **26.** I can organize and maintain information. I can find written or computerized information.

_____ **27.** I can use computers to process information.

_____ **28.** I have an understanding of social, organizational, and technological systems and can operate effectively in these systems.

_____ **29.** I can improve the design of a system to improve the quality of products and services.

_____ **30.** I can use machines and computers to accomplish the desired task.

_____ **Total**

Score your skills for success in the workplace.

150–121   Excellent
120–91   Very good
90–61   Average
Below 60   Need improvement

From the previous list of workplace skills, make a list of five of your strong points. What do you do well?

From the list of workplace skills, make a list of areas you need to improve.

The Planful Decision Strategy

Name _____ Date _____

Read the following scenario describing a college student in a problem situation. Then, answer the questions that follow to practice the planful decision strategy. You may want to do this as a group activity with other students in the class.

Rhonda is an 18-year-old student who is trying to decide on her major. She was a good student in high school, earning a 3.4 grade point average. Her best subjects were English and American history. She struggled with math and science but still earned good grades in these subjects. While in high school, she enjoyed being on the debate team and organizing the African American Club. This club was active in writing letters to the editor and became involved in supporting a local candidate for city council.

Rhonda is considering majoring in political science and has dreams of eventually going to law school. Rhonda likes being politically involved and advocating for different social causes. The highlight of her life in high school was when she organized students to speak to the city council about installing a traffic light in front of the school after a student was killed trying to cross the street. The light was installed during her senior year.

Rhonda's family has always been supportive, and she values her family life and the close relationships in the family. She comes from a middle-income family that is struggling to pay for her college education. Getting a bachelor's degree in political science and going to law school would take seven years and be very expensive. There is no law school in town, so Rhonda would have to move away from home to attend school.

Rhonda's parents have suggested that she consider becoming a nurse and attending the local nursing college. Rhonda could finish a bachelor's degree in nursing in four years and could begin working part-time as a nurse's aide in a short time. A cousin in the family became a nurse and found a job easily and is now earning a good income. The cousin arranged for Rhonda to volunteer this summer at the hospital where she works. Rhonda enjoys helping people at the hospital. Rhonda is trying to decide on her major. What should she do?

1. State the problem.

2. Describe Rhonda's values, hopes, and dreams.

3. What special interests, talents, or aptitudes does she have?

4. What further information would be helpful to Rhonda in making her decision?

5. What are the alternatives and the pros and cons of each?

Alternative 1	
Pros:	Cons:

Alternative 2	
Pros:	Cons:

Alternative 3 (be creative!)	
Pros:	Cons:

6. Only Rhonda can choose what is best for her. If you were Rhonda, what would you do and why? Use a separate piece of paper, if necessary, to write your answer.

CPSIA information can be obtained
at www.ICGtesting.com
Printed in the USA
LVOW02s0256110817
544596LV00006B/28/P